"Readers are invited into a school of transference. In store is a thought provoking study that requests us to look again at that other scene of learning to teach and do so by going to the movies. Stillwaggon and Jelinek are marvelous guides and their book ushers us into fantastical views on the psychical consequences of watching teachers on the silver screen."

**Deborah Britzman**, FRSC and author of *A Psychoanalyst in the Classroom*

"*Filmed School* offers a novel way of thinking about a broad body of often beloved films in connection to the concept of transference. The book lays paths for us to walk towards developing a healthier understanding of teachers and their professional identities, their pedagogical relationships, and, ultimately, their possible influence over students."

**Ronald Chennault**, author of *Hollywood Films about Schools: Where Race, Politics, and Education Intersect*

*Mädchen in Uniform* (1931)

# Filmed School

*Filmed School* examines the place that teaching holds in the public imaginary through its portrayal in cinema. From early films such as *Mädchen in Uniform* and *La Maternelle* to contemporary images of teaching in *Notes on a Scandal* and *The History Boys*, teachers' roles in film have been consistently contradictory, portraying teachers as both seducers and selfless heroes, social outcasts and moral models, contributing to a similarly divided popular understanding of teachers as both salvific and sinister.

In this book, Stillwaggon and Jelinek present these contradictory images of teaching through the concept of *transference*—the fantastical belief in another's knowing that founds a teacher's authority in relation to her students and, to some degree, the public at large. Tracing the place of transference across a century of school films, each chapter demonstrates the persistence of this fantasy in one of the dreams or nightmares of teaching that recurs thematically in school films: the teacher-as-savior, seducer, signifier in a moribund discourse, and sacrificial object. Through these analyses, the authors suggest that something might be missing in our attempts to theorize education when we leave our unthought fantasies of teaching out of the picture.

This book will be of key interest to academics, researchers, and postgraduate students in the fields of educational theory, teacher education, philosophy of education, film and media studies, psychoanalysis, sociology of education, curriculum studies, and cultural studies.

**James Stillwaggon** is Associate Professor of Philosophy at Iona College, USA, where his teaching and writing focus on the place of philosophical ideals in democratic education.

**David Jelinek** is Professor of Art and Art History at Collegiate School, USA. His research and writing focus on the relationship between teachers and students in film. A solo installation of his, Money Down, was exhibited at the Andrew Edlin Gallery in Manhattan.

# Theorizing Education Series
Series Editors
Gert Biesta, *University of Luxembourg, Luxembourg*
Julie Allan, *University of Birmingham, UK*
Richard Edwards, *University of Stirling, UK*

*Theorizing Education* brings together innovative work from a wide range of contexts and traditions which explicitly focuses on the roles of theory in educational research and educational practice. The series includes contextual and socio-historical analyses of existing traditions of theory and theorizing, exemplary use of theory, and empirical work where theory has been used in innovative ways. The distinctive focus for the series is the engagement with educational questions, articulating what explicitly educational function the work of particular forms of theorizing supports.

Books in this series:

### Making a Difference in Theory
The theory question in education and
the education question in theory
*Edited by Gert Biesta, Julie Allan and Richard Edwards*

### Forgotten Connections
On culture and upbringing
*Klaus Mollenhauer*
*Translated by Norm Friesen*

### Psychopathology at School
Theorizing mental disorders in education
*Valerie Harwood and Julie Allan*

### Curriculum Theorizing and Teacher Education
Complicating conjunctions
*Anne M. Phelan*

### Filmed School
Desire, transgression and the filmic fantasy of pedagogy
*James Stillwaggon and David Jelinek*

# Filmed School

## Desire, transgression and the filmic fantasy of pedagogy

James Stillwaggon and
David Jelinek

LONDON AND NEW YORK

First published 2016
by Routledge
2 Park Square, Milton Park, Abingdon, Oxon OX14 4RN

and by Routledge
711 Third Avenue, New York, NY 10017

*Routledge is an imprint of the Taylor & Francis Group, an informa business*

© 2016 J. Stillwaggon and D. Jelinek

The rights of J. Stillwaggon and D. Jelinek to be identified as authors
of this work have been asserted by them in accordance with
sections 77 and 78 of the Copyright, Designs and Patents Act 1988.

All rights reserved. No part of this book may be reprinted or
reproduced or utilised in any form or by any electronic, mechanical,
or other means, now known or hereafter invented, including
photocopying and recording, or in any information storage or
retrieval system, without permission in writing from the publishers.

*Trademark notice:* Product or corporate names may be trademarks
or registered trademarks, and are used only for identification and
explanation without intent to infringe.

*British Library Cataloguing in Publication Data*
A catalogue record for this book is available from the British Library

*Library of Congress Cataloging in Publication Data*
Names: Stillwaggon, James, author. | Jelinek, David, author.
Title: Filmed school : desire, transgression and the filmic fantasy of
    pedagogy / by James Stillwaggon and David Jelinek.
Description: Milton Park, Abingdon, Oxon : New York, NY :
    Routledge, 2016. | Includes bibliographical references and index.
Identifiers: LCCN 2015048452| ISBN 9781138931077 (hardcover) |
    ISBN 9781315679969 (electronic)
Subjects: LCSH: Teachers in motion pictures. | Education in motion
    pictures.
Classification: LCC PN1995.9.T4 S85 2016 |
    DDC 791.43/6557—dc23
LC record available at http://lccn.loc.gov/2015048452

ISBN: 978-1-138-93107-7 (hbk)
ISBN: 978-1-315-67996-9 (ebk)

Typeset in Bembo Std
by Swales & Willis Ltd, Exeter, Devon, UK

This book is for the boys:
Phaedon and Alexandros,
Malcolm and Angus,
who, like the book, took some time to get here, but arrived just in time.

# Contents

| | | |
|---|---|---:|
| | *Series editors' introduction* | xi |
| | *Acknowledgements* | xii |
| 1 | Moving pictures: the fantasy of authority | 1 |
| 2 | First lessons: the origins of the filmic teaching fantasy | 21 |
| 3 | Law, school: impossible relationships in the ideal case | 38 |
| 4 | To save, with love: desire, domination and melancholia in teacher savior films | 57 |
| 5 | Expulsion: the horror of the fantasy made real | 75 |
| 6 | *Down with teachers, up with revolution*: school violence and fantasies of control | 92 |
| 7 | End of class: the death of the teacher and the life of teaching | 113 |
| 8 | End of term: the limits of authority and conclusion | 130 |
| | *Glossary* | 144 |
| | *Index* | 150 |

# Series editors' introduction

*Filmed School* by James Stillwaggon and David Jelinek could be read as an exploration of the ways teaching is depicted in modern cinema using a psycho-analytic lens. Although at one level this is indeed what the book does, provides illuminating insights in modern cinema, its views about education and the ways in which psychoanalysis can be used to make sense of this, this book is actually first and foremost a study of teaching and pedagogy. And while it uses film to bring pedagogy into focus, it does so in order to probe deeper into existing representations of teaching, representations that do not just exist in modern cinema, but in contemporary culture more widely. The book not only opens up a wide variety of understandings of what teaching *is* but also, and most prominently, of what we desire teaching to be – the fantasy of pedagogy, as the authors call it in the subtitle of their book. Stillwaggon and Jelinek not only show what teachers desire about their teaching, but also what students desire about teaching and teachers, and what both desire about the teacher-student relationship. Moreover, they show society's desires about teaching and education more generally.

At one level their study reveals archetypical ideas about teaching, about its possibilities and impossibilities, and about the hopes those who are involved in or concerned about education invest in it. Here they show that many of these ideas and expectations are not new but hark back to discussions that were already central to Greek philosophy. At the same time, however, Stillwaggon and Jelinek pay attention to contemporary themes in education policy, research and practice, particularly to show that archetypical ideas, expectations and fantasies about teaching and its (im)possibility continue to frame contemporary policy, discourse, and practice. While there is much to learn about philosophy, psychoanalytic theory, and 20th century cinema, it is the careful, thoughtful, and insightful sustained analysis of teaching and our relationships with teaching that makes this book highly original and highly relevant for anyone involved in or concerned about contemporary education. The careful way in which Stillwaggon and Jelinek unfold their insights and the clear way in which they have structured their argumentation, makes this book a very welcome addition to the *Theorizing Education* series.

Gert Biesta
London, April 2016

# Acknowledgements

This book started at the Pratt Institute, when we were introduced as Master's student and thesis advisor by Amy Brook Snyder, the chair of Art and Design Education. Amy's elective, entitled *The Teacher in Art and Fiction*, introduced us to many films that occupied our earliest conversations. She helped give birth not only to this book, but also to a great friendship. Thank you, Amy.

Pratt is among several academic institutions that have supported our efforts as writers and teachers. This book was completed thanks to a generous sabbatical year from Iona College. Barnard College and Teachers College at Columbia University, Hofstra University, and Iona have all served as supportive environments for the development of these ideas, and James extends thanks to those who encouraged him to teach this scholarship in its development: Fred Neuhouser, David Hansen, Eduardo Duarte, Alex Eodice, and Pat Antonacci. David gives thanks to Vassar College, especially professors Harry Roseman and Jesse Kalin; Saint Ann's School—in particular Gabe Howard and the late Stanley Bosworth; and Collegiate School, an institution that not only supplied him with marvelous students for the past quarter-century, but also was generous in supporting research—both in terms of time and financial assistance—for this project.

Our book is the product of a decade of intermittent research, writing, and presentations. Some of our published work has been reprinted and reworked here.

Parts of Chapter 4 were originally published as "The mined mind: Domination, desire and melancholy in *The Corn Is Green*" in *Philosophy of Education 2008*, edited by R. Glass and reprinted with permission from the Philosophy of Education Society. The original publication can be found at http://ojs.ed.uiuc. edu/index.php/pes/article/viewFile/1395/145.

Parts of Chapters 1 and 3 were originally published as "Legal, tender: The deferred romance of pedagogical relation in *The Paper Chase*" in the journal *Studies in Philosophy & Education* and are reprinted here with permission from Springer.

Parts of Chapters 1 and 5 were originally published as "A note on the scandals: The role of filmic fantasy in reproducing teaching and its transgressions" in the collection *Art's Teaching, Teaching's Art*, edited by Tyson Lewis and Megan Laverty and reprinted here with permission from Springer.

Parts of Chapters 1, 2, and 5 were originally published as "Annotations on a scandal: Desire, transgression and the filmic fantasy of pedagogy" in the journal *Educational Theory* and are reprinted here with permission from John Wiley & Sons.

Thanks to our editors, especially Gert Biesta and Chris Higgins, who helped us develop these papers toward a body of scholarship, and to our editors at Routledge and Swales and Willis, Clare Ashworth, Thomas Storr, Heidi Lee, Sarah Sleath, and Kay Hawkins who have helped turn that body of scholarship into the current text with their encouragement.

Without the support of reviewers, editors, colleagues, friends, and family this project would never have been realized. We list some who made critical contributions, as we also acknowledge that we can't acknowledge everyone. For anyone accidently left off, please know you have not been left out, and we'll buy the popcorn next time at the movies.

Thanks to John Knapp for his generous and wise legal counsel and for bringing us to see the new restored print of *The Third Man*. Gabriel Acri read an early draft of Chapter 1 and provided research support on *Rock 'n' Roll High School*. Thanks to Timmy, TJ, Viv, Kate, Jen, and Brodie for their impromptu roundtable discussion on John Hughes's films, to Falabella for being a film snob, and to Dan for buying James his first copy of *If . . .* when it was only available on VHS at one video store in Manhattan. Thanks to Tiphaine McGrath and Dan Chisholm for translating sections of *La Maternelle* and *Zero for Conduct*. Alan Sklar ran the finest movie rental store, Alan's Alley, and introduced us to *Term of Trial*.

Thanks to Denise Young: David's favorite picture.

Thanks to Sophia Sarigianides for helping James develop ideas by always requiring more of an explanation of an idea than he is willing to give.

Thanks to Aleka and Asimo and Kaitlyn for creating writing time where none could be imagined.

Thanks also to our colleagues who have inquired about and cheered on and critiqued our work as it has developed: Elizabeth Hollow, Jessica Hochman, Doris Santoro, Terri Wilson, Rodino Anderson, Darryl De Marzio, Paul Farber, Jennifer Logue, Nancy Lesko, John Broughton, Deborah Britzman, and especially Maxine Greene.

And to our parents, for teaching us about transference.

Finally, to all those that made the films: directors, cinematographers, actors, and writers. No matter how many times we watch *The Paper Chase*, our excitement is palpable. Will James Hart succeed in Professor Kingsfield's class? Will Morgan Evans win a scholarship to Oxford in *The Corn Is Green*? What will happen to all those students on the roofs at the conclusion of *Zero for Conduct* and *If . . . ?* Here's to the long lineage of films depicting teachers and students, from two current teachers and perpetual students, one of whom taught the other.

# Chapter 1

# Moving pictures
## The fantasy of authority

A scene from *Jonah, Who Will Be 25 in the Year 2000* (1976) opens with a shot from the perspective of a student sitting in the middle of a crowded classroom. Students shuffle and giggle as an administrator enters the room and stands at the desk, announcing that the history teacher has retired and introducing Mr. Perly, an unknown who will be teaching the class. The class's nervous, adolescent giggling explodes into laughter when the administrator departs and Perly hoists an enormous briefcase onto the desk and removes a cutting board, a metronome, a butcher's cleaver, and several feet of blood sausage.

"Remember, my father was a butcher and my mother sang operetta very well," Perly exhorts the students, enforcing a point that is both hyper-personal and yet stated as if it bears some significance for the students in the classroom. Setting the metronome upon the desk and appropriating the sausage in its greasy coils as a metaphor for time, he launches into an impossibly broad lecture about repetitions in history that allow for prophets and historians to see beyond their own historically bound consciousness. From hysterical laughter the students turn to rapt silence and the camera angle turns 180 degrees, panning across the faces of the students, amazed and attentive (except one, who sleeps). Both teacher and students portray the fantasied image that film is intended to deliver: the student fantasy of a teacher who is both personable and knowledgeable is matched by the teacher's fantasy of students who are taken aback, moved, and set aflame by what the teacher has to say.

At first, the content of Perly's lecture seems entirely replaceable: in *To Sir, With Love* (1967) Mr. Thackeray achieves the same adoration (though not as immediately) with a lesson that involves making a salad. But the fact that Perly's lecture focuses on gaps in time is reinforced by a brief segment cut into the scene in which a man gets out of bed, retrieves a gun from a dresser drawer, considers shooting himself, but shoots a clock instead. The segment trains our focus back on the fantastical significance of the teacher's lecture: that the study of history reveals an escape from the tedious suffering of time. The lesson of the film recapitulates the teacher's words: "In total synthesis, time disappears." Even the monotony of the classroom can be overcome through the ideal meeting of the teacher's fantasy (students who desire to know what the

## 2  Moving pictures: the fantasy of authority

teacher knows) and students' fantasy (a teacher who knows what students want to know). This escape from time is not only possible but manifest: thanks to editing, the entire lesson takes about eight minutes, leaving out all the pauses, repetitions, and awkward exchanges common to real classrooms and ending with the students' thunderous applause.

On the one hand, we can easily recognize that this scene is nothing like a real classroom, or at least nothing like its pretended objectivity as a filmed school activity: the scene is played for the sake of drama rather than for learning. On the other hand, positioned as we are in the place of the student, seated quietly and—much like the students in the film—looking up at the teacher who captures our vision and our imagination, we the audience find ourselves subject to two forms of unspoken authority. The first is the authority of the screen, or of the *auteur* we project beyond the screen that allows us to suspend disbelief and enjoy the fantasy of the film by giving ourselves over to it. The second is the authority of the teacher on the screen, or the fact that when an adult speaks from the front of a classroom, most people can be expected to pay attention, because paying attention to the teacher is the one attitude that is taught in every school and every grade level.

When the authority of the film chooses the authority of *this* teacher over any other, the combined effect is often nothing short of a confirmation of a cultural ideal of teaching that is as widespread as it is impossible to realize. In *Jonah*'s departure from reality, the film conforms to and reproduces this fantasy of teaching, at least as old as Plato's dialogues, that shapes our imaginary expectations of real classrooms, not despite its impossibility but because of it. According to Jacques Lacan, the famed self-proclaimed inheritor of Freudian psychoanalytic thought whose ideas play a large role in the present text, images play an "orthopaedic" role in the life of the psyche (Lacan, 1977, p. 4), establishing objectivity in both the world and ourselves and covering over the cracks and gaps and imperfections of our all-too-human existence. In so doing, our imaginary relations to the world also provide us with an ideal to live up to, and if we have some awareness of the difference between ourselves and our ideals, they may even provide us with a path of self-overcoming on which our desires might lead. Images do not present us with a sense of what we are but with an impossible ideal of what we might be—a phenomenon that leads Boothby (1991, p. 21) to conclude that, "alienation not only begins in the imaginary, the imaginary is somehow alienating in its very essence." Boothby follows by quoting Lacan (1981, p. 166) on the same point: "In the order of the imaginary, alienation is constitutive."

According to Slavoj Žižek, the famed popularizer of Lacanian psychoanalytic thought whose work applying psychoanalysis to popular culture serves as an inspiration for the present text, the fact that so much of our identity is tied up with the promise offered by alienating, impossible fantasies means that the images on the screen are *more* real than the everyday reality we live and breathe, because of their role in providing normative structure to our otherwise meaningless experiences. "If you are looking for what is in reality more real than reality itself, look into the cinematic fiction" (*The Pervert's Guide to Cinema*, 2006).

In short, images matter, because they have the capacity to shape the way we see the world and, as a result, what we desire. While filmic images flit instantaneously upon the screen as a mere moment, perhaps barely catching our attention, and are certainly dismissed as the fluff that passes the low bar of Hollywood producers, even our critical discourses cannot dispel the attraction to the moving quality of motion pictures or the weight that they exert, insofar as the images that make it to the screen are manifestations of a truly public imaginary, and express the social and political spirit of their time often better than contemporary works of fine art. Images of teaching seem to matter a great deal. Despite the fact that films set in schools are rarely among the top grossing films at the box office and mostly disappoint expectations of critical acclaim and industry awards, one only has to look as far as phrases such as "carpe diem," or "Bueller . . . ?" in order to gain a sense of the weight that school films carry in our society and the way they reflect prevailing views of schools and teachers alike. Teacher candidates regularly report their call to teach as a vocation heard in the heroic representations of teaching they have seen on the screen, even though they just as often claim that they understand these images are merely fictional ideals. Weber and Mitchell (1995) have studied this influence in a more formal manner, reporting on research in which the image of the teacher held by schoolchildren worldwide conforms remarkably to the way it is presented in Western film and television narratives.

School films both reflect and reproduce the status of teaching in the public imaginary at a given historical moment, while remaining heavily influenced by visions of the teacher inherited from a long tradition of historical figures and convenient caricatures. While the filmic teacher has traditionally been portrayed as a figure of everyday heroism or at a piously resigned distance from the world, more contemporary visions of the teacher seem divided: on the one hand, maintaining a traditional view of the teacher as a hero, and on the other, keeping up with the scandalous place that teaching and public schools in particular have taken in the public imaginary. Journalistic narratives of teachers failing to raise student achievement in poor districts, changing students' grades on standardized tests to meet achievement benchmarks, collecting large salaries while on administrative leave, engaging in sex acts with one or several students, and revealing too much about their personal lives on social media have recently reintroduced teachers to the public imaginary under a new and unflattering light. Some of this scandal is strictly political, while other forms of teacherly indignity seem clearly personal. But one shared element among these various scandals is that their capacity to generate attention is directly tied to the morally impeccable place that the ideal of teaching has traditionally held in society. Like reading a news report that a nun has laundered money in order to feed a gambling habit, the disconnect between the public's ideal expectations

## 4 Moving pictures: the fantasy of authority

of teachers and their somewhat banal moral failures gives rise to the titillating experience of public outrage.

If Lacan's (1977) orthopaedic understanding of the imaginary is correct, and films produce desires in their audiences, not only in the context of the theater during the film's running time, but also through frames of reference that extended into daily interactions, we may expect that at times the publicly held ideal of the teacher—precipitated through the heroic *and* transgressive fantasies of individual teachers—will produce behaviors that cut violently against the moral grain of schools and society. Teachers' attempts to realize the fantasies of teaching they experience on the screen and to satisfy the problematic desires that these fantasies produce results in a rift in the symbolic order evaded in fantasy: the dream becomes a nightmare (*The Pervert's Guide to Cinema*, 2006) as the conflict between fantasy and the social order offers us a glimpse of the drives that underlie human interactions. The public fascination inspired by teachers' disgrace lies precisely in the horror of this conflict: how can our rule-bound society give rise to motivations for which it cannot account?

One of the primary concepts offered by this book is the idea that both the problematic heroization of teachers and the public fascination with disgraced teachers come from the same source, namely a fantasy cultivated in most school-aged children, and maintained uncritically by most adults, that the teacher actually knows all the things that the child needs to know in order to grow up happy and successful. Freud termed this fantasy *transference*, and both he and Lacan saw it as instrumental to the analyst–analysand relationship, while also posing distinct threats to the relationship it founds. Significant to their studies of the analytic relationship and to the present study of pedagogical relationships on film, the student's misrecognition of the teacher as someone who is presumed to know everything worth knowing sets the student moving in the teacher's direction, desiring everything that the teacher has to teach.

At the same time, because desire is a slippery aspect of human subjectivity, the student's or analysand's desire can be mistakenly directed toward the teacher or analyst. The reason why the psychoanalytic concept of transference works so well both in pedagogical and analytic contexts is not only because analysis is a form of pedagogy. More importantly, and as Lacan (1961) makes clear in his seminar on the topic of transference, the idea of transference is borrowed from a long tradition of thinking on erotic education initiated by Plato in his *Symposium*. In this dialogue, which we discuss at length in Chapter 2, Plato not only defines eros as the principal emotional function by which the human psyche takes its shape, but also provides an example of educational failure, in the character of Alcibiades, launching a tradition of philosophy that privileges desire as both a promising and problematic condition of pedagogy.[1]

In giving voice to Alcibiades' desire for his teacher, Plato provides an unexpected rationale for our inherited cultural interdiction against teacher-student intimacy, as the fulfillment of the desires sparked by transference. If the student comes to know his teacher too intimately, revealing the teacher's desires, weaknesses, and limitations, then the student's fantasy of the teacher's knowing status would be doomed, as would the student's desire to learn what the teacher knows. From Lacan's (1961, p. XI 14) commentary that "the lure [of transference] is reciprocal," we can also surmise that there is something in the unfulfilled character of the student's desire for the teacher (or for whatever it is the student believes the teacher knows) that benefits the teacher as well.

The structural tension that Plato invests in pedagogical relationships, in which both teacher and student look to one another across an impossible distance, lends itself to various forms of narrative drama as well. In more recent expressions of this narrative tradition, films featuring teacher–student relationships prove fertile ground for exploring educational desires, producing images that both define and defile our understanding of what education ought to be. But if these narratives contribute to what real teachers and students expect from a pedagogical relationship, it is easy to see how the work of teaching and learning might be confused with the interpersonal aims of other human connections—maternal, friendly, or romantic—and leave teachers lost, or uncritically convinced of what they ought to be. The power of school films lies in their capacity to offer an ideal narrative of educational desire to teachers and students alike, shaping their desires and, in turn, the way they see themselves. Professor Henry Higgins makes a similar point about the powerful relationship between the imaginary, discursive identity, and desire at the outset of *My Fair Lady* (1964), asking rhetorically, "What could ever matter more than taking a human being and turning her into another human being by creating a new speech for her?"

## A semi-critical cultural playlist

While the fantasy of transference and the erotic motivations of the student help us to understand the ease with which teachers are established in the public imaginary as heroes, as well as the scandal that attends their moral failures, a question might remain about what we should do with this understanding of pedagogical relationships and the image of the teacher they produce. Britzman (1986) identifies one of the more educationally significant consequences of transference as a widespread cultural phenomenon. As teachers serve as one of our earliest transferential objects, away from our original fascination with parental authority and projected onto various trusted persons in the world, they remain locked in that imaginary place, just as our parents do, even as we become educated toward their imagined authorial position. Despite the fact that we move beyond individual teachers' authority, developing our fluency within various symbolic orders, the authority and imagined integrity of teaching maintains its status over and above those who have had the experience of being a student. In an imaginary relation largely untouched by the transformational work of educational growth, the teacher maintains her aura of completeness and knowing.

## 6 Moving pictures: the fantasy of authority

Studying the effect of this imaginary investment in teachers' authority on the developing professional identities of student teachers, Britzman articulates this challenge as a paradox: how does one become a teacher through the practice of being a student? As student teachers have learned to identify as students in order to succeed in school, and as being a good student entails setting one's own desires in relation to another's authority, performing the prescribed identity of the good student seems to preclude the practice of those traits associated with being a good teacher. The oppositional divide between these identities is so clearly evident to so many students preparing to become teachers that it leads Britzman to formulate a set of "cultural myths" that shape student teachers' understandings of teacher identity.

The first of these myths, "everything depends on the teacher" (Britzman, 1986, p. 449) distracts students' attention from the fact that the teacher's authority is bound up in her place within the structure of the school. Far from being the originator of her own authority as this myth suggests, the teacher's identity is an extension of the authority of the school granted by society and manifested through the students' desires. Grounding this individualized notion of the teacher's authority in her relation to codified forms of knowledge, Britzman identifies a second myth, "the teacher is the expert," (Britzman, 1986, p. 450) placing the teacher at an endpoint of learning that cannot be attained through the processes of schooling in which student teachers are engaged.

Perhaps most important to the current study, Britzman's third myth calls upon pre-service teachers' belief that "teachers are self-made" (Britzman, 1986, p. 451) or naturally suited to their work. This last belief obviates the need for teacher training and illuminates Britzman's principal concern, which is that in looking for some basis for their own authority, students merely pattern themselves after their own elementary or secondary teachers—an act of repetition that perpetuates both undesirable pedagogical practices and the cultural myths that naturalize these practices.

But new teachers' autobiographical experiences are not the only source of cultural myths and problematic repetitions. Cinematic representations of teachers have been investigated according to a wide variety of research agenda, including the portrayal of cultural stereotypes (Burbach and Figgins, 1993; Beyerbach, 2005), the articulation of postmodern educational theory (Cohen, 1999), and the exercise of power in the classroom (Bauer, 1998). These critical analyses' focus on the idea that media distorts rather than reproduces existing norms of teaching allows our imaginary investments in pedagogical relationships and teacher identity to go largely untheorized, and often results in a celebration of the problematic ideals these analyses are intended to critique. Ayers (1994, p. 156), for instance, claims that, "Outstanding teachers need to question the common sense—to break the rules, to become political and activist in concert with the kids. This is true heroism, an authentic act of courage." Ayer's words are more soundbite than analysis, but in his rush to create a message with easy assent, he makes the mistake of relying on precisely those outlaw characteristics that mark all "good" cinematic teachers and thereby define our common sense of what good teaching is. Good teachers questioning common sense, breaking the rules, and siding with the kids can be found in nearly every school film.

The problem with endeavoring a critical project on popular representations of teaching analogous to Britzman's "implicit institutional biographies" (Britzman, 1986, p. 443) is that most writing on the presentation of teacher identity in popular media is simply celebratory or judgmental (Dalton, 1995, 1999; Keroes, 1999), treating the teachers on screen as if they were actual teachers rather than filmic fantasies, using films as exemplary of actual pedagogical problems and solutions and thereby misreading filmic teachers' erotic pursuits and authoritative gestures as worthy of praise or blame. No one would ever get away with a scholarly publication critiquing *Spider-Man* on the grounds that the idea of a human being climbing walls is implausible, but somehow when it comes to the portrayal of teachers we forget that films are not intended to provide a window on reality, but on ourselves. What we are looking for in film as a revelation about ourselves is not an objective truth about the world, but, as Martha says in *The Children's Hour* (1961) "the lie with the ounce of truth"—a fantasy that reveals more about its participants than any objective facts could.

Other scholarly work (Farber *et al.*, 1994; Chennault, 2006) turns in the direction of using school films as a way of looking at cultural norms focusing on the representation of various demographic groups as indicative of the place of minoritized and marginalized groups in the public imaginary. These studies are useful, insofar as many films set in school are concerned with anxieties about youth cultures, but their treatment of teacher identity and pedagogical relationships is limited, as it is secondary to their focus on the representation of cultural attitudes and expectations about the social and political work of schools.

Theorists of the cultural images of teaching echo Britzman's ideas about the popular myth of the teacher as omnipotent, omniscient, and self-made, but these images also reinforce impossible paradoxes of practice for the novice teacher who seeks to create personal connections with her students within relationships that are defined by the structure of the school as an institution of social reproduction. This extension of Britzman's concerns suggests that popular images of teaching are not to be merely celebrated or easily dismissed, but might be approached as texts offering insight into the assumed characteristics of teachers that maintain a normative force in our social imaginary. In addition to the examination of implicit institutional biographies that Britzman recommends as a means of understanding how our ideas about teaching have been influenced by those teachers who have exercised authority over us, we might also engage in a study of media representations in relation to the institution of schooling as a means by which pedagogical relations and teacher identity might be better understood through their filmic portrayals. The goal of our study is not so much a critical engagement with the public images of teaching, aimed at becoming

**8** Moving pictures: the fantasy of authority

free from ideological influence, as seems to be the ultimate goal of psycho-analytic film theorists, such as Metz (1986) and McGowan (2007). Pulling the curtain back in order to interrupt our unthought relationship to teaching seems neither possible nor desirable. The point is not to undo the influence that these particular images have on our teaching, but to look at them and the way we see ourselves through them from an oblique angle that isn't offered by our ordinary relationships to public images.

Just as Britzman's work suggests the development of a critical lens through which we may read pedagogical authority through the personal experiences of those subject to authority, we consider here what it might mean to read against the grain of the teacher's authority as it is manifested through popular media. It may be disappointing to hear that as rational adults we must continue to negotiate with media influences; we typically think of media as something we turn on and turn off, rather than something that turns us on or provides the conditions of possibility for our actions. But the moving power of the movies is precisely the reason both teachers and students bring them into the classroom consciously and unconsciously: having been moved, we seek to move others. We know that popular media shapes the way our students see the world; if we can grab hold of the media, or work within its expectations and norms, we might be able to use it to shape our students. The greater question that lies within the fundamental teaching fantasy of influence is whether we are capable of coming to understand the influence that media, among other sources, has already had upon us before we have the opportunity to manipulate it for our own purposes: how it has us before we have it.

In this book, erotic relationships in school films serve as a handle by which media representations of teachers may be grasped and analyzed and our own identifications with these representations might better be understood. Desire works as a basis for our analysis on a number of different registers. At the simplest level, desire can be employed in analysis of school films because of its pervasive, uncanny presence across a wide variety of films set in schools, offering a common ground upon which these films may be described alongside one another. Second, if characters in school films serve as points of identification for viewers, the desires of these characters are important as the site of viewers' identifications. In other words, as Slavoj Žižek suggests (*The Pervert's Guide to Cinema*, 2006), films may give us our desires by giving us characters who exemplify what is good to want.

Third, as a way of understanding the pervasive presence of desire in school films, education has traditionally been linked in some fashion to the cultivation of desires for the good. Desire as the basis for human growth and learning through the realization of one's own ignorance is at least as old as its manifold portrayal in Plato's *Symposium* and has had a constant, if varied place in educational thought ever since. More recently (Gallop, 1995; Britzman, 1998; Logue, 2008), psychoanalytic theories of desire in education have been employed as a means of moving beyond current positivist models of educational growth, de-centering the subject of education in relation to its objects of desire. The idea that schools, as authorized cultural voices, promote and produce desires in the young has been clearly articulated by a number of contemporary theorists (Felman, 1982; Brooke, 1987; Davis, 1987; Schleifer, 1987) using the work of Jacques Lacan, whose emphasis on the agency of language in producing human desires—and in turn, producing the human subject *as* subject to those desires—further begs the questions of authority and pedagogical relations at stake in teachers' identities.

As a result of this framing, this book necessarily focuses upon what might appear to be an idiosyncratic selection of both the history of thought on the subject of erotic subjectification, as it manifests itself through Platonic, Freudian, and Lacanian texts, as well as the history of pedagogical relationships in film. On the subject of film, this means that we have focused on a selection of films that not only respond in some significant way to the history of thinking on pedagogical eros that precedes them, but that also have some seminal influence on the mirrored cultures of film and education that have followed. As a result, some films that have received a great deal of popular and critical attention, such as *Goodbye, Mr. Chips* (1939), and *Stand and Deliver* (1988) are hardly mentioned here, whereas others that have received similar attention, such as *To Sir, With Love* (1967), are also at the center of our study. Similarly, many films that do not play a central role in our culture's conscious understanding of its relationship to education, such as *The Corn Is Green* (1945) and *Zero for Conduct* (1933), serve as central focal points precisely because their influence, while less visible, has nonetheless been significant. The measure of these films' significance is the familiarity of their themes despite the relative anonymity of their titles.

While we use the term "school films" throughout the book to designate those cinematic sites that reflect and reproduce our society's shared, impossible ideal of teaching, it should be noted from the outset that this shorthand does not refer to a film genre or type, but instead includes a wide variety of films that happen to share the common feature of representing teachers and students. Our review of films includes an existential drama (*Jonah, Who Will Be 25 in the Year 2000* (1976)), a *Bildungsroman* (*The Paper Chase* (1973)), a dark comedy (*Election* (1999)), and a thriller (*Notes on a Scandal* (2006)). This fact is significant to our study, because despite the diversity of films that portray teaching, the teachers portrayed throughout maintain their relationship to an imaginary ideal, exposing desires in their students, in the audience, and at times in themselves that offer both pedagogical promise and personal peril.

## An overview of the book

This book is not a single, sustained argument about one text or one idea developed in a linear progression. Neither is it a loose collection of essays. Rather, we invite the reader to consider the book like an apartment with multiple, connected rooms all adjoining a central foyer. If this foyer is the fantasy of transference, the various rooms that one might find through it are the readings of school films available through this central concept, turned one way or another, yielding stories of desire, transgression, domination, rebellion, repetition, and death. What this means is that the succeeding chapters might be approached in a number of different directions. For those who have had less exposure to the idea of desire as a constitutive force in the emergence of subjectivity, in Platonic or Lacanian scholarship, the best way to read would be to follow the chapters as they are presented, developing a more nuanced understanding of the theory in each chapter as it coincides with different themes in popular film narratives. For those who need no introduction to Lacan or Plato, the remaining chapters in this book can be read in almost any order, based on the reader's interest in various topics or specific films, without any significant loss of continuity.

We should also note that, unlike many other books on film, we do not include any stills from the films we discuss, aside from that which appears at the front of the book. In an age when most readers of this book will have immediate access to the films we discuss through a variety of media, the film still seems stilted—providing a narrow reference to those who have seen the film in question and decontextualized image for those who haven't. In lieu of stills, we will curate a number of video playlists on YouTube corresponding to various chapters and offering a more vivid connection to the films we discuss.

Finally, we would like to draw attention to the fact that we will try to avoid a typical move made in many academic texts that seek to apply theoretical frameworks to contexts other than those where they were first thought, and will not attempt to summarize in advance Platonic or psychoanalytic notions of fantasy, desire, or, as will be applicable to later chapters, of the Lacanian real. While we see the work of other scholars who include such summaries in their introductory material as well-intentioned and sometimes helpful, the attempt to summarize often produces two problems with the aim of solving one. Namely, for those familiar with Platonic or psychoanalytic theories of desire, fantasy, identity, etc., any summary we could offer here would only offend, as it would result in omissions of aspects of the theory that one scholar or another would find inexcusable. At the same time, it would likely alienate any educated, casual reader by providing an overly summarized account of a more nuanced idea.

In order to avoid these easy pitfalls, we prefer to follow the direction given to us by the positive responses we have received from some reviewers, editors, and audience members at conference sessions over the past ten years. Given the notorious complexity of psychoanalytic theory and Lacan's deliberate avoidance of definitional signposts, we have been encouraged to work within the ideas that frame this text rather than to report them, to analyze in plain language, wherever possible, rather than reproduce jargon, and to show rather than tell. Lots of good books have been written explaining, consolidating, and coming to terms with Lacan, and anyone looking for an education in his brand of psychoanalytic thought need look no further than the secondary sources cited in this text for a thorough introduction to his teachings. In our opinion, we are not the authors who are showing the connection between popular film and psychoanalytic theory; it is the filmmakers themselves who do this, albeit unknowingly. Our job, in a classically Platonic sense, is simply to show where these convergences come up between ideas and film, holding a mirror to the mirror of our social norms. Some readers unfamiliar with Lacan may have their vocabulary stretched a bit, but not unnecessarily: new terms will be tied to new concepts useful to understanding the films at hand. By the end of this book, or by the end of any chapter of this book, the reader may have learned something more about psychoanalytic theory, something more about the way pedagogy is portrayed in film, and something more about the relationship between education, social norms, and becoming human. The account of any of these three categories will, by necessity, be incomplete, and may jar with established interpretations of philosophical and psychoanalytic theory. We look forward to the discussions that these disagreements bring about.

In what follows, we offer a brief discussion of the succeeding chapters' contents.

## Chapter 2. First lessons: the origins of the filmic teaching fantasy

The value of popular film as a site for thinking through the tensions of educational relationships reveals itself in a number of early films featuring close contacts between teachers and students. Plot lines of early films featuring teachers and students are clearly erotically charged and replete with scandal and, as such, they extend the historical legacy of Plato's *Symposium* while beginning an adaptation of this tradition to the structural narrative requirements of filmmaking. In Chapter 2, we examine a number of early films as a way of introducing themes that will continue to develop and change through later films that we examine in further chapters.

One of the themes that connect school films is that of forbidden love. Nearly all films employ representations of sexual desire as a means of illustrating a student's passion for learning, but what is strangely familiar to Plato's writing is that this erotic educational drive almost always takes the form of an illicit love. The prevalence of homoerotic relationships in early films featuring pedagogical relationships, including *Different from the Others* (1919), *Mikaël* (1924), *Mädchen in Uniform* (1931), and *La Maternelle* (1933), is one thematic vehicle that both connects to the Platonic tradition of educational eros and alerts film audiences to a secret, subversive element in the student's desire to learn. Similarly common is the introduction of a character who represents the interests of moral judgment, and who stands in the way of education's erotic encounter. This jealous voice of the law takes many forms—the bureaucratic administrator, spiteful students, burned out educators—and threatens the erotic relationship

## 12 Moving pictures: the fantasy of authority

through accusation, threats, and sometimes extortion. At the same time that these unlikable characters provide antagonism in the narrative, they absorb the unlovely necessity of judging the appropriateness of the relationship, freeing the audience to enjoy the fantasy unfolding upon the precipice of transgression before their eyes. One significant exception to this theme is in *La Maternelle*, which resolves its erotic tension through the adoption of the young student by the teacher and her new husband, who happens to be the school's principal. In this case, the reestablishment of the family structure ordains the love between teacher and student by transforming it into a different love altogether.

## Chapter 3. Law, school: impossible relationships in the ideal case

Films depicting educational relationships typically emphasize personal connections between students and teachers over the educational goals that such relations facilitate. In doing so, these films tend to obscure the erotic elements of teaching in favor of the charismatic presence of a particular teacher. At the same time, they raise the question of how teachers stand in relation to their institutional roles in such a way as to inspire students' desires for knowledge. In this chapter, in order to examine the influence of institutional roles in defining teacher-student relationships, we analyze two ideal cases of erotic striving in school films, *To Sir, With Love* (1967) and *The Paper Chase* (1973). In both of these films, the teacher and student have no immediate personal connection, but relate to one another entirely through the transferential fantasy. As with earlier films, the interdiction on close personal relationships between teacher and student is indicated by pairings that were considered socially unacceptable at the time of the film's production. Unlike earlier films, the forbidden distance is not bridged by an alternative personal relationship—a maternal connection, or the sensuality of the arts. Instead, these films portray the problematic structure of transference as a differential of authority between teacher and student that can only be successful in motivating the student when the distance between teacher and student is *not* resolved by some other means. As a result, these narratives allow us to focus on the fantasy of transference and its effects on the desires of the student. The success of the student at the end of each of these films is not that she finally connects to the teacher in a moment of mutuality, but that she moves on, leaving the teacher behind, presumably to inspire another.

## Chapter 4. To save, with love: desire, domination and melancholia in teacher savior films

In the most successful pedagogical relationships, the distance between teacher and student is preserved categorically. Like the paradox of Achilles and the tortoise, the student never achieves her goal of meeting the teacher where he stands, but is driven by her desire to surpass him and even replace him in the hope of gaining his recognition. Yet the fact that the desired meeting never arrives draws attention to additional paradoxical possibilities, including that in which the transferential fantasy through which the student is liberated to some bright future also governs the student's desires in a totalizing domination. The danger of this liberating seduction can best be seen in the popular image of the teacher as a savior—arriving from some other place to improve the lives of poor and marginalized students. *The Corn Is Green* (1945) is one of the earliest cinematic examples of the teacher as a messiah of social reform and *Blackboard Jungle* (1955) contains within it all of the significant elements of more recent films featuring teachers as saviors, including *Dangerous Minds* (1995) and *Freedom Writers* (2007). Yet while the oppressive character of liberatory education is all too present in these films, each presents us with an element of grist in the otherwise well-oiled machine of progress. Beginning with Morgan Evans' melancholic glance over his shoulder as he is carried off to a new life at Oxford, we consider this unresolved attachment as a valuable site of resistance to normalized discourses of educational progress, and consider this more subtle resistance as an alternative to more overtly critical and liberatory educational ideals. As *Corn* provides the template for later savior films, we look for its melancholic stamp across the genre, and find it strangely reversed and undone across more contemporary films.

Chapter 4 serves as a transitional discussion in this book, the point at which the conditions of desire in education reach a saturation point and begin to direct our attention toward the darker corners and more problematic possibilities. While the idea of unfulfilled eros toward an impossibly prized teacher provides a remarkably clear way of describing educational growth, the story it tells is also remarkably limited compared to the variety of narratives that populate school films. To misquote Aristotle, there's one way to be good, but lots of ways to be bad, and some of these latter are much more interesting than being good.

Rules—especially those that govern the fantasy worlds of film—are meant to be broken. While human life has come to be defined largely in terms of linguistic, moral, and other social laws, we know our limits and understand the rules that define us by trespassing, transgressing, and breaking from the expected in an affirmation of the human tendency to refuse its environing conditions. Any totalizing set of rules outlining a way of life carries with it the pleasure of breaking with the rules (what Lacan called *jouissance*) as a way of affirming the idea that we cannot be contained by them. As Camus (1991, p. 11) claims, "Man is the only creature who refuses to be what he is." To this we might add: "and enjoys the perversity of being otherwise."

The limit of our *jouissance* is that in it we reaffirm the power of the rules we break. This limit can be explained further by separating it into subjective and objective terms. Objectively, without the existence of the rules that dictate the operation of the mundane, transgression would not be possible. A breaking that

# 14 Moving pictures: the fantasy of authority

served not only to break with but to destroy existing rules would quickly erode the conditions of its own possibility. Subjectively, the experience of breaking limitations, going beyond the permissible, is experienced as a feeling beyond pleasure, as too much pleasure to be maintained beyond the momentary break. The joy of breaking from the given, of asserting oneself, is accompanied by the fear and dread of becoming detached from the very rules that make sense of the world and the transgressive act itself. Worse, a prolonged experience of *jouissance* reveals to the subject that there is no such thing as a mere negation of rules: the space outside the law is replete with the terrifying insistence of everything that laws are supposed to prevent. It is this unbearable nature of *jouissance* that leads Žižek to claim that the realization of fantasy, the actual suspension of the rules, yields a nightmare. The joy of breaking is thus like a vacation: a journey to a somewhere else that would be unbearable if it were not for the common tedium of the home that waits at the end of the trip.

The limit of *jouissance* is only a real limit, however. That is, it is only problematic insofar as transgression cannot be a regular feature of ordinary life. While our pleasure in breaking can never be brought into the real in any durable way, because of its destructive capacity with regard to the rules that constitute human life, it can nevertheless be maintained in fantasy: an interior affirmation of the self powered by the rejection of those discursive social norms that in turn mark the limits of the subject. Fantasy does not participate in the paradoxical problem of *jouissance* insofar as it has no need of being actualized. Instead, fantasy relies upon the power of ordinary human norms to fuel its existence as an escape from the symbolic order into a separate realm in which rules are suspended. Film involves the fantastical representation of social transgressions. It shows us everything that we cannot or would not dare to do. The power of film is that it allows us to experience illicit transgressions second hand, playing a part in the *jouissance* of the characters on the screen while at the same time protecting ourselves from the fantasy made real, the nightmare.

The hero of the cinema, through whom we vicariously experience the pleasure of breaking the rules, has at least two characteristics that we lack. First, he has the transgressive joy of breaking with the ordinary, the adventure that claims him out of his own life and draws him into a narrative where nothing is actually at stake despite the chaos that threatens him, as ordinary rules have been suspended for the sake of the vacation from human norms. The hero has endured the nightmare, providing him with a position of knowledge to which the audience has no access. The relationship of the viewer to the hero is therefore analogous to that of the child to the parent, the student to the teacher: in each binary, the former looks to the latter as a knowing subject who carries the knowledge that completes human subjectivity. As the child's desires are directed toward the place where the parent or teacher stands in an attempt to achieve the knowledge and authority of the parent, the viewer's desires drive toward the filmic hero, demanding the viewer to create herself in the model of the hero if she is to understand herself.

Moving pictures: the fantasy of authority    15

This process of emulation, this following through of desire toward a filmic fantasy, produces new opportunities and difficulties in various fields of human flourishing, depending on the degree of difference between the conditions of the fantasy and the conditions of ordinary life. A person might find himself buying a fedora or a pistol, not because it fits with the demands or aesthetics of his corporate work life or suburban home life, but precisely because it does not: the synecdochal effect of possessing a piece of the impossible makes the actual more livable. Fantasies that are closer to home, or closer to work, such as those presented in school films, have a potentially greater and more thorough motivating force, at times becoming a prime, if unrecognized, motivating force in choosing a career or making decisions within one's line of work. To that degree, however, these close-to-home fantasies also carry with them a greater threat of confusing the fantasy as a sustaining fiction with a realizable ideal.

## Chapter 5. Expulsion: the horror of the fantasy made real

If films serve as a site where all of the possibilities inherent in our social structures might be played out and considered in terms of their effects upon human subjects, it should not surprise us that at some point our tastes as viewers will extend beyond the beautiful to the traumatic, if only to better understand those structures that shape our beliefs and practices. In this chapter we consider two films in which the teaching fantasy of arousing student eros is made real, but in ways that remind us that the point of fantasy is to remain impossible, playing the part of a productive impossibility. In a highly self-conscious way, *Notes on a Scandal* (2006) draws upon the romantic fantasy of pedagogical relationships depicted in the many films that precede it, providing its audience with familiar scenes of a savior teacher, a student who stands out from the crowd, and an extra-curricular relationship that bridges the distance and humanizes both teacher and student. But, rather than leaving the relationship unresolved as a result of the teacher's embodying the fantasy of completeness, the film portrays a disturbing recognition of the teacher's desires, implicating the audience's desires, too, in the horror that ensues. *Election* (1999) explores the same reversal of existing beliefs about teaching for comic purposes. In exposing the base desires of a seemingly model teacher, it upends the traditional fantasy of the teacher as beyond desire.

## Chapter 6. *Down with teachers, up with revolution:* school violence and fantasies of control

If one possible horrific outcome of the teacher-student relationship is that the teacher and student actually come together, nullifying the world that grounds their productive misrecognition, another frightening but more common possibility is that the student rejects adult authority as arbitrarily grounded in meaningless

## 16  Moving pictures: the fantasy of authority

social structures. For these students, authority is there for the taking, or can at least be gained given the right leverage. As Bauer (1998) has pointed out, school films from the late 1970s and 1980s are largely devoid of fully realized adult characters: *Rock 'n' Roll High School* (1979), *Fast Times at Ridgemont High* (1982), and most of John Hughes' films dismiss the possibility that students might learn anything from their teachers, or any adults. Without the fantasy of transference, the erotic impulses of the youth can become comic in their scattered misdirection, or darkly nihilistic in their lack of socially valued objects.

In this chapter, we consider three films that portray student fantasies of revolution and control—a rejection of the expectations of erotic growth within the social order. *Zero for Conduct* (1933) has often been cited as the inspiration for Lindsay Anderson's dreamy and oddly prescient film *If . . .* (1968). Both portray disaffected students whose fidelity to one another is an effect of their oppression at the hands of brutal school regimes. Both end in violent rebellions against these regimes. And yet, perhaps only because the violence they portray remained unthinkable at their respective times of production, both films retain the charm of a dream. In the post-parental world of contemporary youth culture, the same violence in Gus Van Sant's *Elephant* (2003) appears gritty and too real in comparison to a far more gritty and stark image of student rebellion. As *Zero* and *If . . .* maintain the fantasy of students leading an armed revolution to rule the school, *Elephant* attempts to portray what that fantasy looked like when two students attempted to make it real. While the worlds of *Zero*, *If . . .* and *Elephant* are equally banal, equally oppressive, the audience's sentiments lie with the world of the latter if only because of the horror with which its destruction is portrayed.

## Chapter 7. End of class: the death of the teacher

*The History Boys* (2006) closes with a eulogy after the two teachers who have been battling for the souls of their students throughout the film ride off together on a motorcycle and an accident kills one and permanently maims the other. The death of Hector, the deeply flawed protagonist, is ripe with symbolism. Having recently been caught fondling a student, his life as a teacher is over. Moreover, his manner of teaching literature and history, cultivating Renaissance men from working class kids, has had its day; his institution is more interested in the sharpening of rhetorical skills offered by his much younger, ironic rival, Irwin, who excels at counterintuitive analysis of history. Hector must die, because his teaching is done, but he must also die in order to continue teaching in his students' remembrances of his lessons.

Hector's death quotes and parodies those of Socrates, Jesus of Nazareth, and other controversial teachers whose lessons enjoy long lives in part because of their teachers' early departure. Following these larger-than-life figures, his life and death as a teacher beg the question of whether all teaching is a living toward death, as practiced by Socrates and Jesus.

Teachers throughout the world of school films die in different ways, following in the steps of Socrates either literally, like Hector, by losing their identity as teachers, like *Dead Poets Society*'s (1989) Mr. Keating, or through the loss of their identity outside the school for the sake of their students, as with *Freedom Writers* (1995), *Mr. Holland's Opus* (1995), and *To Sir, With Love* (1967). Higgins (2003) has addressed the loss of professional identity outside of the school in the final scene of *To Sir, With Love* (1967), in which Thackeray tears up the job offer he has been waiting for and decides to remain a teacher. Higgins argues that this scene reflects and reinforces an ascetic moral culture that persists among teachers. One way to complicate Higgins' reading of the scene, however, is by referring to the fantasy of teaching that our study has set out to explore. By stepping into the role of the teacher as the one who knows and by inspiring the desires of his students, Thackeray feels himself memorialized in the influence he bears on his students. According to Blacker (1997) and De Marzio (2007), it is in precisely those ascetic motions critiqued by Higgins that the teacher regains herself *as* a teacher. We extend Blacker's argument in this chapter through Freud's discovery of a drive that works against the human organism's drive to prolong its life, and through Lacan's understanding of the death drive as a way of dying on one's own terms: what Lacan, employing Antigone as an exemplar, refers to as an ethical act.

## Chapter 8. End of term: the limits of authority and conclusion

In closing this book, we turn to Hitchcock's *Rope* (1948) in order to indicate the limits of a teacher's influence over her students' erotic striving. This move seems to contradict its own interest: on the one hand, we seek to marry the filmic focus of our study with the world of educational policy, with the aim of undermining the publicly held fantasy of teaching at the heart of accountability measures. On the other, the means by which we connect fantasy back to the real world is by claiming that teaching has a limited claim on anything beyond the door of the classroom. In order to demonstrate the validity of this seemingly paradoxical claim, we look at *Rope* as an example of two students attempting to live their teacher's lessons beyond the limits of the pedagogical relationship. The horror that ensues in the students' execution of "the perfect murder," based upon their teacher's quasi-Nietzschean teachings, provides an extended counter-example against the fantasy underlying accountability in education, while at the same time directing our discussion to the idea of teachers as outsiders and strangers—those whose lessons do not simply recapitulate the existing social order, but provide their students with the possibility of living within their own freedom. Drawing on Hannah Arendt's (1961) critique of progressive education, we close with an image of the teacher as necessarily fantastical: representing worldly images to her students from an impossible place that they can only hope to inhabit and that will maintain a lasting presence in shaping their desires.

## Note

1 The historical development of the relationship between eros and education can be traced through Augustine, Rousseau, Hegel, Kierkegaard, and Freud, but more recently includes (Britzman, 1998; Brooke, 1987; Davis, 1987; Felman, 1982; Frank, 1995; Gallop, 1997; Stillwaggon, 2006, 2008; Taubman, 1990).

## References

Arendt, H. (1961) *Between Past and Future: Eight Exercises in Political Thought*. New York: Viking Press.

Ayers, W. (1994). A teacher ain't nothin' but a hero: Teachers and teaching in film. In P. Joseph and G. Burnaford (eds) *Images of Schoolteachers in Twentieth-Century America*. New York: St. Martin's Press, pp. 147–156.

Bauer, D. M. (1998) Indecent proposals: Teachers in the movies. *College English*, 60(3), 301–317.

Beyerbach, B. (2005) Themes in sixty years of teachers in film: Fast times, dangerous minds, stand by me. *Educational Studies*, 37, 267–285.

*Blackboard Jungle*, Richard Brooks, dir. (USA: Metro-Goldwyn-Mayer, 1955).

Blacker, D. (1997). *Dying to Teach: The Educator's Search for Immortality*. New York: Teachers College Press.

Boothby, R. (1991) *Death and Desire: Psychoanalytic Theory in Lacan's Return to Freud*. New York: Routledge.

Britzman, D. P. (1986) Cultural myths in the making of a teacher: Biography and social structure in teacher education. *Harvard Educational Review*, 56(4), 442–456.

Britzman, D. P. (1998) *Lost Subjects, Contested Objects: Toward a Psychoanalytic Inquiry of Learning*. Albany, NY: State University of New York Press.

Brooke, R. (1987) Lacan, transference, and writing instruction. *College English*, 49(6), 679–691.

Burbach, H. and Figgins, M. (1993) A thematic profile of the images of teachers in film. *Teacher Education Quarterly*, 2(2), 65–75.

Camus, A. (1991) *The Rebel: An Essay on Man in Revolt* (trans. A. Bower). New York: Random House.

Chennault, R. (2006) *Hollywood Films about Schools: Where Race, Politics, and Education Intersect*. New York: Palgrave.

*The Children's Hour*, William Wyler, dir. (USA: The Mirisch Corporation, 1961).

Cohen, S. (1999). *Challenging Orthodoxies*. New York: Peter Lang.

*The Corn Is Green*, Irving Rapper, dir. (USA: Warner Bros, 1945).

Dalton, M. (1995) The Hollywood curriculum: Who is the "good" teacher? *Curriculum Studies*, 3(1), 23–44.

Dalton, M. (1999) *The Hollywood Curriculum: Teachers and Teaching in the Movies*. New York: Peter Lang.

*Dangerous Minds*, John Smith, dir. (USA: Hollywood Pictures, 1995).

Davis, R. C. (1987) Pedagogy, Lacan, and the Freudian subject. *College English*, 49(7), 749–755.

*Dead Poets Society*, Peter Weir, dir. (USA: Touchstone Pictures, 1989).

De Marzio, D. (2007) Teaching as asceticism: Transforming the self through the practice. In M. Stengel (ed.) *Philosophy of Education 2007*. Urbana, IL: Philosophy of Education Society, pp. 349–355.

# Moving pictures: the fantasy of authority 19

*Different from the Others*, Richard Oswald, dir. (Germany: Richard-Oswald-Produktion, 1919).

*Election*, Alexander Payne, dir. (USA: Paramount Picture, 1999).

*Elephant*, Gus Van Sant, dir. (USA: Fine Line Pictures, 2003).

Farber, P., Provenzo, E. and Holm, G. (eds) (1994) *Schooling in the Light of Popular Culture*. Albany, NY: State University of New York Press.

*Fast Times at Ridgemont High*, Amy Heckerling, dir. (USA: Universal Pictures, 1982).

Felman, S. (1982) Psychoanalysis and education: Teaching terminable and interminable. *Yale French Studies*, 63, 21–44.

Frank, A. W. (1995) Lecturing and transference: The undercover work of pedagogy. In J. Gallop (ed.) *Pedagogy: The Question of Impersonation*. Bloomington, IL: Indiana University Press, pp. 28–35.

*Freedom Writers*, Richard LaGravenese, dir. (USA: Paramount Pictures, 2007).

Gallop, J. (ed.) (1995) *Pedagogy: The Question of Impersonation*. Bloomington, IL: Indiana University Press.

Gallop, J. (1997) *Feminist Accused of Sexual Harassment*. Durham, NC: Duke University Press.

*Goodbye, Mr. Chips*, Sam Wood, dir. (USA: Warner Bros, 1939).

Higgins, C. (2003). Teaching and the good life: A critique of the ascetic ideal in education. *Educational Theory*, 53(2), 131–154.

*The History Boys*, Nicholas Hytner, dir. (United Kingdom: Fox Searchlight Pictures, 2006).

*If . . .* , Lindsay Anderson, dir. (United Kingdom: Memorial Enterprises, 1968).

*Jonah, Who Will Be 25 in the Year 2000*, Alain Tanner, dir. (France: Galimont, 1976).

Keroes, J. (1999) *Tales out of School: Gender, Longing, and the Teacher in Fiction and Film*. Carbondale, IL: Southern Illinois University Press.

Lacan, J. (1961) *The Seminar of Jacques Lacan: Transference VIII 1960–1961* (C. Gallagher, trans.). Available at karnacbooks.com.

Lacan, J. (1977) *Ecrits* (A. Sheridan, trans.). New York: W.W. Norton & Company.

Lacan, J. (1981) *Le Seminaire, Livre III, Les Psychoses*. Ed. Jacques-Alain Miller. Paris: Editions du Seuil.

Lacan, J. (1999) *On Feminine Sexuality, The Limits of Love and Knowledge, 1972–1973* (B. Fink, trans.). New York: W.W. Norton & Company.

Logue, J. (2008) The unbelievable truth and dilemmas of ignorance. In R. Glass (ed.) *Philosophy of Education 2008*. Urbana, IL: Philosophy of Education Society, pp. 54–62.

*Mädchen in Uniform*, Leontine Sagan, dir. (Germany: Deutsche Film-Gemeinschaft, 1931).

*La Maternelle (Children of Montmartre)*, Jean Benoit-Lévy, dir. (France: Photosonor, 1933).

McGowan. T. (2007). *The Real Gaze: Film Theory after Lacan*. Albany, NY: SUNY Press.

Metz, (1986) *The Imaginary Signifier*. Bloomington, IL: Indiana University Press.

*Mikaël*, Carl Dreyer, dir. (Denmark: Universum Film (UFA), 1924).

*Mr. Holland's Opus*, Stephen Herek, dir. (USA: Hollywood Pictures, 1995).

*My Fair Lady*, George Cukor, dir. (USA: Warner Bros, 1964).

*Notes on a Scandal*, Richard Eyre, dir. (United Kingdom: Fox Searchlight Pictures, 2006).

*The Paper Chase*, James Bridges, dir. (USA: 20th Century Fox, 1973).

*The Pervert's Guide to Cinema*, Sophie Fiennes, dir. (United Kingdom: ICA Projects, 2006).

*Rock 'n' Roll High School*, Allan Arkush, dir. (USA: New World Pictures, 1979).

*Rope*, Alfred Hitchcock, dir. (USA: Warner Bros, 1948).

Schleifer, R. (1987). Lacan's enunciation and the cure of mortality: Teaching, transference, and desire. *College English*, 49(7), 801–815.

*Stand and Deliver*, Ramón Menéndez, dir. (USA: American Playhouse, 1988).

## 20 Moving pictures: the fantasy of authority

Stillwaggon, J. (2006). Don't stand so close to me: Distance in pedagogical relationships. In D. Vokey (ed.) *Philosophy of Education 2006*. Urbana, IL: Philosophy of Education Society, pp. 119–126.

Stillwaggon, J. (2008) Performing for the students: Teaching identity and the pedagogical relationship. *Journal of Philosophy of Education*, 42(1), 67–83.

Taubman, P. (1990). Achieving the right distance. *Educational Theory*, 40(1), 121–133.

*To Sir, With Love*, James Clavell, dir. (United Kingdom: Columbia Pictures, 1967).

Weber, S. and Mitchell, C. (1995) *That's Funny, You Don't Look Like a Teacher!* London: The Falmer Press.

*Zero for Conduct*, Jean Vigo, dir. (France: Franfilmdis, 1933).

Chapter 2

# First lessons
## The origins of the filmic teaching fantasy

Nearly 100 years ago, one of the first films to openly address homosexual desire was released in Germany: at its center is the relationship between a music teacher and his student. *Different from the Others* (1919) exists today only in fragments, with one known remaining copy that was not entirely destroyed by the Nazis. But the film's narrative and themes have served to found an entire genre of school films that portray pedagogy as a fundamentally erotic practice that draws out and shapes the desires of the young through the fantasied character of the teacher. *Different from the Others* (1919) and a handful of early films establish a genre that derives not only from a repetition of character types but also from a structural similarity that has remained in place throughout the history of film and continues to inform pedagogical relationships in contemporary films as diverse as *Whiplash* (2014), *The History Boys* (2008), and *La Robe du Soir* (2009).

On the one hand, we can describe this formulaic structure of school films as constituted by three elements: a masterful teacher, a student driven by the desire to transform himself in relation to the master, and a representative of prevailing social or institutional norms that hold the teacher and student apart, enforcing some aspect of the law that condemns the relationship. What holds the genre together across a wide variety of permutations is that without any injustice to these films, we can read the same triangle of characters in the same films in a manner that is nearly oppositional: a master torn by his own desires, a student unwilling to be easily led, and a set of social norms that quietly cheer the erotic union between teacher and student even while officially condemning it, bringing about scandal, castigation, the promise of greatness, and the threat of suicide, mental breakdown, or social ruin.

Insofar as these characters' significance derives from their place in the structure of the film, as opposed to their personal characteristics, they can appear two dimensional, less than fully formed. One of the three central characters often emerges as if from nowhere, as a stand-in to complete the triangular structure. Within the opening minutes of a film, a new teacher or new student is introduced to the school, or a suspicious stranger arrives to pry student and teacher apart. One of the most remarkable characteristics of this genre, however, is that its themes are not entirely novel, but instead present the redeployment of

## 22 The origins of the filmic teaching fantasy

ancient themes regarding eros and education within the contemporary expectations and moral norms of modern society and institutional schooling.

## Transference, Eros and education

The idea that pedagogical relationships are both fundamentally erotic, based on the student's fantasy of the teacher, and only properly educational if those desires go unfulfilled, appears at least as far back as Plato's *Symposium*, wherein a number of attractive younger men and learned older men gather to praise Eros, the god of love, experienced in its most familiar guise as human desire. That this common form of love easily becomes wildly diverse in its manifestations is demonstrated through various perspectives on Eros offered by the dialogue's speakers. As many commentators on the text have offered, part of the reason for Plato's acknowledgment of the variety and uncertainty in erotic pursuits is that the *Symposium* is intended to answer the daunting question of Alcibiades, the promising, beautiful youth who, despite impeccable upbringing by Pericles and tutelage by Socrates, went terribly wrong in his pursuit of greatness, contributing to the fall of Athens itself. Seeking a common thread that might explain the profound potential of human desire as well as its dangers, Plato provides an overarching theory by means of which all erotic types might be understood. Through a recounted conversation between Diotima and Socrates, Plato defines eros as a longing for what one lacks, and as a disordering awareness of one's own incompleteness through that longing. Plato illustrates his understanding through the men present in the dialogue who desire proximity to one another by virtue of what they lack: the old desire beauty and youth, and the young, knowledge and wisdom.

While the idea of mutual, asymmetrical attraction between teacher and student pre-exists their visibility in the *Symposium*, Plato upends traditional pederastic roles of older men pursuing beautiful boys through the dramatic device of Alcibiades' confession of love for Socrates. More than a simple transgression of pederastic norms, Plato's rewriting of pedagogy sets the student in erotic pursuit of what he lacks: a presumed end to learning in the position held by the teacher, at the far end of a curriculum that is nothing short of the sum total of social discourse. From the student's perspective, the teacher is not merely one with the law, in the sense of being completed by it, as one who needs the law to tell him what to do. As a subject presumed to know, the teacher stands beyond the law, in excess of its claims, understanding where the law applies and where it deserves to be broken.[1] The fantasy of the teacher's privileged place in relation to knowledge, what Freud and later, Lacan term *transference*, occasions the student's desire to complete herself through knowledge as well as the teacher's desire to be the occasion of the student's striving.[2]

Lacan's (1961, p. XI 14) oblique definition of transferential relationships, "Wherever there is a subject presumed to know there is transference," receives more extensive treatment in his seminar on the topic, in which Alcibiades' confession serves as the primary point of inquiry. Lacan's claim that the teacher's role involves seducing the student, getting him alone in order "to show him what he lacks" distills Alcibiades' story, in which Socrates appears as a lover, pretending to pursue young men, but then turns the tables, questioning his companions in such a manner that they feel "staggered and bewitched," unable to go on with their lives the way they have lived, and feel they must pursue Socrates as their teacher instead (215c–216a).[3]

Alcibiades is shocked at his own pursuit of Socrates, "as if I were the lover trying to seduce the beloved" (217c), and explains his disordering desires by claiming that Socrates is filled with divine images (215a–b) "so godlike, so golden, so beautiful and so utterly amazing," that they inspire "shame" in him such that "there was nothing for it but to do exactly what he told me" (217a). To illustrate his teacher's fullness with divine spirit, Alcibiades tells of Socrates' bravery during war, his immunity to drunkenness, imperviousness to cold, and his ability to stand still in contemplation throughout the course of an entire day (220a–221a).

Alcibiades' pursuit of Socrates reaches its climax in a failed attempt at seduction, wherein Alcibiades resorts to bluntly offering himself in exchange for Socrates' tutelage. Socrates' reply is equally direct: if his own wisdom is so great, why would he exchange it for mere physical satisfaction (218d–e)? Socrates participates in Alcibiades' fantasy, but not in a disingenuous or mocking spirit. As Lacan (1961, p. XI 14) claims, "The lure [of transference] is reciprocal," and requires both teacher and student to participate in the fantasy in order for it to have an effect. Plato tells the story of Alcibiades and Socrates at the distance of a number of narrative retellings, saving himself from the difficult and revealing task of judging whether he himself believed in Socrates' genius in the way he portrayed Alcibiades' belief.

Since Plato, pedagogical desire has largely followed the same terms spoken by Alcibiades: a student awakened to his own lack through the charismatic presence or enigmatic absence of a teacher whose outward differences suggest an inward genius or completion. The student strives toward this completion, first by getting close to the teacher through variously misguided approaches such as physical proximity, seduction, or mimicry—all of which are featured in the *Symposium*—and later through the self-abnegation of study that Alcibiades fails to undergo in order to become closer to the teacher in knowledge. While the student's desire is motivated by a fiction of the teacher's knowing, in most cases the poetic effect of the fantasy justifies the lie.

## Redeploying the erotic ideal in early school films

Eros as the basis for learning has become a fundamental premise of both high and low cultural attitudes toward education, and presents itself as a regular theme in popular representations of pedagogy. At the centre of these images

## 24 The origins of the filmic teaching fantasy

lies the fantasy of the teacher who, like Socrates, participates in a seduction of the student for the sake of the student's erotic striving toward greater self-realization. Never far from that seduction is the threat of corruption in the student's devotion to the teacher rather than to the ideas that the teacher has devoted himself. As Socrates spurns Alcibiades' advances in an attempt to set his erotic motivations on the right path, the fantasy of transference is often portrayed as an interrupted fantasy, limited by the very social laws that occasion pedagogical practice. In this manner, the audience can enjoy both the threat of transgression in the idea that the teacher and student might come together, while at the same time confident that this moment will never arrive, and both partners in the pedagogical relationship will each turn his attention toward more socially useful pursuits.

The earliest films depicting pedagogical relationships establish desire and fantasy at the heart of academic and social relationships, while at the same time presenting the idea that the most productive educational desires may not be the most acceptable within their given set of social norms. *Different from the Others* (1919) can be taken as a template, insofar as it presents a triangular relationship between three essential elements: an older teacher, the object of a young protégé's fantasy, and a suspicious and critical outsider representing the interested character of the law and social norms, who threatens the relationship.

### Different from the Others (1919)

*Different* tells the story of Paul Körner, a virtuosic violinist, and Kurt Sivers, an admiring musician, who never misses Körner's concerts. After one of these concerts, he approaches Körner with a request for an autograph. The two are shown side-by-side as their hands touch while exchanging a piece of paper. Immediately following, Körner is given another note from Sivers: a calling. As the latter enters, Körner sits at the piano and gestures for the youngster to come forward. Sivers expresses his passionate desire to be trained by Körner. When the teacher agrees by extending his hand to shake, the student uses both hands to hold that of the master. When Körner retracts his hand, Sivers' longingly remain.

Both musicians' families become concerned. Sivers' do not approve of his devotion to Körner, while the instructor's parents try to marry him off to a widow. Undeterred, the two grow closer. Körner even sends his parents to a medical expert who explains that homosexuality is not wrong, despite a German Provisional Code (Paragraph 175) stating that it is punishable. Linked and walking through the park, teacher and student bump into a sinister looking man walking the other way. After looking critically upon the couple, the man proceeds to follow them and comments suggestively, "Handsome lad."

Unhappy that Sivers pays little attention to anything but Körner, the student's parents forbid further contact. With his sympathetic sister Else acting as envoy, Sivers conveys his unwillingness to go on living to his teacher. Meanwhile, Körner is also paid a visit by the man from the park. Franz Bollek does not allow the butler to present a calling card, but instead gestures in the same manner Körner summoned Sivers—with a toss of the head—for the manservant to leave the room. Bollek—a representative of the oppressive law, turning its judgment for his own ends—demands and receives payment to keep the relationship a secret.

Körner himself then visits Sivers' parents and convinces them to allow the lessons to go on. Ecstatic, the student diligently practices for his first public recital. At Körner's home, Sivers relays a sealed letter from Bollek demanding more hush money. A concerned, but oblivious, Sivers watches as his teacher frantically rips up the letter. Körner, with his hand wrapped around his student's back, dismisses the matter as a trifling business concern. The two look into one another's eyes lovingly.

At a gay bar, Bollek reads Körner's refusal. After a successful recital featuring student and teacher, Bollek attempts to burglarize Körner's house. When Sivers discovers him, a fight breaks out. Sivers is overwhelmed, as is Bollek when Körner quickly arrives. Bollek discloses the nature of his relationship with Körner, stating that both he and Sivers are *being paid*. Körner attacks Bollek again and throws him out of the house. Körner attempts to hold and comfort Sivers, whose face displays shock, pain, and discomfort.

Humiliated, Sivers runs away from teacher and family. Despondent, Körner reflects on his past. As a student, Körner's attachment to another male student was frowned upon by their teacher and served as the basis for his expulsion. It is also revealed that Bollek has previously blackmailed Körner: the two first met at a gay dance hall; Körner brought Bollek home; the latter immediately demanded payment. When Körner warns Bollek that he is committing extortion, Bollek brings up Paragraph 175. Körner collapses, devastated, as Bollek grabs more money and exits.

Back in present time, Körner reports Bollek to the authorities, and in response, the blackmailer discloses the nature of the teacher-student relationship. While both men are found guilty of their respective crimes, the medical expert helps Körner receive a highly reduced sentence of one week. Nonetheless, the musician is broken internally, shunned by society, and loses work. Körner sees himself as one of many persecuted gay men, including Tchaikovsky, da Vinci and Oscar Wilde. Körner's father, speaking from the position of the law, offers only one "noble" solution: Körner swallows pills and commits suicide. Once apprised of the situation, Sivers returns. Again the two are linked, with the student's head atop his prone and dying master. Sivers decides against suicide only after the expert implores him to restore the honor of Körner and gain justice, turning his desires away from the intimacy of the lost relationship and toward a responsible, perhaps revolutionary engagement with the social order.

Two elements of the film stand out in the difference they introduce to the longstanding theme of erotic education. The first is the choice of setting the Platonic story in a social context in which homosexual acts are explicitly outlawed. As Pausanius' speech in the *Symposium* makes clear, there is no such

# 26    The origins of the filmic teaching fantasy

thing as a human relationship—even a purely physical one—that is not mediated in some way by the normative and prohibitive functions of social discourses. Here, as in Alcibiades' love for Socrates, the manifestation of desire in pursuit of the teacher produces danger as well as promise—a danger that the messenger might be taken as the object of desire, that the desire for the teacher might be fulfilled and the fantasy of the relationship, at odds with social norms, will place both teacher and student in danger. Surely, the more central message in *Different* is one of social critique, namely that laws such as Paragraph 175 ruin lives and encourage crimes such as extortion, but from the standpoint of Socrates' warning to Alcibiades about the *quid pro quo* exchange of beauty for wisdom, Körner's downfall and death also serve as a statement about the status of the teacher, whose identity depends upon his ability to maintain distance from his student as a way of both maintaining the student's desire and successfully returning the student to the world.

The danger educational eros poses carries over into filmic narratives in their representations of physical relationships between teacher and student as impossible or forbidden. Homosexuality becomes a filmic metaphor for forbidden pedagogical love, because of the place homosexuality holds in contemporary Western society, a site of both taboo and fascination. Like the homoerotic relationship throughout the history of Western culture, the teacher–student relationship fascinates and even inspires, but only insofar as the desire that drives it goes unconsummated, or at least remains hidden.

## Mikaël (1924)

*Different from the Others* (1919) is not very different from other early films addressing love between a teacher and student. *Vingarne* (1916) and *Mikaël* (1924) are both silent films based on the Danish novel by Herman Bang. *Mikaël* is more faithful to the story and title than its Swedish predecessor *Vingarne* (*The Wings*), which is largely lost. These films focus on the relationship between Claude Zoret, a successful painter, and Eugene Mikaël, his beautiful protégé and model. In Zoret's large and lavish studio, Mikaël loving displays the older master's sketches of Algiers, from their earlier time spent together. Upon learning how much they are worth, Mikaël wonders why they aren't sold. Zoret approaches the boy, who looks down, embarrassed. Zoret grabs his hair and shakes it, stating, "We do not sell our most beautiful memories."

In an expository conversation between Mikaël and the Duke de Monthieu, the young man recounts how he became the master's model and surrogate son and in telling their story, reinforces the strength of their bond to one another. Four years earlier, after assessing the youngster's art as lacking, Zoret instead invited him to model. Monthieu points out that the paintings of Mikaël established the master's fame, and that the two are indebted to one another. Just as Lacan diagnoses Socrates' and Alcibiades' relationship as a shared fantasy that works to lure both teacher and student, Monthieu's description of the

The origins of the filmic teaching fantasy   27

master and his model ties them together, not only through their desires for one another but through their desires to be regarded in a particular fashion.

As in *Different*, however, the fact that their tie is based in fantasy is brought to light through the interposition of a figure who represents the social order. Zoret had successfully deflected Mikaël's pragmatic question about the dollar value of their working relationship, reasserting the pricelessness of their fantasy in its place. But the arrival of Princess Lucia Zamikow serves as a stronger intrusion of the symbolic order that their intimate relationship had managed to exclude. Upon finding her calling card, Mikaël looks oddly in the direction of the master and announces aloud that yet another princess wants her portrait painted. "Perhaps you have a monopoly on modeling for the master?" asks Zoret's friend, the journalist Charles Switt, commenting on Mikaël's jealousy. The Princess's capacity to displace Mikaël as the privileged object of Zoret's fantasy similarly threatens to undermine Mikaël's devotion to his master. Situated between teacher and student, while retaining a privileged place in the world outside the horizon of their relationship, Zamikow's desire takes on an objective value much like the money that Zoret had dismissed, but much more difficult for either of the men to ignore. Zamikow becomes an object of desire for both of the men, not only because of her symbolic power but because of the way that her desires confirm for each of them what they had previously sought in one another's more intimate forms of recognition. Zamikow's desire for Zoret's gaze confers greatness upon the painter as Mikaël's devotion did, while Mikaël's jealousy at being displaced as Zoret's privileged object is soon quieted by the attention he receives from Zamikow.

Tensions in the relationship caused by the intrusion of this figure of supposed authority and power take the form of aesthetic deliberations and trade upon relationships between the seer and the seen, just as the politics of the *Symposium* turn on shifts in the relationship between the lover and beloved. At dinner, Zoret announces he will paint Caesar's death at the hand of his adopted son, Brutus. When Mikaël queries how Brutus will appear, he and Zoret glare at one another. After dinner, the Princess arrives. As Mikaël looks on, Zoret tells her he doesn't paint commissioned portraits, but then immediately changes his mind. She and Mikaël appear to smile at one another. The steward reveals to Switt that Zamikow is bankrupt. While Zoret and Mikaël show the Princess around the studio, she admires the nude male paintings, the subject of whom, in turn, admires her. When she leaves, Zoret strokes Mikaël's hair and gives him his "best" painting—*The Victor*, a nude that the Princess also esteems. Further, the master tells Mikaël he will eventually inherit everything, again returning the value of their relationship to its place in a social order of exchange.

Zoret has great difficulty with the portrait of the Princess. Switt is concerned, because the master is not sleeping, while Mikaël is out flirtatiously socializing. Obsessed with the commission, the master dismisses Switt and his insinuations. The Princess arrives to pose. Afterward, she and Zoret decide to

# 28 The origins of the filmic teaching fantasy

have dinner without waiting for Mikaël. The latter arrives, lovingly picks up Zamikow's gloves, then throws them down when he discovers he has been left out. Mikaël sorrowfully tells the steward he feels abandoned by the master.

Having returned to the studio, and with the Princess in pose, Zoret complains that it is "her eyes I cannot capture." The double meaning—the fact that her attention is turned toward his student—is not lost. When Mikaël enters, the apprentice is given the opportunity to surpass the master. As Mikaël paints, the camera cuts back and forth between the aspiring master and the Princess, focusing on their eyes as they gaze at one another. "Yes!" declares Zoret, "Now, it's her eyes. Only youth has the ability." The Princess and Mikaël look admiringly at one another. Once alone, they kiss.

As time progresses, Zoret has more difficulty seeing what's before his eyes: Switt informs him of the ongoing affair, but Zoret remains true to Mikaël, shifting his role from lover to father even as Mikaël repeatedly betrays his former mentor in favor of his new love. On his deathbed, after suffering the torments of losing Mikaël, Zoret declares, "Now I can die in peace because I have seen true love." But the love that he has seen is uncertain. Was it his own love for Mikaël? Mikaël's former love for him? Mikaël's current love for Zamikow? What is clear in the midst of this confusion of gaze, identity, and desire is that, as in *Different*, the private sphere of the teacher–student relationship in which the fantasy of the pedagogical relationship might be maintained, is burst by the intrusion of the world outside.

### *Mädchen in Uniform* (1931)

*Mikaël* reminds its audience of something that Plato's Socrates had already argued, namely that the pedagogical fantasy of transference has an end in the student turning away from the teacher and toward the world, filled with desire to create itself through its engagements in the world. But the pedagogical relationships in *Different* and *Mikaël* both seem doomed by the social order under which each couple struggles; neither offers a way out of the fantasy that spurs learning and into the world that the learning is supposed to reflect.

*Mädchen in Uniform* (1931), as one of the first films to transplant the erotic drama of pedagogy from the mentoring relationship that would have been more familiar to premodern societies into the schooling institutions of the modern world, introduces the possibility of the pedagogical fantasy serving students' success in negotiating their constituting social discourses without fundamentally changing the structure that *Mädchen* inherits from earlier films. The principal characters remain: an impossibly ideal teacher who serves as the object of fantasy for her students, a beautiful and erotically driven student who seeks to connect with her teacher, and a representative of the social order who seems determined to undermine the erotic connection that serves as a seamless signifier of transformative pedagogy. As with other films, the antagonist's judgment and her seemingly vicious attitude toward the erotic pedagogical

The origins of the filmic teaching fantasy    29

relationship help the audience to cheer on a relationship that might otherwise be cause for concern, given the differences in age, power, and knowledge that usually raise red flags with respect to teacher-student romances.

*Mädchen* also underscores the potential danger and secrecy of erotically charged educational relationships in a manner similar to other early films by portraying pedagogical relationships as homoerotic. Set in a girls' boarding school, *Mädchen* "has come to be seen as the first truly radical lesbian film," (Pendergast and Pendergast, 2000, p. 721) the central relationship being between a striking student, Manuela von Meinhardis, and her charismatic teacher, Fräulein von Bernburg.

After Manuela von Meinhardis' mother dies, she is enrolled in a boarding school for the daughters of military officers. Upon meeting her peers, Manuela is warned not to fall in love with Fräulein von Bernburg, a teacher who kisses the girls goodnight but whose moods are mercurial: "One minute she looks at you terribly. Then, all of a sudden, she is very kind, almost uncomfortably so." Indeed, when Manuela encounters Bernburg on the stairs, the warnings play out. "Show me how you look," demands the teacher as she twirls Manuela around, inspects her from head to foot, touching the girl's hair and arms. "I demand absolute discipline."

So too does the school's scowling Headmistress who believes "discipline and hunger" are the best educators. However, when Bernburg finds forbidden student communiqués, rather than report or even read them, she destroys the evidence and delivers only a gentle warning. "I try to be a friend to the children," she explains to a less than understanding headmistress. "How do you maintain authority?" questions the headmistress, "You are their superior and must keep your distance."

Bernburg is not always able. All the students love Bernburg and explicitly discuss their attraction. Manuela, however, receives a promise of fulfillment in the actions and thoughts of her teacher, who discusses the girl at faculty meetings and comforts her in her new school surroundings. Writing about *Mädchen*, Richard Dyer (1990, p. 57) observes:

> The good-night kiss, a maternal ritual, is portrayed with the cinema's conventions for the representation of erotic love: "halo" lighting of the loved one, soft shadows to create romantic atmosphere, the isolation (even, as here, in a dormitory) of the participants through editing and lighting, the extreme close-up on the kiss, itself the supreme signifier of love.

Bernburg visits each student's bed, delivering bedtime kisses on each girl's forehead. When it's Manuela's turn, the girl passionately throws her arms around her teacher, who responds by drawing Manuela's arms down around her waist. Bernburg then lifts Manuela's chin, kisses her solemnly on the mouth, then turns her head and quickly leaves the room while Manuela looks on, brimming with happiness. Bernburg's classroom repeats the actions of the dormitory bedroom

## 30 The origins of the filmic teaching fantasy

as a student recites a biblical passage, "Oh that I had a thousand tongues and a thousand mouths," and the teacher's face is intercut with Manuela's.

Upon learning that Manuela's underskirt is tattered, Bernburg provides one of her own. Thankful and tearful, Manuela is encouraged to admit her feelings. "I love you so, but you're distant," sobs Manuela, who also admits to being competitive for her teacher's attention. Bernburg responds negatively, calling Manuela's ideas "silly" and telling the fourteen-year-old to calm down and display control. But just as quickly, the teacher's tone shifts: she asks Manuela to be more a "friend" and less a "young girl." Bernburg explains that she thinks of Manuela often but must not make the other students jealous. Manuela is relieved and elated. Bernburg's underskirt becomes a symbol of their secret: an object of utmost intimacy that is always present, always hidden, and never shared, because to bring it to light alone invites scandal.

Manuela is also inspired by her recognized but unfulfillable desire; she is cast to play the leading role in Don Carlos. The Schiller play revolves around a love triangle: a prince's betrothed is instead married to his father. The triangulation in the play serves as an imperfect mirror to the triadic structure of the film. If Manuela is Don Carlos, and Bernburg her betrothed, then the looming betrayal promised by the play is not only that the headmistress might step in to separate the two but that Bernburg, because of her institutional position as a teacher, was always already tied to the authority of the school, and never actually available as the fantasied love interest her students took her to be. As a result, Manuela's concerns nervously revolve around Bernburg's response to her performance. After being told she is delightful, Manuela—drunk on celebratory punch—overflows with her anxiety about her connection to Bernburg and announces to her peers that she is wearing her teacher's underskirt. The headmistress overhears the disclosure and forbids Manuela from socializing with the others. In response, Bernburg defends her chosen student to the headmistress—"What you call sins, I call the great spirit of love in all its forms"—but also tells Manuela they can have no further contact, stating, "You're not allowed to love me so much."

True to her place as an impossible fantasy of student longing, Bernburg resigns her post, telling the headmistress she cannot tolerate the draconian environment. Don Carlos has not lost her betrothed to the king, but has nonetheless lost her for good. Crestfallen, Manuela attempts suicide by jumping from the top of a multi-storied staircase. When she faints, unable to go through with the annihilation of her desires, her classmates rescue her. As Bernburg reproaches the principal with words, the students do the same with their condemning looks. The headmistress descends the steps, to the darkness below.

In a break from *Different* and *Mikaël* that will be repeated in later films, *Mädchen* does not allow the symbolic order to fully win out over the lovers and remain unchanged. While Bernburg and Manuela will likely part ways, the fall of the headmistress and the restrictive rules that she represents initiates a new theme in school films, in which an unresolved promise of unruliness and transgression brings the film to a close, leaving the audience to imagine what social

The origins of the filmic teaching fantasy    31

order will come to pass now that the oppressive regime has been conquered. The question arises as inevitable, because of the way that school rules are portrayed as a necessary hindrance to pedagogical love throughout the history of film. If fantasy begets eros and desire is the essence of educational growth, the symbolic order retains an essential place in pedagogy if only because it must come under question in order to foster student striving.

## La Maternelle (1933)

Tracing the lineage that has derived the recognizable image of the filmic teacher–student relationship from its roots in Platonic philosophy, we can note that *Mikaël* returns the focus of the pedagogical relationship, albeit tragically, to its fruition in the student's return to the world in a way that is only suggested by the end of *Different*. *Mädchen*, in bringing educational eros into the institutional structure of the school, not only furthers the idea that the erotic relationship upon which education is founded should prepare the youth for the social world, but also demonstrates that the social world must regularly change and find its authorities cast down in order for the future of society to be realized. *La Maternelle* (1933) takes us another step further, insofar as the age difference between teacher and student portrayed in this film is such that the threat of a consummated erotic relationship is unimaginable. Instead, we are left with the idea that the erotic element of education exists entirely on the part of the student, and that the teacher's purpose is to exist as a safe, nurturing object upon which the student might project her desires. In short, through *Maternelle*, we arrive at the ideal teacher we are accustomed to seeing on the screen: a teacher who reduplicates the student's fantasy by seeming to stand somewhere beyond desire.

Some background scenes in *Maternelle* establish the motivations and character of the teacher at the center of the narrative. At a ballroom, Rose—an attractive, petite blonde dressed in white—dances with a male partner. When she sits down, he places a ring on her finger. In the next cut, Rose is seated again, but she wears one glove, which, like her garb, is black. She is being interviewed by a homely female school superintendent for the post of children's maid, a position that involves maintenance of the building and also the care of the children. The superintendent notes that Rose's father has recently died, leaving her bankrupt, and that her fiancé has left her as a result. Rose has been abandoned by the men that define her, but by that fact is also free from the patriarchal norms of her class. Cut off from a male presence that would give her an authentic place within the patriarchal order, Rose is positioned from the start as one who is, in a sense, disordered and searching for reinscription within the world. She is hired on the spot, against protests issued over the phone from a Dr. Libois, her boss, who would prefer his protégé to be hired instead.

Before Rose enters the school on her first day, the seasoned head maid, Madame Paulin, is already busy washing the floors. Marie Coeuret, a young

## 32 The origins of the filmic teaching fantasy

girl, arrives, and Paulin asks judgmentally if Marie's mother has turned her out of the house again, setting the stage for a reading of the student as abandoned and judged by social discourses in much the way Rose has been. Idly waiting for the school day to begin, Marie notices a mouse caught live in a trap, admires it, and begs Paulin, futilely, not to kill it. The child identifies with the unwanted vermin of the school, but seeks to be recognized in the same compassionate way she relates to the mouse.

When Rose first enters school for work and takes off her outdoor clothes, Marie lifts Rose's gloves to her face in much the same manner as the former fiancé held Rose's hand for a kiss. Other children arrive, as well as supervisor Dr. Libois. He expresses dissatisfaction with Rose's hire, while she scrubs the classroom floors. Rose supports his accusation of clumsiness by accidently spilling water on him; however, Libois's scowl is transformed into a smile when she laughs.

Marie comments to classmates on Rose's beauty, then purposely dirties her face so that Rose, alone in the bathroom, can wash her. Marie admits to being lonely and asks, "Don't you ever kiss the children?" Rose shakes her head no, but—like Libois—quickly shifts tone. She kneels, lifts Marie's chin and places a long kiss alongside the child's lips. The camera sits level with the two faces, placing the two on the same level. Afterward, Rose grasps and adjusts the child's shoulders, demanding that Marie "hold [herself] straight." In the courtyard, Paulin tells Rose to be aware of Marie, who is described as stubborn, antisocial, and of a general bad character. Furthermore, it is disclosed that Marie's mother is a prostitute.

Fulfilling Paulin's warning, a subsequent scene takes place in a barroom, where Marie's mother flirts with a john while Marie sits and scowls. When the man follows them into the street, Marie is sent home alone. In the morning, Madame Coeuret returns only to grab her handbag, kiss her sleeping daughter on the forehead and depart for good. In the classroom, the superintendent explains to Rose that the john is wanted by the police. Rose is asked to accompany Marie home; when she cannot find Marie's mother, Rose takes the girl back to her own apartment. Once there, she gives Marie a nightshirt, carries her to bed, and kisses the girl's forehead.

At school, Marie announces that she sleeps at Rose's. The female superintendent is outraged and summons Dr. Libois. When he questions Rose, her explanation is both selfless and selfish: "I felt I had a duty toward Marie, and I am all alone myself." Libois, though doubtful of the arrangement, is nonetheless sympathetic, commenting that Rose is still an idealist. Marie is less than that: she openly expresses displeasure when classmates receive Rose's attention and attacks one child.

Rose's unorthodox ways are further evidenced when a famous and respected professor visits. In a classroom experiment, a rabbit is presented to the children. They are told the animal will later be eaten. Though the school goes to great lengths to select an experienced teacher to lead the class, Rose accidently takes

The origins of the filmic teaching fantasy   33

over and greatly impresses the professor with her ability to elicit genuine feeling from the children. Despite the professor's accolades, the superintendent is aghast. Compounding matters, it is revealed that Rose holds a college degree, making her overqualified to be a children's maid.[4] Rose is told to resign, but a sympathetic and smitten Dr. Libois reverses the decision.

Marie becomes increasingly jealous, both of her classmates and especially of Dr. Libois. As the two adults grow closer, Marie comments, "Rose doesn't notice me anymore." After Marie witnesses Rose's acceptance of marriage, the child runs home only to be told that her mother "went far away on a boat." Marie then heads to the docks, where she sees a couple kissing on a boat's bow. In the water, the reflected image dissolves and reforms into a montage of other couples, including Rose and Dr. Libois, Marie's mother and the john. The child violently spits and hurls rocks into the water, attempting to dispel the visions and thus destroy the unions. Whether by choice or exhaustion, she too tumbles in.

From this melodramatic climax, the film comes to a quick and overly convenient ending. Marie is rescued by the man on the boat and brought back to the school, to the care of Madame Paulin and Dr. Libois. Paulin had previously encouraged Libois in his patriarchal function, saying, "You've taken Rose— now you must take care of Marie." Paulin instructs him to reach out to Marie and he does: as Marie admiringly looks on, Libois frees a trapped mouse, demonstrating the same compassion she had begged Paulin to show at the outset of the film. Libois then extends his hand to Marie in friendship and is received. Rose enters and questions the child about her tumble into the Seine. When no answer is forthcoming, she adjusts Marie, reminding her to stand straight. They smile and embrace.

## The end of school

*La Maternelle* begins and ends with a proposal of marriage; it is a tightly crafted film that is poetically bookended. Unlike many films related to teachers and students, *La Maternelle* ends happily. Orphaned Marie now has a family. Her prostitute mother is replaced by the beloved Rose, a caring school maid who wins the hearts of children and educators alike. Rose, abandoned at the outset by her fiancée, is to be wed to the school's handsome supervisor and medic, Dr. Libois.

If it is not a marriage made in heaven, or even in Hollywood, it is nonetheless tightly structured. The storyline in *La Maternelle* is neatly wrapped up, a present for audience members to take home: all is well; all is resolved. The reason for this happy resolution, compared to other school films made at the same time, is that the problematic desires expressed between teacher and student as the basis of their relationship are resolved into a non-erotic, maternal love. Transformed by Dr. Libois as the authoritative, if somewhat unsympathetic presence that succeeds in providing Rose with an acceptable social role for a

## 34 The origins of the filmic teaching fantasy

woman, he also makes her eligible to provide motherly love, rather than simply engage Marie in her professionally oriented desires.

There are rarely complete resolutions in films concerning teachers and students, because often the charged nature of the central relationship is unresolvable. In *Mädchen in Uniform*, the overbearing and hated headmistress is defeated. But if she is out of the equation, what will transpire between Manuela and Fräulein von Bernburg? In a sense, their love requires an impediment in order to give it meaning: the headmistress, representing social norms, is not only the embodiment of an interdiction on teacher-student relationships, she also represents the body of beliefs and knowledge that stands between student and teacher - the curriculum, that the student is supposed to traverse in order to achieve the knowledge and authority she supposes to reside in the person of the teacher. Without this character, occupying one of three vertices in the pedagogical triangle described above, we are left with a single, straight line connecting student and teacher, with nothing to talk about but themselves.

The films discussed above identify some of the many forms that the jealous superego character takes in school films—the insensitive headmistresses, spiteful students, uncaring educators—who threaten the pedagogical relationship through accusation, interdiction, and sometimes extortion. At the same time that these unlikable characters provide antagonism in the narrative, they also take on the unlovely necessity of judging the appropriateness of the erotic pedagogical relationship, freeing the audience to enjoy the titillating possibility of transgression unfolding before their eyes.

Even in early films that seem to break with the traditional arrangement of heroic teacher, a student moved by desire, the triangular relationship between teacher, student, and the norms of social discourse repeats itself. In *Rope* (1948), discussed in fuller detail in Chapter 8, a teacher finds himself trapped within his students' horrific attempt to bring his lessons to life. The distorting mirror that the students' actions hold to both their teacher's lessons and his authority leads him to break from his role as teacher as the one presumed to know, destroying the fantasy of transference that has become a nightmare and instead taking the place of the moral watchdog, in this case alerting the police by firing a pistol out into the night sky.

*Lolita* (1962)—another early twist on the theme of desire and education—also ends with shots fired, as Humbert Humbert murders Clare Quilty, similarly drawing the judgment of the law like daylight into a feverish nightmare. Just as teacher and students mirror each other in *Rope*, Humbert and Quilty serve as mirrors to one another's desires in *Lolita*, each serving as moral judge of the other's erotic attachment to the girl. As Humbert travels across the country with Lolita—his adopted daughter, former student, and current lover—Quilty stalks them, threatening to draw attention to the fact that, unlike *Maternelle*, Humbert's adoption of the object he desires has not legitimated their relationship or erased the problematic erotic motivations that brought them together. Quilty too is Lolita's teacher and also becomes her lover, and yet even while he attempts to interrupt Humbert's fantasy, he nonetheless emerges as more of a monster, if only because we know more about Humbert's tragic history. While Humbert conveniently dispatches his primary relationship to the social order with two words (picnic, lightning) the love that defines him as an adult in all of his unforgivable, monstrous abuse of power is a childhood infatuation left unresolved by the death of his beloved.

Later films participate in the same erotic educational tradition while adapting their interpretations of both the promise and the peril of eros to their local historical circumstances. In *The Paper Chase* (1973), the characters of Professor Charles W. Kingsfield Jr. and his daughter Susan Fields compete and compliment each other as erotic objects for James T. Hart, whose feelings for the two are as inseparable as their filial bond. When Hart becomes aware of the relationship between his two loves, he sits in class gazing at his professor as he might be expected to look at his lover, aware of the confusion of his own aims, but totally uninterested in separating the two. In *To Sir, With Love* (1967), the threat of a relationship between teacher, Mark Thackeray, and student, Pamela Dare, is the talk of the teachers' lounge. "She's obviously in love with you," Thackeray is told by his principal, "You shouldn't be surprised." More recently, *Dead Poets Society* (1989), *All Things Fair* (1995), *Rushmore* (1998), *Election* (1999), *The Piano Teacher* (2001), *The History Boys* (2006), and *La Robe du Soir* (2009) have presented problematic and promising erotic relationships between students and teachers.

Yet while the recognition of an erotic element to pedagogy has always included the threat of sexuality as one of many ways in which the teacher-student relationship might break down, theorists and filmmakers alike continue to celebrate teachers and students as lovers who long for one another across the distance of the curriculum. One way in which films accomplish the celebration of pedagogical love, despite its illicit potential, involves introducing a villainous antagonist identified with the discursive and moral order of the school, who opposes the desire between the teacher and student as dangerous. In *Mädchen in Uniform*, the fascistic headmistress stands against the nurturing love of von Bernburg and Manuela, demanding a permanent separation between the two. As with other films, the enemy suffers defeat, in this case her downfall illustrated by being cast down the steps. In *The Browning Version* (1951), the teacher's jealous wife, who paints the student's love as an act of manipulation, finally separates from her husband, leaving him to return to his love of study.

The presence of these antagonists ensures that audiences do not judge teacher-student erotic relationships as they typically might, but instead condemn those who would challenge the love between teacher and student. Judgments are instead placed on the villain, assuring that the danger they perceive reflects their own degraded nature and crooked perspective; the audience's interest, by contrast, derives from wholesome pedagogical motives. The idealized teacher in these fantasies, after all, supposedly stands safely beyond desire, in a state of completeness, as a goal for the student's striving. Instructed by the structure of

# 36 The origins of the filmic teaching fantasy

the film to revile those characters who suspect the erotic character of student-teacher relationships, the audience is simultaneously compelled to yearn for unions condemned in real life. In a similar fashion, films celebrate transgressions of repressive school rules when they are carried out by a heroic schoolteacher who has already been granted the status of knowing what rules may be broken for the sake of learning. In the following chapters, we consider various permutations of these filmic structures, playing upon cultural beliefs about heroic, knowing teachers, students' erotic motivations, and the staid social norms that drive pedagogical relationships by standing in the way of their fulfillment.

## Notes

1 For a fuller account of this educational model based on the student's desire in relation to the transferential figure of the teacher, see Felman, 1982; Brooke, 1987; Davis, 1987; Stillwaggon, 2006, 2008.
2 The teacher, after all, was once a student, and therefore still holds on to the myth of the teacher as one who knows (Britzman, 1986).
3 Citations of Plato by Stephanus numbers refer to Hamilton and Cairns (eds) (1961).
4 In a terrifically humorous moment, head maid Paulin explains to a needful child that "She [Rose] can't help you; she is a college graduate!"

## References

*All Things Fair*, Bo Widerberg, dir. (Sweden: Per Holst Filmproduktion, 1995).
Britzman, D. (1986) Cultural myths in the making of a teacher: Biography and social structure in teacher education. *Harvard Educational Review*, 56(4), 442–456.
Brooke, R. (1987) Lacan, transference, and writing instruction. *College English*, 49(6), 679–691.
*The Browning Version*, Anthony Asquith, dir. (United Kingdom: Javelin Films, 1951).
Davis, R. C. (1987) Pedagogy, Lacan, and the Freudian subject. *College English*, 49(7), 749–755.
*Dead Poets Society*, Peter Weir, dir. (USA: Touchstone Pictures, 1989).
*Different from the Others*, Richard Oswald, dir. (Germany: Richard-Oswald-Produktion, 1919).
Dyer, R. (1990). *Now You See It: Studies on Lesbian and Gay Film*. London: Routledge.
*Election*, Alexander Payne, dir. (USA: Paramount Picture, 1999).
Felman, S. (1982) Psychoanalysis and education: Teaching terminable and interminable. *Yale French Studies*, (63), 21–44.
Hamilton, E. and Cairns, H. (eds) (1961). *The Collected Dialogues of Plato, Including the Letters*. New York: Pantheon Books.
*The History Boys*, Nicholas Hytner, dir. (United Kingdom: Fox Searchlight Pictures, 2006).
Lacan, J. (1961) *The Seminar of Jacques Lacan: Transference VIII 1960–1961* (C. Gallagher, trans.). Available at karnacbooks.com.
*Lolita*, Stanley Kubrick, dir. (USA: Metro-Goldwyn-Mayer, 1962).
*Mädchen in Uniform*, Leontine Sagan, dir. (Germany: Deutsche Film-Gemeinschaft, 1931).
*La Maternelle* (*Children of Montmartre*), Jean Benoit-Lévy, dir. (France: Photosonor, 1933).
*Mikaël*, Carl Dreyer, dir. (Denmark: Universum Film (UFA), 1924).

The origins of the filmic teaching fantasy   37

*The Paper Chase*, James Bridges, dir. (USA: 20th Century Fox, 1973).

Pendergast, T. and Pendergast, S. (2000) *International Dictionary of Films and Filmmakers*, fourth ed. Detroit, MI: St. James.

*The Piano Teacher*, Michael Haneke, dir. (France: Arte France Cinema, 2001).

*La Robe du Soir*, Myriam Aziza, dir. (France: Mille et Une Productions, 2009).

*Rope*, Alfred Hitchcock, dir. (USA: Warner Bros, 1948).

*Rushmore*, Wes Anderson, dir. (USA: American Empirical Pictures, 1998).

Stillwaggon, J. (2006). Don't stand so close to me: Distance in pedagogical relationships. *Philosophy of Education 2006*. Urbana, IL: Philosophy of Education Society, pp. 119–126.

Stillwaggon, J. (2008) Performing for the students: Teaching identity and the pedagogical relationship. *Journal of Philosophy of Education*, 42(1), 67–83.

*To Sir, With Love*, James Clavell, dir. (United Kingdom: Columbia Pictures, 1967).

*Vingarne*, Mauritz Stiller, dir. (Sweden: Svenska Biografteatern AB, 1916).

*Whiplash*, Damien Chazelle, dir. (USA: Bold Films, 2014).

# Chapter 3

# Law, school

## Impossible relationships in the ideal case

Scholars analyzing the teacher-student relationship as portrayed in popular media invariably focus their attention on *To Sir, With Love* (1967) (Dalton, 2004; Keroes, 1999). The film's appeal draws from its emphasis on close teacher-student relations: little formal schooling takes place despite its educational setting and characters. As in the many films that it follows and those that follow its lead, *To Sir, With Love* replaces the "three R's" with romance and transforms the task of education into an interpersonal exchange of sincere beliefs and tastes. The popularity of *To Sir, With Love*, as well as the regular repetition of its character types and themes in dozens of school films, draws attention to the paradoxical place of teachers in the popular imaginary. On the one hand, the teacher is clearly a representative, even an enforcer, of those social laws and bodies of knowledge reproduced in schools. On the other, evidenced by the films discussed in Chapter 2, films set in schools regularly convey the message that the good teacher questions and resists all the expected behaviors of her social milieu and seeks personal connections with students rather than opportunities to indoctrinate the young into norms of social continuity.

While no one would deny that connections between teachers and students are fundamental to learning, and while many theorists have identified some kind of love as the basis of any good teaching, the paradoxical position of the filmic teacher as both authority and transgressive seducer begs the question of what kind of love, if any, serves education. Further, these portrayals of pedagogy beg the question of our unspoken pedagogical beliefs and expectations from the fact that we so often portray teachers and students as unconsummated lovers (hooks, 1994; Frank, 1995; Gallop, 1997; Todd, 1997; Fried, 2003). In this chapter, we look at the structures of pedagogical relations that educe desires between teacher and student in an effort to understand the problematic images of teachers and students in films as well as these images' possible contributions to teaching practices. Following those theorists who claim that the filmic commonplace of the teacher-as-lover reflects an underlying erotic charge in our social expectations of educational relationships, we might question where this charge originates in the educational relationship as an available normative structure. In other words, if artistic images can help us to see the conditions of possibility at play in the work of teaching, how can we understand teaching identity not in the erotic longing of particular teachers and students, but in the relational structures that condition and regulate students' and teachers' desires?

The great strength of *To Sir, With Love* is that it convinces audiences and censors alike that the erotic aims of the pedagogical relationships it portrays have not been realized. Despite Mr. Thackeray's sustained campaign of breaking with standard curriculum and school tradition, his brand of transgression stops short of fulfilling the romantic expectations that he incites in Pamela Dare, his top student, and in his audience. Whether Thackeray is aware of it or not, however, his transgressive, intimately personal approach to pedagogy only serves to mask a more fundamental erotic relationship that he sustains less in his classroom rebellion than in the fantasy that he represents for his students: the worldly success that they cannot imagine themselves or their families to be.

Yet while the romantic and "purely" erotic aspects of pedagogical relationships in *To Sir* can be distinguished, they cannot be finally separated. We accept the idea that, in the end, we cannot show desire except by manifesting it in a few, fairly clumsy approximations of desire as an awareness of one's own lack. In order to explore erotic longing as a fundamental motivation invested in the structures of educational practice, rather than in the negation of these structures through transgressive interpersonal connections, we consider a film in which the teacher–student relationship is stripped of those explicitly romantic and rebellious attributes that signify a personal connection between teacher and student. *The Paper Chase* (1973) does not have a socially sanctioned object of affection as its authority figure; neither does it feature any personal proximity or romantic connection between teacher and student. What it does present is a fundamentally erotic relationship between an authorized master and a yearning novice, mediated entirely by the formal curriculum of the school and the pedagogical roles defined within it. Framed by linguistic and curricular rather than intersubjective and intimate points of reference, desire emerges in *The Paper Chase* as the entry point for student subjectivity in the student's relation to the law, made possible through the teacher's authority.

## The teacher chase

Desire between teachers and students in *To Sir, With Love* (1967)—an idealized fantasy of teacher-student relationships in the swinging sixties—is immediate and obvious. Within minutes of the opening credits, after new teacher Mark Thackeray (Sidney Poitier) has survived a city bus ride in which he has been taken as a potential sexual object for a number of white, working class women, who attempt to engage him in a discussion of their marital engagements, he literally collides into student Pamela Dare as he attempts to navigate his new school. Off-balance, they hold each other in the hallway as teenage boys and girls look on and cackle. This first awkward physical connection will repeat

## 40 Impossible relationships in the ideal case

itself at another level in the film's finale as teacher and student dance heatedly together during the graduation party while the entire school body excitedly applauds, again cheering on the union of teacher and student across differences of age, race, class, and culture as signifiers of the more fundamental difference between their institutional roles and the impossibility of intimacy from within these roles. In *To Sir, With Love*, everybody knows about and comments upon Thackeray and Dare's relationship. "She's obviously in love with you Mark," claims Grace Evans, the Deputy Head of North Quay School, "You shouldn't be surprised."

Neither would anyone be surprised at the scenes that follow Thackeray and Dare's first interaction. Even by *To Sir*'s release in 1967, a requisite "inner city" expository formula seems to have been established, involving exterior and interior shots of the school with mobs of unruly, vaguely threatening youth crowding the schoolyards and hallways. An overburdened, well-meaning bureaucracy, a classroom of indifferent students, and a faculty lounge filled with callous, burned-out veteran teachers completes the generic picture to which Poitier had already contributed as a disaffected youth in *Blackboard Jungle* (1955), and which continues, 60 years later, as a shorthand for middle class concerns about the poor.

What is surprising, despite a thoroughly obvious opening involving students' half-hearted reading out of textbooks, decontextualized lessons about global economy, and increasingly brutal pranks that Thackeray does his best to take in stride, is the turning point in the film, which centers on the burning of what appears to be a menstrual pad on the radiator of the classroom. This strange prank leads to Thackeray's sole outburst. Dismissing the young men from the room, he condemns the young women's:

> foul language . . . crude behavior and . . . sluttish manner. There are certain things a decent woman keeps private, and only a filthy slut would have done this . . . that disgusting object had better be removed and the windows opened to clear away the stench. If you must play these filthy games, do them in your homes, and not in my classroom!

Thackeray expels himself from the classroom to suffer out loud in the staff room, calling his students "devils incarnate" and almost immediately turning around, recognizing that they are "just kids." Suddenly, he is resolved to change not only his pedagogy but his entire curriculum. Returning to the classroom, he neatly stacks the books then throws them roughly in the trash, exciting the interest of the class:

> Those are out; they are useless to you. I suddenly realized that you are not children, that you will be adults in a few weeks, with all the responsibilities that that implies, so for now on you will be treated as such by me and by each other . . . We are just going to be reasonable with one another, we are just going to talk, you and I.

The scene is immediately grasped as a forfeiture of the academic lessons that would normally occasion the pedagogical relationship but here have no real mediating value. An easy and common reading of the scene suggests that Thackeray realizes the courage to engage his students on a personal level, and that he succeeds throughout the rest of the film by continually returning to this risky wager. But what, exactly, does Thackeray have to offer the students at this personal level? The scant clues delivered by the film suggest that he is a somewhat broken, unrealized person, unsuccessful in his attempts to find employment in his field and geographically adrift. The only glimmer of a personal life the film provides is of Thackeray in his bathrobe, ironing his white work shirt before a shabby pantry of a few canned goods. While Evans describes him in glowing terms: "handsome, intelligent, clean, big, brawn," Thackeray's value as a person has already been undercut by a series of racist comments from his most cynical colleague, Mr. West, who refers to him in their first meeting as a "lamb for the slaughter, or should I say black sheep?" and later tells him to use "black magic" and "voodoo" if he is to succeed in controlling his class. Even Thackeray's students judge his color: one student compares Thackeray to his black father, who ruined his white mother's life by marrying her; another expresses amazement at Thackeray's red blood when the teacher throws himself in front of a piece of shrapnel flung at one of his students. The problem of black masculinity has been noted and subtly reinforced by Keroes (1999, p. 75) who claims:

> If Poitier's strength is unquestioned, his sexuality is always under restraint, at once muted and insisted upon by his identity as both a black man and a teacher-father figure . . . The pressure to suppress it is therefore doubly strong. Poitier's ineradicable sexuality is always contained.

Keroes slips beyond the personalization of the teacher to the fantasy that the audience maintains with respect to the actor in describing the racial tensions of the film. In doing so, she repeats much of the anxiety and attendant titillation of filmgoers in watching a black man make claims over white female bodies. But she also shows us that this highly personal reading cannot account for the transformation of the classroom that Thackeray realizes in suspending the curriculum. If everything depended upon Thackeray's persona, the class could easily reject him, as they did his predecessor, who, we learn, sought to be popular with the students.

At only a slight distance from the common, but problematic, reading of Thackeray's success as a matter of intersubjective connection, however, we might instead posit the idea that it is not Thackeray's personality, but the fact that he stands at the front of the classroom in a suit and tie that gives him the authority to throw the books into the garbage and decide that the students need to know *his* views on "life, survival, death, sex, marriage, rebellion." The moment of his emergence as a subject presumed to know comes when some things he happens to know meet up with their desires as young people. But the fact that the

## 42 Impossible relationships in the ideal case

students look to Thackeray as an authority on life, rather than to the housewives on the bus in the first scene who clearly know something about the themes his new curriculum covers, is only a function of his profession. Thackeray's role as an exception to his students' expectations depends upon a structure that is partially obscured by his charismatic presence.

In Thackeray's new curriculum, we learn that "no man likes a slut for long" and that clean clothes and bodies are considered attractive by women. Pamela, while tidying up Thackeray's desk, assumes domestic role play: "a woman's work is never done." In the film's celebration of the teacher's ability to relate to his students and teach them "life lessons," the teacher's responsibility to instruct according to the demands of the school has been quickly forgotten. In films that have followed the model set by *To Sir, With Love*, a similar relationship emerges, splitting student desires from subject matter: frustrated by a lifeless curriculum and apathetic, unruly students, the teacher seems to step outside his institutional role and become a personal figure in students' lives, saving students and teacher alike from their state of apathy through sheer charisma and personal sacrifice. Thackeray's deviation from norms of teacher behavior therefore poses no obstacle to his recognizability as a popular image of teaching: on the contrary, his is perhaps the most common image of filmic teaching identity we have and a likely point of identification and inspiration for many new teachers. The only problem with this identification is that it ignores the relational structure upon which Thackeray's deviation continues to depend, even in its performance of rebellion against that structure.

Thackeray can rail against his role: punching one student, dancing with another, throwing textbooks in the garbage, and yet remain recognizable as a teacher to his students and the audience alike, because the weight of his institutional role counterbalances his individualistic rebelliousness. In the culminating scene of the film, a party where Thackeray and Dare dance heatedly, they never touch—a reminder of the institutional forces that both restrain and constitute the desirous relationship between teacher and student. Some part of Thackeray's identity as a teacher, even as a fictional teacher, is already at play in the public's imagination of educational relationships, and serves to ground our understanding of what he does as respectable and pedagogical even when it threatens to cross the line.

At the party, Pamela makes a request for a ladies' choice dance. With drum and bass beating out a dramatic rhythm, the camera closes in on Pamela's face as she proceeds to close in on Thackeray. The floor clears as Pamela—hand on hip—sways back and forth to the music, with her teacher following suit. The tempo increases as lyrics are introduced:

It's hard not to think about you,
to keep you off my mind.
It's hard to live in the world without you.
And it's getting harder all the time.

Thackeray elevates his dance, twirling and shaking. Faculty and students nod approvingly and clap; so too does Pamela. Student and teacher imitate each others' gestures; the tempo alternating between slow and fast. As the dance comes to a close, Pamela leans in with open mouth, and the camera focus blurs. Although neither dancer touches the other, the dance is unabashedly carnal.

In the end, the two hold each other's hands. "Can I come and see you sometimes, you know next term?" Pam asks. With mixed emotions, a sweaty Sir states that he won't be back at the school; he has been offered a lucrative engineering position. "The dance signals the end of their relation as teacher and student (that's why they can dance at all), but the film acknowledges that this is a connection not easily severed," comments Keroes (1999, p. 79). "Once she graduates, Sir can tell 'Pamela,' as opposed to 'Miss Dare,' that 'she will be a knockout,' and the scene can conclude with a long, soulful farewell, filled with unspoken desire, a longing that must, of course, remain unfulfilled." Thackeray comments, "The whole world's waiting for you; you're a smasher." What Keroes also fails to report is that the film concludes with Thackeray tearing up the acceptance letter and not, ostensibly, because of Pamela. Rather, his second thoughts about leaving teaching come about when a teenage couple crashes rudely into his classroom, the young man announcing, "I'm in your bleeding class next term." The audience approves Thackeray's commitment to reforming another group of hooligans, while at the same time wondering if his trick of playing the exception to the very institutional rules that establish his authority can work again, now that he has officially foreclosed his other professional identity.

Thackeray's role as a teacher and his authority among his students is ultimately anchored by his place within the school's institutional order through his rejection of it and his establishment of himself as an exception to that order. Yet while his authority is dependent upon the structure of order it rejects, his personal charisma serves to obscure his dependence upon the established order of educational relation that gives it credence. In turning to Thackeray the rebellious individual, the lover, as a model of teacher identity, what we miss is an understanding of that educational and erotic order—visible in curricular constraints, classroom discipline, and the asymmetry of teacher-student relationships—from which his transgressive stance derives its power.

These same structural elements of school relations from which the teaching role gains its authority are on full view in *The Paper Chase*—James Bridges' 1973 film about a student's first year at Harvard Law School. Both the audience and the students learn about legal matters in Professor Kingsfield's contract law class. Actual cases are discussed using what Kingsfield calls "the Socratic Method": increasingly difficult questions posed by an all-knowing teacher to a sea of students struggling to gain recognition through their answers while trying to avoid being chosen as the next victim. In contrast to Thackeray the courtier, Kingsfield (John Houseman) is neither young nor attractive, and his students are mostly male, alerting the audience that within

44 Impossible relationships in the ideal case

the heteronormative structures of our cinematic expectations, no romance is to be found in the classroom.[1]

Kingsfield's actions and his expectations for his students follow the same rules that structure the class. There is no fraternization: Kingsfield does not greet his students or carry on discussions after class. Furthermore, his very method and manner of teaching are removed, relying on his institutional authority and command of the law for his pedagogical style rather than on personal connections to particular students. Employing a seating chart complete with photographs is Kingsfield's sole way of distinguishing individual students from one another. The only contemporary character who comes close to Kingsfield is *Whiplash*'s (2014) Fletcher, whom most would agree is an unmitigated monster. Kingsfield, by comparison, is a far more ambivalent character.

Despite the emphasis on curricular content and formalized teaching roles, the relationship between Professor Kingsfield and the principal character in *The Paper Chase*, James T. Hart (Timothy Bottoms)—a soft-spoken, quick-witted Mid-westerner—is charged with desire, and similar in its desirous nature to that between Thackeray and Dare. In both cases, students are called to self-awareness through the presence of a teacher who seems to stand outside the ordinary limits of human finitude. But while we might describe Thackeray's relationship to Dare as a merely romantic story that happens to be set within a school, or a romance that derives its significance from its opposition to school norms, it would be difficult to claim the same about Kingsfield and Hart, as the curriculum of their contract law class and their institutional roles within it thoroughly define their relationship.

While Hart and Kingsfield's relationship stands out as overtly institutional compared to most teacher-student relationships portrayed in film, it is nonetheless charged with a desire that is as familiar in schools as it is rare on film. In order to account for the unlikely love story between Kingsfield and Hart, we must draw out some of the underlying structures of relationships characteristic of schooling, at least insofar as these relationships are projected in and understood through film. In the next section, through an analysis of those institutional and relational structures portrayed in *The Paper Chase* (1973), we explore Kingsfield and Hart's relationship as founded in their respective relationships to the curricular content that separates them.

## Hart's desires

In the first scene of *The Paper Chase* (1973), shortly after the students take their seats and the professor takes his place at the podium, Hart is the first person Kingsfield calls upon and he is unprepared, unaware that readings had been assigned for the opening day.[2] Kingsfield asks Hart to stand and lambastes his assumption that the initial day of law school would be introductory. In the first instance of a theme of silenced speakers that runs throughout the film, Hart is left standing silent before the class. Immediately following, a humiliated Hart runs to the nearest bathroom and vomits, establishing a direct and visceral relation between the intellectual pursuits of the classroom and the physical lives that are informed by these practices.

Hart's humiliation in the classroom and expulsion from it demonstrate a disordering of the subject, a reminder of the subject's limited ability to command either the language in which it is inscribed or the body through which it experiences the world. As Aristophanes explains in Plato's *Symposium*, desire originates in human incompleteness, a lack of wholeness described in his mythical tale as a physical division of the subject ordered by divine law that produces a longing to be whole once again (191d).[3] In our contemporary inheritance of this myth, desire is similarly understood as a product of the human subject's division by the law of language.[4] The pre-oral child's experience of integrity and wholeness in communion with its caretaker, much like the pre-lapsarian humans of Aristophanes' myth, finds itself divided from the source of its own wholeness and contentment by a similarly transcendent law of language that separates the two by rendering the child's needs incomprehensible to its caretaker.

In order to overcome the gulf of language and express itself in terms that would allow its caretaker to make it whole again by fulfilling its needs, the child subjects itself to the language through which it seeks the fulfillment of its incompleteness through the desire of the other. The paradox of language acquisition, in which the child subjects itself to a language that is external to it in order to express those needs it feels internally, forms the basis of all learning relationships, insofar as the autonomy promised at the far end of learning can only be gained through one's submission to a discipline already in play and a forfeiture of truly autonomous actions that would indicate a reunion with one's other half. Once the child engages in the field of language by learning the words that might express its needs, the weight of its desire to be understood and recognized by others "supersedes and all but replaces the original need that drives the relationship" (Lacan, 1977, p. 286). Wholeness is no longer sought in the fulfillment of needs but in increasingly complex account of the self in a language that precedes the subject not only historically but in its capacity to consider its own identity.

Hart's arrival to a class that has always already begun signifies his belatedness to the language of law as well as the law of language—not only because the assignment has been given but because the law of contracts in question predates Hart as its subject, even in his ignorance of it.[5] Hart's ignorance of the language game already at play before his arrival is underscored here by the fact that even his excuse for his condition does not count. As ignorance is the presumed condition of the student, his profession of unknowing cannot be recognized as a valid excuse for his current state, but only makes sense as a communication of his desire to learn—an emptying of the self illustrated in the bathroom scene that follows. Like the Socratic Method that Kingsfield later describes, the first scene has left Hart in a position of *aporia*, literally "without resource" (*a-poros*), emptied and aware of his emptiness. Alfred Geier (2002) has claimed this position of *aporia*—the awareness of one's own lack—as the origin of desire and the foundation for any potential to learn, insofar as such awareness drives the subject in its attempt to complete itself through the world around it. The environment established by Kingsfield's authority to redescribe his students according to the expectations of the law leaves Hart with an awareness of his position of lack, inciting his desire to be recognized by his teacher as a means of completing himself.

Plato's *Symposium* illustrates the relationship between incompleteness, *aporia*, and desire through two young men who are each brought to an aporetic state of confusion over their own understandings of the world. Agathon, who serves as the focus of Geier's claim, stands at the precipice of recognizing his own incompleteness when Socrates brings him to a state of self-contradiction and confusion in trying to speak of Eros (201c). Despite this moment of aporia, Agathon is unable to recognize his incompleteness, because his recent recognition as a great tragedian by the Athenian people has filled him with pride. His desire takes the form of a *philodemos*—a love for the masses who appreciate his work rather than a pursuit of wisdom (194c).

Alcibiades, who erupts upon the scene at the end of the dialogue to drunkenly confess his love for Socrates, has become aware of his own incompleteness as a result of his interactions with Socrates on other occasions. But as his confession makes clear, Alcibiades' desire to complete himself is limited insofar as it does not extend past Socrates himself, who Alcibiades believes holds all the answers to his questions (217a). As in Britzman's (1986) analysis of the cultural myths that define teaching, Alcibiades' faith in his teacher's exceptional relation to the truth obstructs his own realization of that position of knowing.

Neither Agathon nor Alcibiades arrive at the presumed goal of education, present in the *Symposium* in the form of Socrates, who parallels his better-known claim of only knowing his own ignorance in the *Apology* (21b) with a claim early in the *Symposium* that he knows something about Eros (177d). The play between these paralleled claims suggests that the ignorance Socrates knows is no mere emptiness, and that the *aporia* that results from his elenchic examination of his interlocutors can be viewed instead as a fecund source of human understanding, given the constitutive relationship between eros and the human soul (Demos, 1934, 1968). Socrates' parallel claims and his account of Eros reinstate his authority as a speaker while providing us with a more complex view of how authority operates. From this perspective, we can claim that Hart's desire to master the law to which he is subject has been secured in his realization of his belatedness, framed in relation to Kingsfield's authority, but that the fruition of this desire is not in the novice's imagined mastery of the field but in understanding the perpetual pursuits of desire itself.

Outside the confines of school, Hart's desires give rise to another desirous relationship, providing a visible parallel to the desires excited in class, but even at a distance from the classroom the authority of the teacher as an all-knowing presence predominates. Susan Field—a complete stranger—approaches Hart and asks to be walked home one night, afraid she is being pursued. "There's someone following me," she whispers to a startled Hart as she takes his arm on the street and glances nervously behind her, the two walking quickly off camera. Susan's stalker's identity is never revealed and seems to play a merely instrumental role, serving as the occasion of Hart and Susan's meeting, but it is Kingsfield who plays the role of unknown intruder in the scene immediately following. Having broken into the library early to get a book, Hart is again startled by a shadow walking above the glass floor divide. "There's someone else here," Hart informs his co-conspirator, Ford, in words that echo Susan's. Having inadvertently interrupted Hart's burglary—thus protecting the seat of knowledge—Kingsfield looms over the lives of his students, particularly Hart, as the ever-present, all-knowing, and completed subject, identified with the contract law he teaches and, by extension, to the laws that govern all things.

Hart's relationships with Susan and school develop as parallel plots through scenes alternating between the classroom and the bedroom. Yet here, just as in the library, Hart is forever under Kingsfield's watchful eye. For example, when Hart first calls upon Susan after their accidental meeting and subsequently stays the night, she is in the midst of painting the walls of her apartment white. Later in the film, Kingsfield poses a hypothetical question involving a contract between two people whitewashing a house. Conversely, while with his lover, Hart often employs the language of the law: "I am trying to make sense . . . I can't live like this. I need to be organized. Susan, I need a way of living I can rationalize." Even after making love, it is of Kingsfield's class that Hart speaks, in terms that suggest a developing understanding of the relationship between aporia and desire:

> It's very interesting to me how quickly the classes have divided into three factions. One faction being the students who sit in the back of the class, giving up sitting in their assigned seats, preparing the cases. What is it, only October? They've already given up trying. Cowards. The second group are the ones who won't raise their hands or volunteer an answer but will try when called upon. That's where I am right now: living in a state of constant fear. And then there's the third echelon: the volunteers. They raise their hands in class. They thrust themselves in the fray. I don't think they're smarter than anyone else, but they have courage. And they'll achieve the final recognition: the teachers will get to know their names, and they'll get better grades. Past couple of weeks, I've been preparing to enter the upper echelon, and this weekend—if I can get all my work done—I'm going to enter it Monday morning in Kingsfield's Contract Law class.

In contrast to his dismal opening day, Hart has begun to shift his position in relation to Kingsfield and to the class. Hart's awareness of his own lack has become an active desire to "thrust [himself] into the fray," to become

## 48    Impossible relationships in the ideal case

something by virtue of being recognized by the field of law. Come Monday morning, he volunteers and triumphs in Kingsfield's class, leaving his teacher, this time, uncharacteristically mute. In an earlier scene in which Kingsfield describes the Socratic Method, the professor assures his students that "in my classroom, there is always another question—another question to your answer." Yet, when Hart answers, Kingsfield has no further question. The king of the field, identified with the law itself, is rendered mute by a subordinate speaking from the position of the law.

Kingsfield's silence is not a matter of personal expression or lack thereof; Hart has simply brought the case analysis to the point at which the erotic interplay between teacher and student has been momentarily fulfilled, and as a result, stalled. The teacher's silence in this scene calls to mind Thackeray's silence in two scenes of *To Sir*, except that in Thackeray's case he gets to play both the student and the teacher. On Thackeray's first day of school, he and another young teacher are drawn out of the teacher's lounge by loud music. The students are dancing in the hallways and invite Thackeray to join. He is silenced, then stammers out an excuse, rushing from the room. In this early scene, Thackeray finds himself a-poros, without resource, because of his lack of familiarity with the youth culture he faces. At the end of the film, after accepting an invitation to dance with Dare, repeating the earlier scene and demonstrating his savvy, he is once again silenced, this time by his students' demonstration of their appreciation for his commitment to them. In this later scene, we know that Thackeray's silence is not merely a matter of ignorance or discomfort, as it was in the earlier scene. What makes him stumble over his words and rush from the room in an almost exact replication of the earlier scene is that, like Kingsfield's silence in relation to Hart's answer, the end of the educational relationship between Thackeray and his students, premised upon the idea that they must become ready for the world, has been achieved.

Running out of class following his victory, Hart proclaims, "I did it in Kingsfield's class. This is a goddamn dance." His shift in metaphors for classroom discussion, from the military "into the fray" to the ease of the dance, demonstrates that Hart has achieved some kind of mastery over the discourse that once seemed so daunting. While his relationship with Kingsfield will continue to develop over the course of the year, Hart has come to understand something of its erotic kernel, namely that his striving and coming to terms with his own ignorance is the mainspring of his education.

In *Tales Out of School*, Jo Keroes (1999, p. 2) reminds us that, "For Socrates the teacher is the lover, the student the beloved, and the process of dialectic, the path along which knowledge is acquired, an erotic dance they share." Keroes has it partly wrong, at least in terms of the roles she ascribes to teacher and student. Alcibiades' speech at the close of Plato's *Symposium* clearly portrays a reversal of the traditional roles in Greek pederasty, including complaints from Alcibiades that Socrates tricks him into taking on the role of the lover. But Keroes gets the dance right: Hart and Kingsfield engage in a series of strategic and purposeful moves that recreate a tradition of teaching and learning as a play of subjective positions that traces its lineage to the *Symposium*.

Unlike the climactic dance sequence in *To Sir, With Love*, Hart can't literally dance with Kingsfield as a culmination of their educational relationship. Their shared passion is consistently portrayed as maintained across the distance between their respective student and teacher desks, facing one another across the broad expanse of the lecture hall. To break down this distance through a dance sequence or embrace between teacher and student would be to break down the tension in which educational desire is produced. In order to show the fulfillment of educational desire, Hart instead runs to find Susan, whom he then embraces and kisses. His passion is real and Susan is its presumed object, but she is a surrogate. Hart's feelings originate and can only be satisfied in the classroom—in his desire to be acknowledged and recognized by Susan's father, Professor Kingsfield.

## Close to Hart

The connections between Hart's desire inspired in class and its expression in his relationship with Susan become even more entwined when Hart discovers that Susan is Kingsfield's daughter. "It all makes so much sense," he states, uncannily commenting on both his relationship to Susan and Susan's place in the structure of the film. Susan's relationship with Hart cannot be understood on its own: her character is never fleshed out, and they rarely speak of anything other than Hart's relationship to Kingsfield. Instead, her role in the narrative is to serve as the physical signifier of Hart's intellectual/erotic pursuit of Kingsfield, thus providing a safe transfer of Hart's desires toward his teacher.

While the characters of Thackeray and Dare in *To Sir, With Love* excite the possibilities of desire and mutual interest in teacher-student relationships by causing the audience to focus on attraction across social taboos (black/white, sophisticate/novice, adult/child), the suggestion of pairing Hart and Kingsfield reemphasizes the distance and disconnect between teachers and students and the impossibility of their physical relation. One way in which this disconnect is achieved visually is in the pairing of two male characters within a highly heteronormative environment. As Eve Kosofsky Sedgwick (1985, p. 3) writes: "much of the most useful recent writing about patriarchical structures suggests that 'obligatory heterosexuality' is built into male-dominated kinship systems, or that homophobia is a necessary consequence of such patriarchical institutions as heterosexual marriage."

It should come as no surprise then that what is allowed to pass between a male teacher and student of the same sex is highly restricted as in established patriarchal relationships. Ebert (1998, p. 609) notes that "the fundamental relationship in the movie is between Hart and Kingsfield," but this primary relationship is a highly structured and highly mediated one. The only communication that takes place between Hart and Kingsfield is academic; their profound lack of

# 50 Impossible relationships in the ideal case

relationship by any personal standards is reflected in Kingsfield's repeated inability to remember Hart's name or even recognize him outside of the context of the classroom.

The heteronormativity and corresponding diminishment of women's roles in the male-dominated law school atmosphere is captured in a locker room shower scene that is central to the supposed tension between Hart's romantic and academic pursuits. Classmates Thomas Anderson and Franklin Ford III stand on the left and right of Hart who remains silent throughout. Hart shaves; the other two wash. The shot is cropped from the waist down: the common shower imposes the dual norms of male-centered discourse and heterosexuality by showing the audience that all of the action in the men's room happens above the waist.

*Anderson:* I'm telling you, Hart, the worst thing a law student can do is get involved with a girl. Affairs by their very nature are time-consuming.

*Ford:* On the contrary, it's the best thing you can do. Nothing makes you hornier than studying.

*Anderson:* My father warned me about that . . . he said the celibate mind is sharper, retains more information.

*Ford:* Look, the only sensible thing to do in a mess like this is find a woman that doesn't make any demands and hang on. Hang on like hell. You grab onto her boobs and don't let go.

Even Ford, tied as he is to his pre-linguistic identification with maternal needs satisfaction, hints at the dangers of desire in the form of a demanding woman. Physical connections are acceptable, but beware of a woman who has desires of her own rather than simple, yielding nurturance. The film's portrayal of femininity as a sort of a trap or distraction that lies outside the realm of manly vocation allows the men engaged in the discourse to remain on the level of equals. So long as both regard women as the beloved/passive object, they can assume the position of the lover/active subject. Susan's place as Hart's beloved and Kingsfield's daughter "makes so much sense," because without her we are forced to recognize the erotic association between Kingsfield and Hart.

The established masculine and feminine roles in *The Paper Chase* are reinforced by the tagline used to promote the film: "You have to choose between the girl you love and the diploma you've worked for all your life. You have 30 seconds."[6] The supposedly mutually exclusive objects of the girl and the diploma are in fact complementary objects, both from the perspective of the symbolic relationship between Susan and Kingsfield and from their actual relationship as father and daughter. In order for Hart's desire to be fulfilled in a physical manifestation that we can see upon the screen, he needs an object that is both outside the domain of Kingsfield's classroom while still related to it. Susan Field, *nee* Susan Kingsfield, stands outside the law, in that she has rejected her father and his kingly position. Nonetheless, she remains his daughter, just as she remains a subject of the law even in her alienation from it.

"I can see the resemblance," Hart remarks as romantic music begins. While Susan feels, "It was much nicer before not having any background," a cheerful Hart is far from uncomfortable: "I wouldn't say that." Susan sounds the student: "I'm going to ask you a question. You came back here [the bedroom] because I'm Kingsfield's daughter." "That's not a question; that's an answer," Hart replies, making no secret of the connection between his desire for her and his desire to be recognized by Kingsfield. Indeed, while these lovers do talk, their talk is not that of lovers. If anything, the structure of their dialogue—with questions and answers—is most suggestive of Kingsfield's Socratic classroom, only here Hart is master. The conquest of the position of authority and the conquest of the authority's property go hand in hand. The challenge that Hart faces is how to win both.

## King of Hart

The goals of succeeding in Kingsfield's class and winning the heart of his daughter are deeply intertwined. The success that Hart seeks, the goal to which his desire drives, is not to be one with Kingsfield, in the sense of making love to him, but of being recognized as his equal, or of achieving the same position with respect to the law. Entering an empty classroom, Hart demonstrates the direction of his desire by posing as his professor: walking up to the podium, he looks out over the silent seats to see his own seat from the perspective of the teacher before a janitor exposes Hart's desires by turning on the lights.

Until this point in the film, Hart's understanding of himself and his place in relation to the law is dominated by his presumption of Kingsfield's privileged position in relation to language. As in Alcibiades' confession of love at the end of Plato's *Symposium*, Hart believes that Kingsfield's authority derives from a place beyond human incompleteness—a belief that serves initially as both a goad and a limit to his own learning. Kingsfield is a model for law students to emulate, but as a model that attains perfection he equally frustrates their progress by making their goal seem like an imitation of Christ: noble, but impossible. The seeming conflict between school and love that Hart articulates in his need for a "relationship [he] can rationalize" reflects his desire to stand in relation to the rational principles of the law in every aspect of his life.

When Hart breaks into the law library a second time to study Kingsfield's first drafts and student notes, he gains a new perspective, noticing that, "They're just notes, and they look just like mine." Kingfield's place as the idealized subject presumed to know is taken down a notch: how can the one who knows be so similar to the one who stands in ignorance? In the purloined notes, a young Kingsfield himself questions the ultimate subject presumed to know:

> Can we make a contract with God that is binding to man? I am almost the living extension of the old judges. Where would they be without me?

52  Impossible relationships in the ideal case

> I carry in my mind the cases they wrote. Who would hang their pictures if there were no law students? It's hard being the living extension of tradition.

The realization that Hart makes here is that Kingsfield's authority is not based upon a privileged place in relation to the law or to language—a difference that would, strictly speaking, be impossible to overcome from the position of the student. Instead, Kingsfield's authority is derived from a privileged place in relation to the hierarchical structure of Harvard Law School, a less impossible distance to overcome, but one that suggests a path of self-overcoming along which the ignorant initiate may at some point arrive at the position of the master.

To hold the same authority as Kingsfield also means to hold some sort of control or parental dominion over his daughter. At least one other has tried in the past, but has failed in both respects. Philip Field, Susan's estranged husband from whom she seeks a divorce, was also one of Kingsfield's students, but he has since dropped out of law school and lost the heart of Kingsfield's daughter. In marrying Philip the failure, Susan has given up her claim to being a Kingsfield and has instead merely become a Field—the field over which Kingsfield holds patriarchal dominion, the field of law. While she has been demoted to the status of a subject of the law, her soon-to-be ex-husband has left the country, living entirely outside the law over which her father continues to hold mastery. Philip's brotherly love lacks the drive necessary to follow through; Hart must prove that his erotic approach can prevail.

Hart seeks to succeed where Philip has failed by taking on both positions at once: making love to Susan in Kingsfield's bed while remaining Kingsfield's best student. Descending the stairs with goblet in hand but without clothes, Hart performs the conquering hero as he enters Kingsfield's study—the presumed seat and origin of the law. Casually spinning a heroically sized globe, he has the world in his hands. Susan enters while Hart wonders, "Do you think he would mind me drinking in his special room?" "I think you're behaving just the way he wants you to behave," she says, "Picking up his little silver mementos . . . I think he'd like it just to have you fondle his things." "I feel like he knows me," Hart imagines. However, a moment later he is forced to escape out the back door when Kingsfield prematurely returns. "Well, he just said he hoped it wasn't a law student," Susan later relates. Kingsfield continues to succeed at maintaining the separation from his student, but Hart is getting close.

When Hart later denounces Kingsfield in class as a "son of a bitch," it is not Kingsfield's relation to the law—the name of the father—that is criticized, but his relation to his mother, the nurturing relation that stands outside of the law. In recognizing Hart's outburst by claiming it is the "most intelligent thing you've said all day," Kingsfield not only reinforces the separation between the subject and the maternal relationship, but in doing so recognizes Hart as speaking the language of the law. Hart feels vindicated by this recognition, and in identifying once again with Kingsfield as the representative of the law obeys his command, voiced as a form of permission, "You may take your seat." Hart smiles as he returns to his place: somewhere between the lawlessness of stealing the king's position in the field and being rendered incomplete in comparison to Kingsfield's authority, Hart realizes that it is recognition he seeks.

Hart's smile in response to Kingsfield's command serves as a mirror to their first interaction, in which Hart was expelled from the classroom and sickened by the words of his teacher. In that opening scene, Hart sought recognition in a personal sense, a connection with his professor outside the language of the law and the hierarchical structure of the teacher-student relationship. Through his resistance to personal contact and enforcement of the institutional structure, Kingsfield brings Hart to seek recognition within and according to the law: he inspires in his student the desire to complete himself in the image of his teacher as a knowing subject.

In discovering the path from student to teacher, Hart's search for recognition is no longer defined exclusively in terms of anxiety. In the final scene of the film, having suffered through final exams and sitting on the beach at Kingsfield's summer home with Susan, he produces an unopened envelope containing his final grades. In an act that demonstrates his developing status as a knowing subject who needs no reassurance of his mastery of legal language, he folds the envelope into a paper airplane and tosses it out to sea.

## To chase, with love

In contrast to films like *To Sir, With Love* (1967) that seemingly operate outside the curriculum in an effort to emphasize the relational and romantic aspects of educational relationships, *The Paper Chase* (1973) presents a picture of educational erotics in which the curriculum is understood to be the primary determinant in the relationship between teacher and student. On the one hand, the curriculum precedes both teacher and student, setting each in relation to the other according to his place in the structure of the school. On the other, the language of the curriculum sets out all the possibilities for the relationship, including forms of recognition and interaction. While most popular films set in schools portray the teacher forging a personal relationship with students, emphasizing the fact that all institutional education takes place through the work of individuals, the personal distance Kingsfield keeps from his students reminds us that the desire which drives educational relations is not fundamentally an emotion directed toward a particular individual, neither is it a desire that can be fulfilled within the institutional roles established in the school setting.[7] Instead, the lack of fulfillment of our educational desires engages our energies in a continuous pursuit of our own identities through our understanding of the world around us.

In *To Sir, With Love*, in order to portray the teacher as both institutionally authorized and personally accessible, good teaching is presented as an act that uses its official position to break down the very curricular language

54  Impossible relationships in the ideal case

that gives the teacher authority. As a result, Thackeray becomes an impossible composite of the subject presumed to know, whose distance from the student inspires desire, and the lover whose proximity allows the fulfillment of desire. His paradoxical position is captured in scenes in which he stands at the teacher's desk, in the position of knowledge, while throwing away books and introducing more sensual and immediate objects from outside the school, in relation to which he and his students can drop their institutional roles for more "authentic" communication.

Thackeray's reliance on extra-curricular attachments for his identity is established early in the film, as he teaches while waiting for a letter of employment from an engineering firm, and serves as the backdrop for two culminating events in the film: a field trip to an art museum and the class's attendance at a funeral for a schoolmates' mother. But Thackeray's teaching cannot actually manifest itself in the real world: once outside the limits of the school he is one among his students, no longer a teacher. The impossibility of Thackeray's position is signified in the final scene by his tearing up of a letter offering him a job outside the school. But in tearing up the letter and renouncing his connection to the pursuit of his dreams outside the classroom, we are forced to ask if he hasn't become like the other teachers who populate the school.

Thackeray's paradoxical position is partly resolved in the narrative structure of *The Paper Chase*, in which, to make Hart's desires visible and his interpersonal connections more human, the film introduces a secondary, extra-curricular relationship between Hart and Susan. Outside of the law but nonetheless related to it, Susan allows the audience to comfortably experience Hart's desires, for she—unlike her father, who takes the institutional role of the teacher—is young, attractive, and of the opposite sex. Nonetheless, Hart's relationship with her revolves around conversations about law, school, and primarily the ever-present father figure. Just as Susan suddenly and improbably appears in Hart's life—coinciding with his entry into contract law—she never materializes as a completely credible character in the film. Instead, she provides Hart and the audience with a person on whom to place feelings that originate in other arenas.

Susan and Kingsfield complement and complete one another; Hart's feelings for the two are, as they are, deeply related. After learning the identity of Susan's father, Hart sits in class aglow, smirking as his eyes linger lovingly on the professor. To look at his face alone, one would think Hart to be in the bedroom; certainly, he never displays such sentiment for Susan. In fact, the classroom is the only place Hart expresses anything approaching love. He is allowed such expression in class because he is sleeping with Susan, because he sees her face in the father, because Hart is the conquering hero of property and position of authority. We are tempted to suggest that if we take Susan out of the story—and she is barely in it to begin with—we will better understand Hart's erotic pursuit of Kingsfield.

Yet it is precisely at the point at which we try to remove Susan from the picture that the necessity of her presence becomes evident. Without Susan,

Kingsfield's relationship to Hart becomes a stark, totalizing presence without any room for Hart to retain that which is his, outside the language of the law and the order of the school. In *Whiplash* (2014), as a contemporary example, Andrew's loss of control to Fletcher is signified by his breaking off his relationship to Nicole. Just as Thackeray draws his superiority as a teacher from outside the bounds of the curriculum, in some ways usurping his students' pursuit of their own lives by providing them with a romantic object that coincides with their subject presumed to know, the re-ordering of Hart's desires according to the order of the school depends upon his ability to remain Hart despite the changes he must undergo. Despite her relationship to the professor, Susan is not a relationship Hart can rationalize. She is instead the desire that is irreducible to the claims Harvard Law School has made on Hart.

What remains unresolved in this chapter, and perhaps must remain unresolved at least in part, is that aspect of the human subject that maintains itself despite the claims made on it by desire, whether by attachment to objects of desire that are contrary to its expected growth and development, by rejecting the authority of the subject presumed to know, or by a simple, ascetic refusal of desire that provides the subject with enough inertia to resist change. If education is ultimately the act of shaping students' desires toward the right things, than this resistance is the greatest challenge to teachers who assume the institutional roles that precede them in an effort to inspire students' learning. In the next chapter, we focus on this resistance in precisely the place where we would expect to find it least: the teacher savior narrative.

## Notes

1 That our expectations as an audience are clearly shifting is evidenced by more recent films such as *The History Boys* (2006), in which same-sex relationships between teachers and students are condemned (and quietly celebrated) for their transgression of professional rather than sexual norms.
2 Bottoms returns to the genre of the school film three decades later as the equally unprepared principal in *Elephant*, Gus Van Sant's dramatization of the Columbine attacks, discussed in Chapter 6.
3 Citations of Plato by Stephanus numbers refer to Hamilton and Cairns (eds) (1961).
4 The ego, whose strength our theorists now define by its capacity to bear frustration, is frustration in its essence. Not frustration of a desire of the subject, but frustration by an object in which his desire is alienated and which the more it is elaborated, the more profound the alienation from his *jouissance* becomes for the subject . . . even if he achieved his most perfect likeness in that image, it would still be the *jouissance* of the other that he would cause to be recognized in it. (Lacan, 1977, p. 42)
5 Other films have achieved the same sense of belatedness through their characters literally showing up late to class as Hart does later in the film, beginning at a school with a long tradition, or entering upon a school where problems are so established that no academic progress can be made.
6 http://imdb.com/title/tt0070509/
7 Alternatively, some school films attempt to provide a conclusive ending while acknowledging that the very fact that the film is set in a school means that the story is not over.

## 56 Impossible relationships in the ideal case

Consider, for instance, the device used in *Animal House* (1978) and later in *The History Boys* (2006), in which the audience is given information on how each principal character's life turns out.

## References

*Animal House*, John Landis, dir. (USA: Universal Pictures, 1978).

*Blackboard Jungle*, Richard Brooks, dir. (USA: Metro-Goldwyn-Mayer, 1955).

Britzman, D. (1986). Cultural myths in the making of a teacher: Biography and social structure in teacher education. *Harvard Educational Review*, 56(4), 442–456.

Dalton, M. (2004). *The Hollywood Curriculum: Teachers in the Movies*. New York: Peter Lang.

Demos, R. (1934). Eros. *The Journal of Philosophy*, 31(13), 337–345.

Demos, R. (1968). Plato's doctrine of the psyche as a self-moving motion. *Journal of the History of Philosophy*, 6(2), 133–145.

Ebert, R. (1998). *Roger Ebert's Video Companion*. Kansas City, MO: Andrews McMeel Publishing.

Frank, A. W. (1995). Lecturing and transference: The undercover work of pedagogy. In J. Gallop (ed.) *Pedagogy: The Question of Impersonation*. Bloomington, IN: Indiana University Press, pp. 28–35.

Fried, R. (2003). Passionate teaching. In *The Jossey-Bass Reader on Teaching*. San Francisco, CA: Jossey-Bass.

Gallop, J. (1997). *Feminist Accused of Sexual Harrassment*. Durham, NC: Duke University Press.

Geier, A. (2002). *Plato's Erotic Thought: The Tree of the Unknown* (Vol. 3). Rochester, NY: University of Rochester Press.

Hamilton, E. and Cairns, H. (eds) (1961). *The Collected Dialogues of Plato, Including the Letters*. New York: Pantheon Books.

*The History Boys*, Nicholas Hytner, dir. (United Kingdom: Fox Searchlight Pictures, 2006).

hooks, b. (1994). *Teaching to Transgress*. New York: Routledge.

Keroes, J. (1999). *Tales Out Of School: Gender, Longing, and the Teacher in Fiction and Film*. Carbondale, IL: Southern Illinois University Press.

Lacan, J. (1977). *Ecrits* (A. Sheridan, trans.). New York: W.W. Norton & Company.

*The Paper Chase*, James Bridges, dir. (USA: 20th Century Fox, 1973).

Sedgwick, E. K. (1985). *Between Men: English Literature and Male Homosocial Desire*. New York: Columbia University Press.

Todd, S. (1997). Introduction: Desiring desire in rethinking pedagogy. In S. Todd (ed.) *Learning Desire: Perspectives on Pedagogy, Culture, and the Unsaid*. New York: Routledge.

*To Sir, With Love*, James Clavell, dir. (United Kingdom: Columbia Pictures, 1967).

*Whiplash*, Damien Chazelle, dir. (USA: Bold Films, 2014).

# Chapter 4

# To save, with love
## Desire, domination and melancholia in teacher savior films

The promise of desire in driving student growth toward an impossible fantasy of knowledge cannot be raised in a democratic society without also raising the issue of domination. As the films discussed in the preceding chapters suggest, educational growth, or the development of rationality as the capacity to operate within a particular discourse of human flourishing, only ever appears as the effect of an imaginary attachment to a goal that cannot be reached. The critical distance that it would take to launch a critique of one's own investments in a discourse seems equally unreachable. This issue seems especially the case in situations involving teachers who represent dominant social classes and poor, marginalized, or otherwise underprivileged students who stand to benefit from their tutelage under the influence of those with greater cultural capital: the seduction of power may prove stronger than either party's capacity to call it under critique. As a result of this blindness, we may be too quick to view education as a social panacea, a liberatory project, or a tool to lift all boats.

As in other political genres, those doctrines that have promised the most radical new freedoms and realizations of human potential in their pedagogical plans have often been most severely critiqued for their hidden ideological content. The "unmasking" of modern education as ideologically suspect marks a "crisis of legitimation" (Peters, 1996, p. 10, in St. Pierre, 1997, p. 279–280) in contemporary discourses on education, as the oppositional pole to which one would swing in rejecting emancipatory, modernist educational projects is presumably a conventionalism no less ideologically based and sustained in domination.

But if this crisis weighs heavily on the shoulders of educational theorists, the fantasy world of cinema proceeds almost entirely unaware of its ideological assumptions. Themes of freedom and domination that have caused so much dispute among scholars for centuries are reconfigured in teacher savior films, drained of the bile and uncertainty that attends political disputes over education: white teachers save black students from the failures of ghetto schooling, and outsider teachers save white students from the bourgeois values of their own culture.

Presented with this paradox of pedagogical emancipation and domination, however, perhaps we come to experience a bit of relief: not from the interest in

## 58 To save, with love: teacher savior films

educational freedom as such, but from the task of imagining freedom as something we might create. Instead, we might be drawn to mine the resources of more conventional approaches to education for forms of liberty and human flourishing that may have gone overlooked.[1] Recognizing a split in the history of pedagogical theory, between what might be called metaphysical and critical approaches to the question of freedom and domination in education, the first step we make in this chapter is to question this split by arguing that both rely on dominating student subjectivity within a particular set of values. Considering domination as a fundamental aspect of education, we analyze *The Corn Is Green* (1945) as an example of educational domination for the purpose of individual freedom, and consider the erotic relationship between its protagonists Ms. Lilly Moffat and Morgan Evans as the basis of that domination.

*The Corn Is Green* operates entirely within traditional educational themes, yet achieves a rare degree of ambivalence regarding the ideals represented therein. Staged as a story of emancipatory education, the film portrays the teacher, Lilly Moffat (Bette Davis), as a messianic savior who descends upon a Welsh mining town to free a chosen student, Morgan Evans (John Dall), from the darkness of the mines by drawing him instead into the light of an Oxford education. Teaching has been described as a "profound calling" (Bauer, 1998, p. 302) in analyses of the film, a mission to reshape the world and the will of the student through a series of replacements: the light of the schoolroom for the darkness of the mine, the word of truth in the composition book for pastimes of drinking rum and fighting, and ultimately the replacement of Moffat herself for the local girls who threaten the undoing of her work.

This last replacement stands out, both for its sacrificial symbolism and for its pedagogical use of student desire. Erotic striving holds an ambivalent place in educational thought: it serves alternately as a means to achieve and to overcome domination. In *The Corn Is Green*, desire plays an equally doubled role in its relation to domination, both drawing the teacher and student together and pulling them apart. At this complex intersection between domination and desire, however, a third category of educational relation emerges—a melancholic relationship to the lost object left out of the curriculum—that opens a dimension of possibility, a different sort of freedom, internal to the dominance of discourse.

### Learning and liberation

One position on freedom in education, rooted in a metaphysical belief in the power of the word as the truth, might be understood as a positive freedom, in the sense marked by Berlin (1969) insofar as it considers the liberty of the individual as a function of his place within learned truth. Another position, known widely in its manifestation as critical pedagogy, could be called negative freedom, again in Berlin's sense, insofar as it holds that education is a means of dominating young minds toward a reproduction of oppressive social norms, and only in breaking from the *status quo* can the individual find freedom.

To save, with love: teacher savior films 59

Historically, both of these models have relied on students' erotic striving as part of their normative message but, as one might guess, in contradictory ways. The positive model holds that desire is a fundamental, irrational aspect of the human psyche that drives the individual to subject herself to reason: desire is the way we learn. According to the negative model, in which the rationales of the discourses taught by schools have been poisoned by power and human error, desire represents that aspect of humanity that does not conform and that presents a way out of educational tyranny: desire is the way we unlearn.

If desire allows a break from the *status quo*, however, critical pedagogies beg the question of what lies *outside* current conceptions of education. The implicit assumption in all critical forms of pedagogy since Plato's cave allegory is that there is a truth outside of the received wisdom, but the majority of people simply lack access to it. If this is the case, then critical pedagogies begin to look quite a bit like their metaphysical precursors, insofar as the desire that breaks the student from ignorance is at the same time directing him toward some greater truth. The negative freedom sought in critical pedagogical theory is an *emancipation from* that takes place under the auspices of a more primary *domination by*.

Ellsworth (1992) calls out the implicit metaphysical system at work within critical frameworks by noting that contemporary critical theorists rely on supposedly transparent, neutral notions of rationality in their attempts to obscure their own political commitments. Her critique may attribute more self-understanding to critical pedagogy than is due, and it certainly lacks some degree of self-reflection itself in supposing that Ellsworth's own commitments are all on the table for examination. But taken as a descriptive account rather than a critique, Ellsworth's redescription of critical pedagogy as a metaphysics that is blind to its own commitments posits a significant point about the domination common to all education. Specifically, it shows that the naturalization of some particular concept, perspective, or set of values is a primary condition of educational domination: students become subject to a discourse by taking a perspective for granted. Moreover, the naturalization of the teacher's authority in terms of her privileged position within the given horizon of values provides a model for students' desires—an empowered way of being in the world worthy of emulation.

Ellsworth's critique helps us to understand the seemingly contradictory claims made by Socrates in Plato's *Republic*. While many critics have tried to square the apparent incompatibility of Socrates' descriptions of education in Books II-III and VII by claiming they belong to different classes or different aspects of the soul, the claim of ideology in every pedagogical practice means that in both the subject's indoctrination into common social norms and in the access to a higher truth that founds social criticism, eros, and ideology are at play.

When the protagonist of Plato's cave allegory is freed from his shackles and makes the steep, rough ascent of education into the light of the sun, what he gains in his negative freedom from the shadows and false knowledge of the

# 60 To save, with love: teacher savior films

underground is only made possible through the effects of a new domination. The only difference between the oppressive force of the shadows and the liberating force of the sun is that the latter is really the truth.

Some contemporary scholars have argued that in the absence of a substantial view of the truth, or without a meaningful correspondence theory of truth, the aim of education should not be a specific, authorized content, but instead ought to focus on the process by which truths are generated and disseminated. Burmester (1997) points to the relational dynamics in Plato's *Phaedrus* and David Mamet's *Oleanna* (1994) in order to show that pedagogical outcomes depend on a host of relational connections between teacher and student:

> *For* my students, I aim to provoke (from the Latin meaning "to challenge or cause to take action"), to seduce (to persuade through passion), and finally, to awaken their incipient sense of wonder at the world and the language that creates this reality. *From* my students, I ask to *be* provoked, to *be* seduced, and to find wonder in their original ideas and perspectives.
>
> (Burmester, 1997, pp. 2–3)

Burmester's position on the co-construction of knowledge has become fairly standard rhetoric in pedagogical discourse at all grade levels. It is also entirely disingenuous as her own claims about justice in pedagogical relationships make clear:

> In a just relationship, power flows evenly back and forth, in flux. It is shared *between* both, rather than belonging to one or the other. In this way it is both balanced (just) and *social*—created and maintained by the class rather than one individual. Further, when power is equal, the distinction of teacher and student begins to dissolve, and in many ways to become inter-changeable.
>
> (Burmester, 1997, p. 3)

Justice, traced back to its root in the Ancient Greek *dike*, can certainly be linked to the idea of balance without much distortion. But the leap from justice-as-balance to justice-as-equality reflects a very late development in contemporary democratic thought—one which applies to individuals' status under the law, but which has little or no application in pedagogical relationships, which are founded upon the authority of the teacher, even when the teacher strives to create a relationship based on reciprocity. Burmester's emphasis on flow and equality is an appropriate ruse in motivating students, but it is fundamentally dishonest with respect to Burmester's own authority to, for instance, choose the *Phaedrus* and *Oleanna* as texts, to focus on the production of truth in a pedagogical relationship, or to operate her classroom under assumptions of equality. Remarkable in Burmester's analysis is that she fails to recognize the strong parallels between her own described practices and those of Mamet's professor,

John, who attempts to use his power as a professor to liberate his students, only to be taken down by a student who takes his teaching seriously.

Plato has another way of putting the same point, namely to describe the false beliefs that dominate his cave dwellers in terms similar to those employed by Burmester. The world of the cave, after all, is also a dialogical vision in which the prisoners determine the significance of the shadows on the walls in discussion with one another, without any reference to a "real" object that would found a discussion on whether the truth corresponds to the world. Their interactions and authorizing discourses are entirely democratic, which is why they have both power over the protagonist when he returns, despite his superior learning, and a good reason to kill him.

## Major and miner

The conditions of domination in films about education are most often borne by one individual, whose single-minded determination serves as a stand-in for the social categories in which human identity is defined. Lily Moffat sums up her determination early in the film:

> When I was quite a young girl, I looked the world in the eye and decided I didn't like it. I saw poverty and disease, ignorance and injustice, and in a small way I've always done what I could to fight them.

Moffat's missionary positioning is a direct reference to Plato's premodern brand of critical pedagogy: her aim is to draw poor boys up from the mines to allow their bodies to play in the light of the sun and their minds to play in the light of reason. That light, though alien to the people of Glensarno, is nonetheless perfectly evident in Moffat's appearance, which serves to redescribe the local culture in terms of her privileged gaze. Her self-presentation, the arrival of her books, her demands made on locals, and the power associated with her upbringing are enough to convince her students of a superior way of life, another discourse outside their own, in which Moffat is clearly a powerful figure.

In order to transform her students according to the order of appearances in which they have already recognized her superiority and authority, the next step is to allow them to be recognized in the same way by becoming like her in body and taste. Seemingly incidental scenes and exchanges display elements of Moffat's insistence on students' personal as well as pedagogical habits. Washing the black coal soot from their faces, instruction on the use of a nail file, money spent on new suits and speaking according to an Oxford manner are all examples of a performance of scholarly demeanor intended to reflect inwardly on the character of her students. The scholarly order inscribed upon their bodies works upon their identities: to speak in school is to espouse the attitudes and beliefs appropriate to scholarly ways of knowing, to replace their habits and instincts with those of the teacher.

Reinforcing her students' identification with their new behaviors, appearances, and values, the same recognition they have extended to Moffat is returned to them as a demand. As a delayed reply to Morgan's accusation: "You aren't interested in me," Moffat states bluntly, "I don't understand you." An interest in Morgan as he was before Moffat rescued him from the mines is so far outside her purposes that the accusation does not make sense to her. Moffat recognizes her student *as* a student, but her gaze excludes any reference to who he *was* except in the negative. Moffat's refusal to recognize Morgan except in the role of the student, on his way to where she stands, means that there is to be no negotiation or compromise between his way of life and hers. In order to be recognized, to gain an identity, he must not only behave as she demands, but shake off the constraints of his current state and take on her interests, her beliefs, her concerns as his own. It is not only his knowledge that must be changed but his desires.

## Seducing a miner

Morgan's emancipation from the mines requires his subjection to the Oxford order that Moffat represents according to the force of his own desire. Films traditionally represent the protagonist's desires by a love interest, and while films about educational relationships are no exception to this rule, the presentation of desire between teachers and students tends to take on remarkable shapes in order to suggest the presence of desire without suggesting pederasty. Moffat and Morgan's relationship is exemplary: there is a clear sense of attraction and longing between the two, but in order to show Morgan's desire on the screen another character must emerge with whom Morgan can enact the passion that he and Moffat cannot.

When first introduced to Lily Moffat, Morgan is part of a group of boys freshly emerged from the mines, smiling and singing. Coal dust covering his face and clothes, Morgan's mouth is no cleaner: "Please Miss, can I have a kiss?" She beckons, as if she will comply with his request, then bends him over and swats his backside instead, shifting from lover to mother. Significant to this scene is the fact that Morgan first offers himself to his teacher through his body. While his first words to her are disobedient, his body bends easily to her punishment as a malleable object that might be transformed by her attention. Under Moffat's discipline, Morgan is indeed reborn: he forgoes the mines for private lessons, sports new clothes and a clean face. His recognition by Moffat, the authorized representative of the empowered discourse, leads him to seek her attention and her approval, even as he raises her status well beyond his grasp. Even when he falls back upon his old habit of drinking rum, his mind is still on his new passion: with chalk in hand, Morgan practices his Latin, declining *amo* on the wooden counter of a bar. Love and language have become inseparable through the intervening discourses of learning.

Moffat confesses her love for Morgan in a similarly displaced manner, speaking to her assistant of her desire to be closer to her star pupil: "It is odd to have spent so many hours with another human being in the closest intellectual communion . . . I know every trick and twist to that brain of his . . . and yet not to know him at all."

While Moffat can affect her student's striving, her pedagogical purposes define the limits of her relationship to Morgan: her knowledge stops short of the carnal. She does not "know" Morgan and therefore cannot control him except at a distance. As Moffat describes herself as having a "figure that ensures cleverness and an age that excludes marriage," the love interest that commonly signifies the protagonist's desire must remain platonic. The sexual attraction that represents Morgan's erotic striving must appear in the form of another woman.

After a fight in which Morgan lets Moffat know that he is tired of being known as "the school mistress's dog," of having his identity altered by being addressed as "Mr. Evans" instead of "Morgan," the stage is set for the entrance of an object of desire who knows Morgan in ways Oxford cannot. Up until this point in the film, Bessie Watty's character has developed as no more than a disobedient, recalcitrant child whose noisy interjections serve as the backdrop for Morgan's hard work. As Morgan carries out his fall from grace, however, Bessie falls in her escape from a second-story window directly into his path. Like Milton's Lucifer, she is reborn in her fall, suddenly emerging as the object that satisfies the desire between Morgan and Moffat.

Recalling Moffat's refusal to recognize Morgan as anything but a student: "I don't understand you," Bessie's recognition is of everything in Morgan that goes unrealized in the school: "What a man wants is a little bit of sympathy." In their joint exodus from the school, Morgan and Bessie invoke an Adam and Eve in reverse, returning from the school as the site of knowledge to a low-walled garden, a point of innocent origin. The empowered language of the school disappears as she sings to him in their mother tongue—the "native" language that Moffat cannot speak—as a chorus of Welsh miners echoes their song in the distance. Under a tree in the couple's new Eden, the apple that represents Moffat's promise of academic knowledge is replaced by a rum bottle and her words are replaced by a song.

In realizing the desire between Moffat and Morgan, Bessie's kiss undermines all that Moffat has been struggling to attain, reducing Morgan to acting on untutored drives, or, according to a way of life over which Moffat has no control. Bessie's place as a fantasy object for both Moffat and Morgan explains the structure of the educational relationship. While Moffat would like to have the interest in Morgan that he accuses her of lacking, she cannot because her desire for Morgan would be for precisely those aspects of him that differ from herself, specifically for his native character. To fall in love with Morgan would be to appreciate the very characteristics Moffat seeks to obliterate in him. Bessie accomplishes Moffat's desire for her, but as that part of Moffat's character that

## 64 To save, with love: teacher savior films

must be stilled in order for Moffat to dominate Morgan's understanding of the world, Bessie emerges in the film only to be destroyed.

Morgan returns to his studies, but his dalliance with his former life has had greater consequences than he expected. While Bessie's role is on the one hand no more than a fantasy object where Morgan and Moffat come together, on the other she also serves to represent the fertility of the teacher-student relationship. Like the representation of Morgan's educational desires in extra-curricular pursuits, the fertility of his intellectual pursuits is represented by precisely that which would undo his future as a scholar and Moffat's success as a teacher: the symbolic realization of their love has become its potential undoing.

The battle for Morgan's identity takes place entirely in his absence and ignorance. While he sits for his scholarship exams at Oxford, ostensibly determining his own fate off screen, Bessie flaunts her pregnancy in front of the intellectually fertile, but physically barren Moffat. "You couldn't see what was going on under your nose," Bessie taunts, speaking of her own tryst with Morgan, but alluding to Moffat's unrecognized desires, "Well you can't manage him any longer 'cause he's got to manage *me* now." Moffat threatens to kill Bessie if she does not vacate before Morgan arrives, but settles for paying her off, quieting the drives she cannot destroy.

In a final sequence of convergences, Morgan returns from his exams, his scholarship at Oxford is confirmed, his fatherhood revealed, and Moffat agrees to raise his child as long as he agrees never to return to Glensarno. Morgan's ties of love to his home and the girl he would otherwise be obligated to wed are severed completely by new ties to Moffat. By taking Bessie's place as mother—the symbol of her desire as well as her competition—Moffat has closed the circle of Morgan's desires and her own. She has become not only the object of his educational desires but in keeping with her name, Lily, now also the virgin mother of his child.

The conditions under which Morgan learns of his fatherhood are telling: a telegram arrives via a local woman from Glensarno. "I've never seen a telegram," she announces and asks Moffat to read it aloud: Morgan has been accepted. The woman immediately runs out to tell the town. Up to this point, Morgan has made clear his plans to renounce the scholarship, but only to a handful of people connected to the school. Through Moffat's reading of the telegram, employing her learning against his decision—Morgan has had the opposite decision made for him. He will not be able to disappoint an entire town that has been anxiously awaiting the news. Moffat—speaking for herself and the town—explains that Morgan's duty is to the world, that is, the world of Oxford, and not to the child. His face, which moments before displayed angry conviction, is soft, malleable, and attentive. Before he speaks, Moffat has already achieved her aims.

Once this is accomplished, Moffat again assumes an intimate position, sitting down by his side. "Look at me Morgan. For the first time we are together. Our hearts are face to face unashamed. The clock is ticking and there is no

To save, with love: teacher savior films   65

time to lose." Moffat instructs Morgan that he has no duty to Bessie but only to the world. If Morgan is "standing at the crossroads," it is clear which path leads to salvation. He must go forth, achieve great things and renounce all else, but Moffat's words are as odd as her assumptions. Can Morgan, a good and moral person, simply forget his own child? What is the implied shame: the pregnancy, the bribery, or the love between teacher and student? After all, why are their collective hearts emphasized?

Responding to the news of the scholarship, a mob gathers outside Moffat's door, cheering for Morgan, waiting to bring him to the train station, to expel him finally from his hometown. He is lifted onto their shoulders as the music rises to mark the triumph of the teacher and the film closes.

## Don't look back

As the townspeople triumphantly carry Morgan off to the train, he glances back briefly as Moffat looks longingly in his direction. Watching at the window, Moffat's face displays deep sorrow, which is peculiar given that Morgan has fulfilled her expectations, acted at her command, and that their relationship has been consummated, through Bessie, in her impending motherhood. Her sadness is not a matter of the power she wields but its result: his future and hers, brought together in the educational moment, are now moving in opposite directions. Morgan's education and his future have been thoroughly dominated by the knowledge and values of his teacher. He has placed himself under his teacher's command to the point of agreeing that he will never return to his hometown again. But in doing so he has occupied the Oxford position once held by the teacher while she in turn has taken the position of a humble villager in Glensarno. Each has been changed by their highly mediated erotic encounter, and each dominated by the educational relationship to the extent that both go forth with conviction that what they do is right. Why, then, do both look back at their former positions one last time before the closing credits fix each in place?

Part of the reason is that the film is over. The finality of Morgan's choice never to return is foreshadowed in an earlier statement in which he expresses his dissatisfaction with the limitations of his small-town life:

> Since the day I was born, I've been a prisoner behind a stone wall, and now someone has given me a leg up to have a look at the other side. They cannot drag me back again. They cannot. Someone must give me a push and send me over.

Morgan recognizes the wall as that which separates him from the life of power and knowledge that belongs to learned people like Moffat. Seen from the other side, however, the same wall excludes those with an Oxford education from participating in the provincial life of the miner and the villagers. The push over the wall that Moffat offers is an expulsion from his own life as well as a leg up. Having abided by Moffat's commandments, Morgan has been banished from his former life, even forsaken. Far from any clear sense of emancipation, the result of his education is an ambivalence about his place in the world.

The finality of the choice that closes the film, accompanied by the longing across the widening gap between teacher and student, underscores the fact that despite each character's transformation both Moffat and Morgan find themselves still quite attached to the roles of teacher and student they once occupied before their desires were realized. While the specific knowledge and attachments that defined their place in their old roles have no place in their new lives and have been forbidden to them by their pact, something of those former roles holds inside each of them that cannot be eradicated by their new positions.

The unlikely, mirrored structure of Moffat's and Morgan's new identities leaves each with an aspect of his or her identity that will remain inexpressible in each character's new role, and yet cannot be so easily given away in favor of new possibilities. Freud appropriates the term "melancholia" to name the internalization of and identification with that which one cannot bear to lose and yet cannot find the words to mourn, drawing upon a rich history of philosophical and literary ideas about the subject's inability to be transformed by its context (Freud, 1957a). By establishing melancholia in relation to the "normal affect of mourning" (p. 243), Freud underscores the significance of the subject's erotic attachments to its objects in constituting its identity, thereby demonstrating that any obstacle to the subject's ability to develop new desires and attach to new objects effectively shuts down its ability to grow and function in the world in a manner consistent with the normative expectations of its social environment.

The difference between a subject's ability to mourn a lost beloved object and its tendency toward melancholic refusal depends less on the subject's attachments to the object than on its objective value within social discourse. As contemporary theorists such as Butler (1999) and Eng (2000) have pointed out, the subject's withdrawal into a private world of its own suffering can be viewed as a refusal of the linguistic order in which the subject's beloved object has no public value and therefore does not count as a loss. In Freud's words, "The difference is that the inhibition of the melancholic seems puzzling to us because we cannot see what it is that is absorbing him so entirely" (1957a, p. 246). For Morgan, his forsaken attachments to Glensarno, the Welsh language, and his untaught way of life are hardly losses within the privileged discourses of Oxford. The very idea that one would have to give something up in order to become educated would likely be unthinkable for Morgan's professors and classmates.

In order to describe the work of melancholic attachment in *The Corn Is Green* and the films that follow its pedagogical pattern, some distinction must be made between Freud's two related theoretical constructions and a third idea that might be called "cultural melancholia" in the somewhat paradoxical

To save, with love: teacher savior films   67

sense that unspeakable loss might be shared by members of a discourse. While Freud's two versions of melancholia differ in their constitutive value for the subject, cultural melancholia might be said to extend the constitutive effects of unmournable attachments to a discourse as a whole and allows us to see how melancholia can take on normative social weight.

Freud (1957a) initially discusses melancholia as a distinct pathological state, involving the "cessation of interest in the outside world, loss of the capacity to love" (p. 244) and to be transformed by new erotic attachments—a condition that Kristeva (1982) seamlessly and without qualification equates with depression. But Freud later (1957b) reconsiders melancholic identifications as essential to character development, allowing him to account for the fact that the human psyche is not endlessly mutable according to its context, but exhibits the capacity to stand out from the immediacy of its own experience. Three characteristics of Freud's later understanding of melancholia stand out in considering Morgan's position. First, the resistance that Freud describes as "character" is not a total, systemic inhibition, but allows some aspects of the subject to continue growing through its erotic attachments to new objects in its environment while others remain true to the past. Second, the fact that the subject, in its divided state, continues to operate in the world, the unspeakable element of the psyche takes on a less pathological, and potentially even a positive role, as it introduces an irreducible grain of sand into an otherwise perfect adapting machine. Without its melancholic attachments, the subject would have no integrity and discursive practices would dry up in an endless reduplication of the word without any difference. Finally, in its new guise, melancholia seems to be a common or even a universal phenomenon, affecting various individual subjects more or less depending on the difference between their early, unspoken attachments and the opportunities that their discursive environments offer for representing these attachments in commonly recognized forms of mourning.

While Morgan will go on to participate in new horizons of meaning at Oxford, to be further dominated by the purposes embedded in Oxford's academic and social discourses according to his own erotic striving, his forbidden and inexpressible attachments to his home will become rooted in his identity as an aspect of the self that cannot be transformed by new desires. The melancholic object serves as a stumbling block to Morgan's success as a student, insofar as his success is defined by his total transformation by the discourses of the school. But it also serves as a stumbling block to the totalizing forces of the school, a blot or stain upon Oxford's discursive horizon that prevents Morgan from dissolving into his new environment.[2] Distinct from both the premodern, positive freedom of belonging to the truth and the modern, negative freedom of escape from limiting social discourses discussed at the outset of this chapter, melancholic identification presents a mechanism of educational freedom based in the subject's erotic attachments to and domination by multiple discourses. Morgan's sense of expulsion and loneliness in relation to both his hometown and the scholar's life ahead of him is reframed in a potentially

## 68  To save, with love: teacher savior films

positive light: his commitments to both discourses prevent total identification with either and, through his imperfect participation, both might be reshaped.

### Loss in the savior curriculum

The fact that Morgan's more localized form of melancholia is applicable, in some way, to every human subject suggests that groups of people might share unmournable losses in common. The idea of a shared melancholic attachment at first seems to contradict melancholia's relation to mourning, as a shared sense of loss seems to be at the center of any mourning ritual. Beyond this fact, a collective sense of unmournable loss would seem to have an opposite place in relation to language, strengthening the communal ties of a discourse as it works around those absences that cannot be spoken. The first of these concerns can be addressed with the clarification that mourning rituals not only demonstrate a shared loss but provide it with context and meaning. Even with the mention of two of the most prominent historical examples of shared melancholia, the Holocaust and the World Trade Center attacks of September 11, 2001, it is clear that a loss does not gain in meaning or accommodate mourning simply because it is shared. To the contrary, the unspeakable character of each of these losses— not only the loss of human life but the feeling that we have lost something of our humanity through these traumatic events—has provided a sense of solidarity precisely in people's inability to ascribe meaning to the events.

Britzman's (1998) work on *The Diary of a Young Girl* is instrumental in founding not only the idea of a cultural melancholia but also the curricular means by which a shared sense of unspeakable loss is reproduced from one generation to the next. Answering the second concern raised above regarding the place of melancholia in language, Britzman's analysis confirms that unspeakable losses shared by a community serve to strengthen the ties of discourse that circulate around the unspeakable loss, just as the individual psyche works to insulate and protect the internalized object from any further loss in language. According to Britzman, the value of Anne Frank's diary is in its capacity to align contemporary students' affective connections to past losses that define current social commitments, despite the text's contested origin. While the text itself might be seen as a means to mourning, Britzman (1998, p. 133) recognizes that, with respect to Anne Frank, "our pedagogy still resides in the ambivalent fault lines of mourning and melancholia, in our desire to remain loyal to the dead."

While Britzman's work takes Anne Frank's diary as a curricular object that stands beyond our capacity to critically analyze it, we can imagine that the complex of discursive limits around September 11, 2001 would be an equally appropriate object for the same demonstration, requiring attention to "how this demand to remain loyal shuts out insight into the conflicts, ambivalences, and desolations that are part of the work of mourning" (Britzman, 1998, p. 133). By sharing an untouchable loss that, as a group, we agree is beyond our collective capacity to put into words, we bind ourselves to one another more strongly in the discursive productions we must produce in order to elide our constitutive lack. In other words, if everything else in the universe can be discussed, dissected, debated, and turned into words the better to be mourned and let go, the handful of objects or events that are immune to critique or revision maintain their hold as central aspects of our identity. Just as Freud posits the subject's earliest attachments as constitutive of its character precisely because these attachments are prior to and thereby immune to the transformative power of language, those cultural attachments that cannot be critically examined prove to have the greatest hold on our collective consciousness. The two phrases most commonly associated with September 11, 2001 and the Holocaust—"never forget" and "never again"—seem like convenient bumper stickers, but they nevertheless remind us that the only way of preventing a loss from repeating itself in history is to maintain that lost object in our presence forever, to make sure that the phenomenon of suffering never ends so that we never have to experience it anew.

While Morgan exemplifies Freud's second, more positive view of melancholic attachment as constitutive of character, the clichéd image of the teacher savior that has developed after the model of *The Corn Is Green* serves as an always imperfect illustration of social commitments that are founded on shared unmournable losses. The opening scenes of *Blackboard Jungle* (1955), *To Sir, With Love* (1968), *Conrack* (1974), *Dangerous Minds* (1995), and *Freedom Writers* (2006) present the culture of impoverished youth as a deliberate form of resistance, or a stubborn attachment to an impoverished, undesirable way of life that refuses to be lost to the nominally nobler purposes of the school. In this genre, however, the possibility of students' melancholic resistance has already been taken into account by the discourse of the film itself, insofar as the teacher quickly adapts her approach to teaching in order to fit the audience's expectations of the poor minority students who populate the imagined classroom.[3]

Highlighting this co-opting of student resistance is a requisite scene or series of scenes in which the heroic teacher fails in his or her first attempt at connecting with students. LouAnne Johnson (*Dangerous Minds*, 1995), for instance, walks out of her first meeting with her students, calling them "rejects from hell," echoing Thackeray's reference to his students as "demons." Once this monolith of student resistance has been registered, the teacher returns with a new purpose, often signified by a new wardrobe and a new manner of speaking, and begins the 10- or 20-minute montaged task of meeting students "where they're at." The end goal of this revised pedagogy is not anything near what the poor students' privileged white peers would call success; instead, the savior teacher's goal is to achieve a much more basic identification with the normative beliefs and values underlying the official curriculum: the unspoken commitments of a culture.

In place of the wistful suggestion of melancholic identification on Morgan's face as he is carried away from his home, more recent teacher savior films suggest another, distinct operation of melancholic attachment that manifests itself culturally rather than individually. The lessons these films teach is that success in the classroom and the world of privilege for minoritized students requires giving up one's own unmournable identifications in favor of the ineffable losses that define authorized discourses. LouAnne Johnson unlocks the barriers that keep her students from white standards of literacy by providing them with a path to appreciating white music and poetry. Bob Dylan serves as the metonymic lost object that represents a fantasy of "the sixties" maintained by the Baby Boomer generation. By keeping Dylan alive, inscribing him as a sort of American poet, white America allows itself to continue its everyday path of segregation and oppression while identifying with a rebellious folk ideal. The soundtrack to *Dangerous Minds* functions in a similar fashion, with many of the songs based on 1960s and 1970s motown samples (Stevie Wonder, Jackson 5) immediately familiar to the white listener, coupled with moralizing lyrics thinly disguised as an authentic poetry of resistance yet penned specifically for the film.

Normalized melancholic identification is also at play in *Freedom Writers* (2006), in which the greatest shock of the savior teacher, Erin Gruwell, is her realization that her poor, marginalized students who live under constant threat of gang violence are ignorant of the Holocaust. For Gruwell, understanding their ignorance provides a key to understanding and perhaps overcoming their oppression, as participation in an empowered discourse requires an emotional tie to the losses embedded in that discourse. If succeeding culturally means aligning oneself with the values embedded in cultural practices, then shaping Gruwell's perspective is the idea that her students are in the wrong, because they suffer the wrong unmournable losses.

Gruwell's great success comes in shifting her students' gaze away from the suffering and oppression in their own neighborhoods—a loss that is genuinely invisible from the perspective of American meritocracy and equality—to the suffering and oppression of Eastern European Holocaust victims, who count as oppressed objects in the discourse of empowered America in ways that poor students and their families cannot. Through this shift, students and teacher alike discover a cure for their own suffering: the students learn the affects that attend a performance of cultural power, while Gruwell is allowed to avert her eyes from the unspeakable problem that defines her work, but remains entirely beyond the school's or the teacher's capacity to address. Illustrating the failure of such a normative melancholic curriculum, and highlighting Britzman's insight in reading Anne Frank as a lost object that founds cultural solidarity, North African immigrant students in *The Class* (2008) go on strike while reading *Diary of a Young Girl*, clearly refusing the French national curriculum's authorized narrative of historical loss, because of its focus on the trauma suffered by Europeans, to the exclusion of the past and current sufferings of colonized North Africans.

The problems of the savior teacher film have not gone unnoticed by scholars writing on educational matters, but the resulting critique is often under-researched and, as a result, fairly thin. Writing about *Dangerous Minds*,

Giroux makes an unsupported and wholly incorrect claim that "Hollywood films about teaching have a long tradition, but rarely do such films use the theme of teaching merely as a pedagogical tool for legitimating a conservative view of 'whiteness'." (1996, p. 47) A brief review of teacher savior films corrects this claim, providing a vivid portrait of whiteness in a powerfully conservative guise. Conroy's (*Conrack*, 1974) first words to his poor, black students are "I want you to take a good, long look at me," after which he spends most of the first class meeting talking about his Irish lineage, his white appearance, and finally his name. Conroy succeeds with the students where their previous teacher has failed them because, as she explains to him, as a white man, he does not understand what black children need. Morgan arrives at Moffat's school with a black face and leaves with a white face, reflecting his radical change from a member of a disposable group of marginally British subjects to an Oxford man. Even Thackeray—another marginalized subject of the British Empire who has gained entree through his education—reinforces the dominance of white culture through his dress, speech, eating habits, and sense of appropriate moral outrage.

## The lost teacher

As so much of the curriculum of teacher savior films is about directing the attention of both the film's students and the film's audience to a society's shared losses, it is not surprising to find filmic teachers and real teachers too stuck on lost objects such as the pre-electric Dylan, the innocence of the folk music movement, and its connection to the Civil Rights movement as a social phenomenon without any moral ambiguity, or Anne Frank, a representative of the millions of slaughtered innocents, and the similarly unambiguously heroic fight against the Nazis. Faced with radical social inequalities and new forms of oppression that do not command the same degree of assent with respect to their causes, it is much easier for teachers on the screen and in classrooms to look to history in order to provide clear examples of national identity, personal responsibility, or moral righteousness. Yet as Freud makes clear in his earliest writings on melancholia, hanging on to objects that are no longer with us can be detrimental to our capacity to form new desires and move on with our lives. Savior teachers' regular return to past losses as a way of relating to, or perhaps avoiding, their students' current suffering, begs the question of whether these teachers themselves suffer a kind of unspeakable loss.

A third, less direct take on melancholia in education that returns to Freud's initial formulation and addresses the question of teachers' melancholic relation to teachable losses comes from *Half Nelson* (2006), a self-conscious, oppositional departure from the teacher as savior films that make up its genre. Dan Dunn, its protagonist, offers scattered, pseudo-Hegelian lessons on the dialectics of history to his inner-city middle school students by day and commits himself to a self-destructive descent into cocaine and crack addiction by night. The film's narrative is intercut with speeches from students about historical events, specifically around the subject of social injustice, but Dunn's curriculum is a heroic vision of the Civil Rights era obliquely celebrated by LouAnn Johnson's focus on Bob Dylan. Dunn believes he is providing the students with the tools to dismantle the structure of their own oppression, but no suggestion of transference, or even the relevance of his lessons to his students enters the scene. Students roll their eyes, laugh, and occasionally connect, but none of them seems to take his nostalgic curriculum as either personally or academically relevant.

The film features elements that situate it carefully within the heroic teacher tradition of *The Corn Is Green*: an unorthodox teacher who attempts to engage the emerging intellectual eros of his students, the expulsion of the official curriculum, a favored student, and a menacing figure who would stand in the way of the pedagogical relationship. But even from the first of Dunn's weak classroom presentations, the fabric of the fantasy begins to fray. By the time the favored student, Drey, catches Dunn smoking crack in the girls' locker room after basketball practice, the sense of disappointment and discomfort has become unbearable to the point at which it is clear that the film intends to bury the ideal of the messianic teacher.

Attempting to engage his students on oppositional historical forces, Dunn asks the students, "What keeps us down?" The students call out various answers: "prisons," "white man," "schools," and Dunn agrees to all of these. "Aren't you the machine?" one student asks. Caught off guard, Dunn attempts to deflect the question, dramatically calling out, "Oh no you *didn't!*" and getting a laugh out of the students. A moment later, he accepts the association, realizing that it can be subsumed within his understanding of dialectics without implicating him personally. "But if I'm part of it, so are you. We all are." The student's point effectively dismissed by way of diffusion, Dunn turns back to an appropriation of his students' alienation and slang in order to show how connected he is: "You guys hate coming to school, right? Holla back if you heard me."

Dunn's rhetorical trick of turning everyone into perpetrators and victims, while eliding any real response to his students by mimicking their habits of speech for a laugh, avoids the question of what role he is supposed to play in relation to his students. Snorting cocaine with two young women at a bar after work, Dunn rambles some fragments of trite expressions: "What am I supposed to teach them, you know? That's the point. If you can help one student, no, if you can change one person . . . ," as if he has already accepted the futile position he plays.

Dunn is not as repulsive as his father, a self-satisfied former anti-Vietnam War demonstrator who attempts to engage his son with stale racist humor: "Teach me some ebonics. Is that what they've got you teaching in that zoo?" But Dunn's failure can be summed up in the fact that he believes that his rambling misunderstanding of Hegel's philosophy of history is superior to the curriculum he has been provided by the school. The film's inclusion of his parents helps to flesh out Dunn's commitments insofar as they show his attachments to impossibly idealized political movements of the past. With no way of realizing the nostalgic ideals he has learned from his parents, from politicians and the movies, his solution is to remain within a destructive cycle of negation and denial without any hope of negating the negation that moves Hegelian dialectical theory forward.

Dunn's melancholia—his inability to move forward due to his inability to let go of his parents' generation's supposed moral achievements—suggests a deeper ambivalence in American culture about re-opening the unfinished question of race due to the fact that the lost ideal of the 1960s is too beautiful to give up. Unlike Morgan, whose relationship to his unmourned losses promises to give him distinction in his new environment, Dunn's melancholia is not matched by any desire to succeed in his new environment because, according to the racist culture in which he lives, he stands superior to it. As a result, Dunn finds himself awash in a mix of idealistic excitement and crushing grief, visualized through the ups and downs of his drug addiction.

*Half Nelson* seems to suggest that just as Dunn perpetuates a system of criminality and violence toward poor and marginalized communities through his drug use, his practice of teaching as a privileged, white, post-college practice of *noblesse oblige* sustains an economy premised on divisions between rich and poor. His remarkable failure reminds us that the ends to which filmic teachers educe the desires of their students are not always objectively positive, but may simply reflect the teacher's own needs and, as a result, may not serve the student or his community at all. Looking again at Morgan, we may be able to see that he is unwittingly subject to Moffatt's unresolved desires to attend Oxford, and that his attendance to her losses might be a greater loss to his own community, as they have lost one of their brightest stars to academic purposes beyond their interest or comprehension. More importantly for the purposes of this study, Dunn's failure and its relation to his family history and his own unresolved losses open the question of what the teacher wants, or what kind of fantasy the teacher is chasing in engaging with students. In the next chapter, we turn to the question of the teacher's desires by looking at films in which the fantasy of the teacher as a completed subject, presumably beyond desire, falls apart in its quest for fulfillment.

## Notes

1 Our culture's concern with students' freedom in education is no more than an exposition of a conflict within our notion of an educated self: an individual whose freedom is predicated upon his subjection to the authority of traditional knowledge.
2 Slavoj Žižek (2001, pp. 94–96) suggests that melancholia, redescribed as Lacan's *objet petit a*, is precisely that which creates authority in a discourse, as it prevents the individual from being absorbed entirely by the discursive mechanism already in place.
3 The fact that these films are often "based on a true story" draws attention to their formulaic character and the power of the popular imaginary to normalize not only film but ordinary human experiences.

## References

Bauer, D. M. (1998) Indecent proposals: Teachers in the movies. *College English*, 60(3), 301–317.

Berlin, I. (1969) *Four Essays on Liberty*. New York: Oxford University Press.

*Blackboard Jungle*, Richard Brooks, dir. (USA: Metro-Goldwyn-Mayer, 1955).

Britzman, D. (1998) *Lost Subjects, Contested Objects: Toward a Psychoanalytic Inquiry of Learning*. Albany, NY: State University of New York Press.

Burmester, B. (1997) When "Phaedrus" meets "Oleanna": Teaching composition as social justice, or reconsidering power (im)balances between students and teachers. Paper presented at the Annual Meeting of the Conference on College Composition and Communication (48th, Phoenix, AZ, March 12–15, 1997). http://files.eric.ed.gov/fulltext/ED409565.pdf.

Butler, J. (1999) *Gender Trouble: Feminism and the Subversion of Identity*. New York: Routledge.

*The Class*, Laurent Cantet, dir. (France: Haut et Court, 2008).

*Conrack*, Martin Ritt, dir. (USA: Twentieth Century Fox Film Corporation, 1974).

*The Corn Is Green*, Irving Rapper, dir. (USA: Warner Bros, 1945).

*Dangerous Minds*, John Smith, dir. (USA: Hollywood Pictures, 1995).

Ellsworth, E. (1992) Why doesn't this feel empowering? Working through the repressive myths of critical pedagogy. In C. Luke and J. Gore (eds) *Feminisms and Critical Pedagogy*. New York: Routledge. p. 90–119.

Eng, D. L. (2000). Melancholia in the late twentieth century. *Signs: Journal of Women in Culture and Society*, 25(4), 1275.

*Freedom Writers*, Richard LaGravenese, dir. (USA: Paramount Pictures, 2007).

Freud, S. (1957a) *The Standard Edition of the Complete Psychological Works of Sigmund Freud* (Vol. XIV). London: The Hogarth Press.

Freud, S. (1957b) *The Standard Edition of the Complete Psychological Works of Sigmund Freud* (Vol. XIX). London: The Hogarth Press.

Giroux, H. (1996). Race, pedagogy and whiteness in *Dangerous Minds*. *Cineaste*, 22(4), 46–50.

*Half Nelson*, Ryan Fleck, dir. (USA: Hunting Lane Films, 2006).

Kristeva, J. (1982) *Black Sun: Depression and Melancholia* (L.S. Roudiez, trans.). New York: Columbia University Press.

*Oleanna*, David Mamet, dir. (USA: Bay Kinescope, 1994).

Peters, M. (1996) *Poststructuralism, Politics, and Education*. South Hadley, MA: Bergin & Garvey.

St. Pierre, E. (1997) An introduction to figurations: A poststructural practice of inquiry. *Qualitative Studies in Education*, 10(3), 279–284.

*To Sir, With Love*, James Clavell, dir. (United Kingdom: Columbia Pictures, 1967).

Žižek, S. (2001) *Enjoy Your Symptom! Jacques Lacan in Hollywood and Out*. New York: Routledge, pp. 94–96.

# Chapter 5

# Expulsion
## The horror of the fantasy made real

In recognizing the power of transference in shaping pedagogical relationships and the subjectivities that emerge from these relationships, the threat of eros, as well as its promise, remains ever present. It does not take a great deal of imagination to project the suggestion of a sexual relationship onto situations where none has been suggested, as Bauer (1998, p. 307) seems to in her analysis of *Dangerous Minds* (1995), claiming the "sexual ambigu[ity]" of a scene in which a student "takes refuge" at a teacher's house in order to escape death. In this particular case, we might claim that Bauer reads a bit too deep, but not because her approach to viewing is corrupt or perverse. School films have been presenting images of erotic tension so consistently and for so long that it is difficult to stop looking for love in school films. Žižek, speaking on "one of the great achievements in Western Civilization," *The Sound of Music* (1965), in the film *Slavoj Žižek: The Reality of the Virtual* (2004), provides some insight into the ways films fulfill our unrecognized fantasies while upholding the authority of the law:

> Officially, as we know, it's a story about small, anti-Fascist democratic Austrians. At the political level, that is to say; I mean leave out all the singing aspect. Small, honest democratic Austrians fighting, resisting the Nazi occupation of Austria in '38. But look at the movie really closely . . . You will discover a quite different reality: a kind of virtual reality of the officially depicted narrative reality . . . Austrians are depicted in the movie . . . as kind of smallish, beautiful provincial Fascists; their idiocies emphasized as local folkloric dresses and so on. They are presented directly as anti-intellectual, rooted in a narrow lifeworld and so on. Now look at how the occupying Nazis are presented. They are mostly not soldiers but managers, bureaucrats, exquisitely dressed with short moustaches, smoking expensive cigarettes and so on. In other words, almost a caricature of [a] cosmopolitan, decadent, corrupted Jew. So, that's my point: at the level of simple narrative reality, we get one message: democratic resistance to Nazism. But at the level of—let's call it virtual texture . . . we get practically the opposite message: which is honest Fascists resisting decadent

Jewish cosmopolitan take-over. And incidentally, maybe this is one of the reasons why this movie was so extremely popular: while officially agreeing with our democratic ideology, it at the same time addresses our secret Fascist dreams.

*To Sir, With Love*'s penultimate scene, setting two of the most beautiful people to appear on film in 1967 dancing wildly inches from one another, under an unspoken but absolute rule that they may not touch, fulfills the conditions of Žižek's (2000) observations perfectly. While the official moral restriction on romantic relationships between teachers and students is reinforced by signifiers of clothing, age, and ethnicity, its opposite is celebrated, even if it remains unrealized, in the camera's ability to cast the two as a couple, with the entire senior class, faculty, and administration cheering them on. As a result, the audience gets to experience the dance as something much more exciting than it actually is, insofar as it suggests a rupture in the function of the law.

All the same, *To Sir*'s moral refusal to realize the erotic relationship between Dare and Thackeray leaves open the possibility that another narrative—filmic or otherwise—will set out to deliberately break the taboo around pedagogical relationships, motivated by iconoclasm, titillation, or simply an aesthetic imperative of novelty. Two films, one titled *The Teacher* (1974) and another titled *A Teacher* (2013), both serve as clear examples of this will to overcome the limits set by the past, as each takes the explicit sexualization of the teacher as its primary aim. While the former is a nearly unwatchable B-movie and the latter a dark independent film, the two films fail in precisely the same manner, namely by labelling one of their central characters as "the teacher," but doing little else to imbue her with a sense of discursive authority or completeness. Without this stature, the film has no moral tension to break, as the figure designated as a teacher has no noble distance to lose. In both cases, the character is undoubtedly sexual, but only doubtfully occupies the role of the teacher, and so the sexuality carries none of the scandal that might make it interesting.

Richard Eyre's *Notes on a Scandal* (2006) seems to wade somewhere in the same, deliberately murky waters as other films in which teachers and students get too close, while at the same time reassuring its audience that there's solid moral ground somewhere, if only in our naming the relationship a scandal from the outset. In its initial moves it seems to offer nothing new to the long-standing tradition of narratives featuring teachers and students in love initiated by Alcibiades' confession of love for Socrates.

By placing the film in relation to the tradition that precedes it, however, significant differences and new connections emerge between *Notes* and its context: both the all-too-human films in which teachers go too far and the heroic films in which they don't. As we have seen in preceding chapters, the more innocent narratives comprised by the genre of pedagogical love stories concern themselves primarily with students' educational self-becoming and treat erotic longing as a force both necessary and necessarily sublimated within the task of learning. The less innocent narratives use schools as a familiar stand-in for the authority of social norms—a contrast with the rebellious intimacy of the lovers. In *Notes*, as suggested even by its title, the primary concern is not teaching or learning or sex, but the scandal that stands as a looming threat within our existing pedagogical discourses.

While *Notes* introduces itself through recognizable, idealistic images of erotic education—a heroic novice teacher, a lost child, and restrictive curricular rules that must be broken in order for "real" learning to occur—these elements are deployed in a manner that demonstrates their moral and educational ambivalence. *Notes* accomplishes its transgressive break with the moral norms of educational practice by exploiting a tension already present within traditional ideals of teacher and student identities, namely, the idea that while erotic attraction constitutes the pedagogical relationship—by bringing the teacher and student into one another's proximity—it also threatens to destroy that same relationship by closing down the distance that makes educational eros flourish.

By focusing on this structural tension, the film emphasizes the fact that both teacher and student are lured by the fantasy of transference, albeit in different ways. The student's fantasy of the teacher as the subject presumed to know produces desires as it reveals what he lacks in comparison to his teacher, and provides a model he might follow. For the teacher, who is not the all-knowing subject her student believes her to be, the fantasy of transference covers over and orders her lacks and gaps, providing her with a sense of her own authority capable of inspiring her students.

*Notes* makes a break from its tradition by representing many of the narrative elements of an erotic school fiction such as *To Sir, With Love* while at the same time discouraging its audience from finally succumbing to the transferential fantasy they are bound to expect. Revealing the teacher as incomplete, like the student, *Notes* breaks down the categorical difference between the two, rendering their relationship devoid of pedagogical significance. Yet this apedagogical relationship would not have the added element of scandal if it were not for the fact that celebrated teachers in history and fiction are often recognized for their revolutionary pedagogy: as illustrated by our analysis in previous chapters, great teaching takes place beyond the law. As the ideal teacher is regularly defined in opposition to an existing lifeless curriculum, her iconoclastic practices appear as altruistic rather than self-serving. When the teacher's rebelliousness seems to be motivated strictly by its negation of the law, however, the upshot is what Lacan refers to as *jouissance*: a transgressive, thrilling enjoyment in breaking with the symbolic order; a form of pleasure that exists not *despite* its lawlessness but *because of* it.

*Notes* provides a more complex picture of teaching identity than most of the filmic images that occupy the popular imaginary, but this complexity is only possible because it draws upon these popular images, which contain all the convolutions and paradoxes of teacher identity in more inchoate manifestations. In effect, what *Notes* achieves is a fulfillment of the erotic pedagogical

## 78 The horror of the fantasy made real

relationship promised in so many of its predecessors. In fulfilling this fantasy, however, it reveals the horror of the fantasy made real.

## "Only you": the fantastic image of the teacher

*Notes* follows many school films with familiar establishing shots, creating expectations about the story to come. An asphalt inner-city schoolyard, mobbed with unruly teenagers making their way into the halls signals a familiar image of the school as barely containing a threat of undisciplined energies. In the midst of the mob, above the fray, the new teacher, Bathsheba Hart, arrives by bicycle, invoking Jean Brodie and Lily Moffatt, two heroic if unorthodox teachers who are each portrayed arriving at school by the same mode of transportation, as if from nowhere. Her arrival by bicycle tells us that Sheba is not of this desperate place, yet is practical, down to earth, and ready to cultivate order in the swarming chaos.

Unlike the genre that it quotes with this opening scene, however, the view from on high with which *Notes* introduces the viewer to the school does not belong to an omniscient or impersonal narrator. The viewpoint from which the audience takes in these familiar scenes is that of Barbara Covett, standing on a balcony above the school's entrance hall, who offers us not only her vision but her commentary on the children she teaches: "Here come the local pubescent proles. The future plumbers, shop assistants, and doubtless the odd terrorist too. In the old days, we confiscated cigarettes and wank mags. Now it's knives and crack cocaine. And they call it progress."

An insider to the school, Covett at the same time stands above it—both in her clear superiority to the bland teachers who surround her and more so in that she is the narrator of the story through her diary entries. Covett negates the fantasy of teaching typically featured in school films, and as a critique of this fantasy she promises to demonstrate its limits, revealing the embarrassing desires that fantasy sometimes succeeds in covering over. Through her writing, in volumes marked "Ruled," suggesting her relation to the moral codes reproduced through schooling, she nonetheless addresses her audience in a spirit of intimacy: "People trust me with their secrets. But who do I trust with mine? You, only you."

Covett's initial assessment of Hart underscores her image as the outsider teacher while maintaining Covett's superiority as one who knows better: "Hard to read the wispy novice. Is she a sphinx or simply stupid? Artfully dishevelled today. The tweedy tramp coat is an abhorrence. It seems to say 'I'm just like you'. But clearly she's not." Sheba has neither the ability nor the experience to be a typical teacher, but as the genre of film to which her role refers features only heroic, radically different teachers, the audience does not want to see a typical teacher. As in the celebrated teaching films that precede it, *Notes* promises a teacher drawn from fantasy: willing and able to transgress the staid, lifeless rules of the classroom; sacrificing herself for the sake of her students' success. As in other films, Sheba's bland, inert colleagues introduce themselves through

# The horror of the fantasy made real   79

a faculty meeting in which the flatness of their characters suggests, at best, the middling background to her brilliant difference; at worst, a group defined by not only mediocrity but jealousy toward the atypical newcomer.

Tracing the borrowed narrative arc with which *Notes* begins, Sheba's altruism quickly meets mob resistance, and she is rattled by her students' behavior and the attention she receives as one who has not yet achieved the authority invested in her role. Sheba's colleague notices her class is out of control, but rather than step in as an authority he reports the scene casually to his colleagues in the staff room: "It's like bloody *Lord of the Flies* in there. Boys screaming, 'Get your tits out for the lads'. Girls too. It's carnage . . . [Sheba's] completely lost it . . . she's screaming, 'Stop it you little fucking bastards!'" Covett, as the representative of the law, rushes to Sheba's aid, restores order to the classroom, draws apologies from the offenders, and comforts Sheba.

In the midst of her growing despair over her teaching ability, Sheba sits at a café with her colleagues—Covett and "Fatty" Hodge. Covett points out froth from a cappuccino on Sheba's nose: a blot on an otherwise perfect image. Hodge, attempting to comfort Sheba, counsels her with a deflated idea of pedagogy: "Console yourself with the gems. That's when it's satisfying."

Hodge's advice might be taken as merely a confirmation of her lazy mediocrity, reminding the audience of their expectation that the exceptional teacher is surrounded by lesser teachers who fail to challenge their students. But Hodge's implicit confession that teachers seek satisfaction in their students is perhaps more than the audience wants to hear, as the idea of a teacher satisfying her desires through her students jars with the fantasy of the teacher as beyond want and therefore always acting in students' interest. Contrary to Alcibiades' depiction of Socrates as complete and beyond desire, Hodge's pathetic advice on teaching confesses a gap she seeks to fill through attending to her better students.[1]

Faults in the perfect picture of the filmic teacher continue to emerge as the action of the film moves farther from the school setting. Covett, invited to Sheba's house for Sunday brunch as a reward for restoring order in her classroom, maintains the audience's expectation of Sheba's superiority. Upon arriving, however, Covett's ideal image of Sheba's life is deflated by the casual banality of the occasion. After brunch, secluded in a garden shed, Sheba's admission, like "a novice confessing to mother superior," that "marriage and kids don't give you meaning," both presages her later confession while at the same time revealing the feeling of emptiness that led her to teaching: "Shouldn't have kidded myself I could teach . . . and I am so desperate to get out and do something."

With Sheba's confession of her incompleteness, all of the parallels and quotations that *Notes* has carefully placed, linking Sheba to heroic film teachers, begin to unravel. Unlike the teachers regularly encountered in film, and despite her respectable home, Covett learns that Sheba suffers from the same feelings of imperfection and desire that plague ordinary people like herself. The fact that Sheba has been using teaching to escape her domestic desperation demonstrates her participation in the same impossible notion that Alcibiades

# 80 The horror of the fantasy made real

held: the teacher as all-knowing. Sheba seems to believe that by standing in the place of the mythic teacher, the subject presumed to know, she would also solve the problem of her own desires.

Like the image of failed teaching offered in the character of Fatty Hodge, Sheba has come to teaching seeking fulfillment: she seeks recognition as the "wonderful teacher" Covett promises her she will be, and is now poised to fulfill her desires by consoling herself with the gems. This interplay between juxtaposed images of teaching fantasies and teaching desires set *Notes* apart from its precursors in a way that complicates the familiar image of the teacher as beyond desire that is readily available in popular media. While other films have offered glimpses of the teacher as a desiring being, whether to provide dramatic tension or to humanize the hero, *Notes* allows these moments of desire to take on their own weight, combining with and eventually destroying the selfless fantasy of heroic teaching with which the film begins.

According to the psychoanalytic schemata developed through the work of Freud and Lacan, fantasy, or the image-making faculty of the human psyche, serves the purpose of smoothing over the ragged edges of the desiring self, of promising a self-completion toward an ego ideal. Desire, by its nature, must always go unfulfilled, at least insofar as desire itself is never satisfied, but each particular desire for some object is always replaced by another. The limitations on the subject's ability to fulfill its desire posed by both natural and human laws support and maintain the very desires they refuse: by leaving desire unmet, they ensure its continuity, as well as the striving of the subject who yearns to fulfill them. Fantasy, on the other hand, can be seen as standing in opposition to the laws that produce and promote desires, insofar as imagining a completed self suggests the possibility of overcoming the laws of human limitation, of having fulfilled one's desires without regard for the limits that constitute subjectivity.

Sheba's mistake stems from a fault in the popular fantasy of teaching. On the one hand, our society—especially as portrayed in film—promotes the idea that anyone can teach (especially Sheba's subject area of art) and that outsiders to teaching may prove to be better teachers than jaded veterans; on the other, the teaching role retains a great degree of power and authority for anyone who has been a student. The result is that many, like Sheba, see teaching as a powerful, self-completing role that can be taken up without any restrictions upon the desiring self.

## The scandal and the law

By the time Sheba sits down for coffee with Covett and Hodge, *Notes* has reached the point in the genre of teacher success films where the audience might expect a great shift in pedagogical approach, a montage of late-night preparations demonstrating a rethinking of teaching identity, or a radical change in wardrobe and attitude. As the camera has chosen this teacher over others, the film promotes the idea that her lack of ability, her lapse in authority in controlling her classroom, and her doubts about herself are momentary shortcomings required by the arc of the narrative. This fantasy has been interrupted by Sheba's confession of desire, of incompleteness, but at this point in the film, just as it is too late to prevent the as yet unacknowledged scandal from taking place, it may also be too late to change the heroic fantasy that the film has promoted with the help of the tradition that stands behind it.

While *Notes* reintroduces its characters through the following scenes in ways that are clearly scandalous, this reintroduction clashes with the expectations cultivated in earlier scenes. This conflicted portrayal lends complexity to the film's characters, but also highlights serious paradoxes in the teacher's identity as a socially-constructed category, as well as conflicts between the teacher's identity qua teacher and her identity qua human subject.

Covett—and through her eyes, the audience—discovers Sheba and Steven's affair through a series of cuts between two simultaneous scenes: a Christmas pageant in the school's auditorium and the shadows of the art room. Covett sits in the audience of the pageant holding a seat for Sheba, who doesn't arrive. Abandoning the seats in frustration, Covett searches for Sheba and, peering through the window of the art room, finds her sexually engaged with her student, Steven. For the moment, shocked by the scene, the audience may not notice that Covett fails to interrupt the crime. What is not lost to the viewer, however, is Covett's sinister, spying gaze framed in the window, suggesting her implication in the act.

Covett's spying is not the only mirror held to the new discovery; however, neither is she the only one held complicit in the crime. While Covett has left the auditorium, the pageant there continues, and the cuts between the two scenes juxtapose the teacher's seduction of her student with students on stage singing "Glory to the New Born King." Covett spies in fascination and horror while the rest of the school body cheers and claps. As the paralleled performances in the auditorium and the art room come to a climax, an image of the Headmaster fills the screen, cheering enthusiastically, "Very Good! Well Done!" Hodge—who had earlier instructed Sheba to find her gem—conducts the chorus onstage and, symbolically, the actions taking place offstage. Thus, instructed by the film, and following a long tradition of erotically informed pedagogical relationships, the audience finds itself encouraged to cheer for student and teacher to come together. Like Thackeray and Pamela Dare dancing wildly at the climax of *To Sir, With Love* (1967), like Morgan and Moffatt symbolically wed by a child in *The Corn Is Green* (1945) and like Hart and Kingsfield similarly brought together by their mutual connection to Susan in *The Paper Chase* (1973), Sheba and Steven seem to inevitably arrive at their moment according to their respective positions as characters in a school film.

Interestingly, at the very beginning of *Notes*, it is Covett's admonishment of Steven that both precedes and oddly parallels the pageant song. The first time we are introduced to Steven he scores a goal playing football. He points to Sheba and takes off his shirt. When Covett tells him to put it back on,

## 82 The horror of the fantasy made real

he explains that he just scored the winning goal. "Glory be," she sarcastically replies, in distinct wording that foreshadows the coupling of Steven and Sheba: even their most fierce opponent becomes yet another supporter.

Barbara's passionate pursuit of Sheba for the details of the affair mirror the audience's enthusiastic desires to know, but the answers Sheba gives are disappointing. "I hadn't been pursued like this for years," she claims, echoing her earlier complaint about spending the last ten years as a mother, but contradicting evidence the film has provided regarding the school community's interest in her, further emphasized by Covett's earlier commentary on how all the faculty and students "flock to her, even limp little Brian."

"It began to feel like a secret and secrets can be seductive," is Sheba's next explanation, recalling her private lair where she discloses to Covett her desires for meaning and purpose beyond the everyday life of the home. The seductive secrecy of Sheba's desires reflects the fact that they cannot be spoken within the normative expectations of a homemaker's work, yet it is precisely this opposition to her social expectations that impels her toward the forbidden relationship: "Something in me felt entitled. I've been good all my adult life. I've been a decent wife, dutiful mother . . . This voice inside me kept saying, 'Why shouldn't you be bad. Why shouldn't you transgress? You've earned the right'."

Sheba's excuses and attempts to explain her actions to Covett sound naïve, suggesting that, like her biblical eponym, she has been seduced by forces beyond her control into a scandal whose repercussions are beyond her comprehension. Far from the audience's expectations of the teacher's wisdom, Sheba seems like a fool, and, as the film later reveals, she has been fooled by Steven's story of abuse at the hands of his father. "You wanted a sob story; I gave it to you. Made you feel like Bob Geldof," he teases, mocking the very savior complex that the film uses to establish audience expectations.

Unlike Sheba, Steven does not seem in need. Athletic, confident, and handsome, with unblemished skin, he appears older and far more confident than his 15 years. The representational drawings he first shows Sheba are technically sophisticated and already fully formed. "These are good; you can draw," is all Sheba can offer. During the one art lesson the film depicts, it is the student who explains da Vinci to the teacher. But Steven, like Sheba, also bears a biblical name that suggests his innocence, even his martyrdom. When Sheba expresses concern that their affair may be made public, he only worries about being expelled from school: "Whatever shit you're working out—you know, your husband, your kid, you, I don't know. I can't help you." Other than their beautiful bodies, both teacher and student have nothing to give one another. "It was supposed to be fun," summarizes Steven. And, in turn, his attempts to be a seducer come off as alternately silly and vaguely disturbed. As his mother reminds Sheba in a violent confrontation after she discovers the affair, "He's just a boy!" If Steven is a martyr and Sheba a seduced innocent, how can the audience resolve their confused feelings of intense curiosity and moral outrage?

The horror of the fantasy made real    83

Two aspects of Sheba's confessed motivation stand out as guideposts in understanding *Notes'* moral manipulations. One is that she does not express any desire for Steven. Instead, following her own schoolgirl longings, she wishes to stand in a place of excess—a fantasy quickly perverted into a wanton impulse of transgression without gain. The second is the "voice" that supposedly impels her to act. If she has been good, if she has internalized the word of the law, what voice speaks to her from inside? Throughout the film, the voice that has guided the audience through the scandal has been associated with the rules. Covett's voice has represented the law and even claimed a purer interpretation of the law in defying the Headmaster's orders. As with other films that make up the background of assumptions that *Notes* takes as its guide, the institutional character of teaching provides an imperative task for the heroic outsider through an act of transgressive negation.

Despite her identification with the law, Barbara Covett is, by her name, also a covetous, barred subject, who jealously seeks to use her position of confidence to pressure Sheba into an intimate relationship: "A magnificent opportunity here . . . secure the prize long term forever in my debt. I could gain everything by doing nothing." *Notes* encourages its audience to reject the authority of law by portraying the law itself as a vulgar, unlovable, desiring being—showing its limits by addressing its wants. When she charges Sheba to "Take some responsibility," Covett's plotting diaries have already been discovered and read, undermining her authority to instruct. Instead, she falls back on language similar to Steven's: "I gave you exactly what you wanted." Displaying the limit of the law encourages its negation while indicating a preferred place of transgressive pleasure outside of the law. While the audience knows that they cannot morally support Sheba and Steven's relationship, their rejection of Covett creates an alliance with the lawless transgression of these blind innocents: an untenable and unsettling fulfillment of teaching's filmic fantasy.

In short, *Notes* provides a horrifying image of a teacher–student relationship by fulfilling a publicly held fantasy that has always been played out in an unfulfilled fashion under the limiting character of the law. A cursory analysis of the film might tempt the belief that what is lacking in this scandal is some final authority, some true representative of the law who is not motivated by her own fantasies. The response offered by *Notes*, however, is that such a belief in authority is itself nothing more than a schoolgirl fiction and that the law is itself incomplete. *Notes'* critical look at the fantasy of transference, that serves not only as the foundation for the representation of the teacher in film but for the place of the teacher in the social imaginary itself, underscores the fragile character of authority, while uncovering a more subtle aspect of its nature.

The fragility of authority, as it is unmasked in *Notes*, lies just beneath its convincing surface, and consists in the inevitable fact that no teacher could ever live up to the impossible ideal impressed upon our cultural norms. At some point, every teacher will have to be a person, and some interruption of the myth, whether in the form of the insistence of the body or the weakness of the spirit,

## 84 The horror of the fantasy made real

will inevitably break through. This analysis is important, but if *Notes'* analysis of transferential authority remained at this level, it would do little more than note the fictional character of our teacherly ideals. Any person walking out of *Freedom Writers* (2007) might achieve this same level of critique, and feel a little deflated and a little clever at the same time.

What makes *Notes'* undermining of transference far more damning is the fact that it helps us see how the fantasy of teaching and the symbolic order that stands as the backdrop of this fantasy serve to undermine one another. On the one hand, transference serves as a negation of the symbolic order, the law, insofar as the teacher is understood to stand *beyond* the law, occupying a place from which the application of the law or its negation might be authorized coherently. But if the individual who breaks the law is found to be subject to the law, in the form of desire, returning to Sheba's feelings of incompleteness, of want for meaning, this claim of the law over the ideal not only destroys the ideal but also the student subject's fiction of his own ego—that which holds the subject together as a coherent narrative that is more than just the competing demands of social norms and bodily drives. But if fantasy and law tend to undermine one another, what *Notes* leaves in its often crude and disturbing physicality is that the only real element in the pedagogical relationship is a thinly veiled insistence of the body.

Following the later Lacanian topology of the Borromean knot, in which the imaginary, the symbolic and the real are connected to one another in such a way that the removal of any of the three would also result in the dissolution of the bond between the other two, the problem of transference can be seen in the fact that it spans the imaginary and the symbolic, providing a fantasy of mastery in relation to the law. The relationship is not strictly paradoxical, but it opens the way to its own undermining insofar as the negation of the law implied in fantasy renders the master's mastery inconsequential. The filmic teacher's iconoclasm, breaking the rules that give her authority in order to have a more "authentic" relationship with her students, perfectly illustrates this problem in enacting transferential relationships.

From a Lacanian standpoint, it makes sense that transference has its problems. Based on the topography of the Borromean knot, we can see that the imaginary and symbolic are not linked to one another except through their independent relationships to the real, or more precisely, through the specific opposition to the real that each represents. Just as the symbolic and the real undermine the imaginary as the foundation of the ego, and as the real and imaginary falsify the claims of the symbolic, so too are the imaginary and the symbolic tied together in a denial of the real, which finds its ideological negative in the problematic ties of transference.

Defined in this oppositional manner, the real is what remains when the organizing principles of the imaginary and the social laws of the symbolic order are both removed. The real is unintelligible to the human psyche, because it is the raw there-ness that is made habitable through the objectivity conferred by the imaginary and the order of things described in language. Strictly speaking, that which is unimaginable and unsymbolizable cannot be experienced, but Lacan allows that a trace of the real may be seen in inexplicable scenes of trauma. Among school films, the very best example of a film that confronts the problem of the real is *Picnic at Hanging Rock* (1975), in which something goes terribly wrong, but no one, including the audience, ever gains any knowledge or understanding about what happened.

The film opens with Miranda, one of the girls who will disappear on the rock, reciting: "What we see and what we seem are but a dream. A dream within a dream." Miranda's recitation contains a reference to the Lacanian real, insofar as it begs us to consider what lies outside the confines of the dream. The same move from constructed, safe space into the unknown is undertaken by a schoolgirl field trip into the wilderness to see a geological formation. The scientific purpose of the trip highlights the limits of human knowledge, as the light of science is held up against an infinite darkness that surrounds it. Whatever it is into which the girls disappear, the only knowledge it generates is in the unspeakable horror produced in those who remain.

In the tradition of school films on which *Notes* bases its particular twist, we can see the shadow of this brutal presence in the forms of teachers' ignorance, institutional chaos, and the ever-present drives. *To Sir, With Love*'s Thackeray signals the threat of the real in the insistence of his bodily drives when questioned about his choice of a single orange when eating lunch at school:

> When I eat . . . do I love to eat! I love wine, but I just can't have a glass. I want the whole bottle. So I avoid wine, and pastrami sandwiches, and baked potatoes with butter and bacon, and strawberry shortcake, and cheesecake. But I like to eat light for lunch.

As if to underscore the metaphor being built around Thackeray's appetite by seemingly changing the subject, his colleague responds to his gluttonous litany by asking, "How's the Dare girl?" "No problems," he counters, without missing a beat.

In Sheba's case, her attempts to establish her authority as a teacher by humanizing herself, becoming friendly with her student, instead erode the rule upon which that authority is based until the law has been surpassed, the fantasy of mastering the law has been rendered moot, and the only element that remains connecting the two individuals is their respective animal drives and the way each person's drive circulates around the other's body.

## From the sublime to the ridiculous

The history of school films leading up to *Notes on a Scandal* (2006) extends and makes visible a set of much older culturally held beliefs about teachers, students, and their respective motivations. From Plato's *Symposium* through

*Dead Poets Society* (1989), students are understood to be moved by a more or less sublimated erotic attraction to a teacher they believe to have some piece of knowledge they lack.

*Notes'* exploration of a failure of the pedagogical relationship, despite the presence of various recognizable elements from this erotic educational tradition commonly associated with good teaching, reveals both the value of transference as a motivating fiction and its complex opposition to the drives it helps to sublimate in the production of human subjects and the reproduction of human norms.

The popularity of the school film attests to the widespread lure of transference. As Britzman (1986) explains in relation to teacher training, even those who study pedagogy as a practice continue to be swayed by impossible fantasies about the knowledge and authority of the teacher. Certainly this belief is not held with respect to all teachers: the exception to the rule provides the rule of the exceptional teacher. But even those who leave school without the slightest degree of admiration for the real teachers they encountered seem to fall for the impossible fantasies of teaching that are exchanged and enlarged through the filmic imagination.

What filmic fantasies typically encourage their audiences to forget, and what *Notes* viscerally recalls to mind, is that when social conventions place the teacher beyond desire, and by extension beyond the authority of the law, the institutional norms that undergird the teacher's authority paradoxically fall with it. While Lacan (1961) insists that transference is a fantasy shared by analyst and analysand, or by teacher and student, the lie must have its limits: a fact that leaves two unlovable alternatives regarding the teacher's understanding of her own motivations. Certainly, contemporary cultural norms do not admit the obvious and yet seemingly perverse fact that a teacher desires and seeks to experience her students' desires in order to give her own professional life meaning. The alternative, however, explored in *Notes*, is clearly worse. If the teacher believes in her student's valuation of her as a subject presumed to know, if she participates in the fantasy of teaching in such a way that she actually believes herself to be beyond desire, then she will inevitably fall into the moral hubris of believing in the altruism of everything she does, giving license to pursue the satisfaction of desires she fails to recognize and drives she does not want to know.

*Election* (1999), which portrays the problem of teacher's desires in a darkly humorous narrative, begins with a statement that reflects this dangerous hubris and lack of self-knowing. A narrated claim on the part of Jim McAllister, the protagonist teacher, that he did in fact live a fantasy of teaching as a contribution to the civic good, would feel false and unreflective even if it were presented on its own. In contrast to this narration, and highlighting its willful ignorance, however, a montage displaying McAllister's body, his clothing, his car, even his lessons distinguishing ethics from morals betray a mediocrity that undermine the optimism of his words. Even before his life unravels, the more

The horror of the fantasy made real  87

quiet failure of his teaching fantasy can be identified in the person of Tracy Flick, McAllister's overly ambitious student who, without the desire that a teacher dreams of inspiring in his students, is able to rattle off answers to the questions that tire McAllister himself. Flick's determination without desire threatens to ruin McAllister's teaching fantasy, and, as a result, he seeks to command a greater authority than his teaching position allows.

Unlike Sheba, who attempts to realize her teaching fantasy by inspiring the educational desires of one student through friendship, McAllister's transgressive attempt to realize his teaching fantasy is more complex. Frustrated with his wife's sexual demands that are too tied to the goal of pregnancy, he attempts an affair with Linda Novotny, the wife of a fellow teacher who has been fired for pursuing an affair with Flick. The audience realizes McAllister's conflation of fantasies in a scene in which he makes love to his wife. The camera assumes McAllister's perspective as he looks upon his wife's face. She demands, "Just like that, yeah! Fill me up! Fill me up! Yeah! Fill me up!" as, through McAllister's fantasy, her face transforms into that of Linda Novotny, who repeats the same phrases. Suddenly, however, the face transforms again to that of Tracy Flick, who screams, "Fuck me hard, Mr. McAllister. Harder! Harder! Fuck me, Mr. McAllister. Fuck me hard. Harder! Fuck me! Please!"

McAllister's tangle of frustrated desires and illicit fantasies can be summed up in the transposition of faces that appear on the screen, all making the same demand. His perception of his own impotence in relation to his wife's demand to "fill [her] up," his inability to take up the authorized place of the father, leads him outside the symbolic bonds of the marriage bed and into a fantasy of domination in which his drive can be exercised without any worry over whether and how children might come about as a result of sex. But the object McAllister chooses in order to escape from the social order is already too telling, and already ties him back to the social order he wishes to escape through the fantasy of teaching that gives his professional life meaning. In his fantasied partnership with Linda Novotny, McAllister places himself in the position of Linda's husband, Dave. At the same time, as McAllister takes Dave's place, he also imagines himself as the teacher who excites Flick's desires, the teacher who holds the promise of filling Flick up in a way that McAllister cannot.

Like Sheba Hart, McAllister's fantasies of serving as the object of desire for both his colleague's wife and his student turn to horror when he attempts to make them real. His attempt to rig the school election—a confused ploy to regain the power he never had as a teacher—ultimately brings an end to his teaching position.

Both McAllister and Sheba end up ruined by their attempts to realize the fantasy of the ideal teacher, and their appearances late in their respective films give clear visual cues that each has lost the symbolic status associated with teaching. Each suffers a moment of appearing in public, dishevelled, incoherent, and seemingly mad. Their portrayals closely match the mental instability often ascribed to real teachers who step outside their ordinary roles and engage in romantic affairs with students.

Debra Lafave, a Florida teacher arrested for having sex with her 14-year-old student, demonstrated these characteristics in a televised interview (Lauer, 2006) in which she claims that at the time of the affair she did not know what she was doing was wrong. Self-described as a "modest person" who wanted to teach in order to protect students from the very situation that she perpetrated, her defense was simply that her actions were due to "a fog I was in." Yet the fact that Lafave drove over 100 miles to have sex with her student in the back of her car, and reportedly told her student that, "One of the things that turns me on is knowing that I should not be having sex with you," suggest an unrecognized wish to escape those professional limits that constitute the teacher-student relationship. As with her filmic counterparts, Sheba Hart and Jim McAllister, once these boundaries were successfully evaded, the relationship that ensued could no longer maintain its pedagogical significance. While her defense attorney successfully redescribed Lafave's behavior as the result of a bipolar disorder, the circumstances of her transgression beg the question of how the popular ideal of teaching portrayed in school films encourages teachers to measure their worth in terms of the personal connections and pedagogical desires they ignite in their students. When these elements are conflated through the filmic ideal of breaking the school rules in order to reach the student, the teaching fantasy may easily become a nightmare.

Žižek (2000) takes aim at the bipolar disorder defense of teachers accused of statutory rape by claiming that the medicalization of their motivation removes desire from its all-too-human context, thus depriving the individual of her humanity as a way of explaining something, which in other contexts needs no explanation. He cites Mary Kay LeTourneau as an example of someone who, despite her diagnosis of bipolar disorder and subsequent treatment, returned from prison to commit herself in marriage to her victim: an act that is clearly outside the bounds of the manic mood swing suffered by bipolar patients. Yet Žižek's otherwise sound critique of medicalized desire swings too far in the other direction, citing LeTourneau's behavior as an authentic, ethical act of personal volition against the conditioning forces of contemporary society that would have us betray our desires in order to fit a prescribed norm.

Žižek's claim misses the mark on two levels. First, it neglects the symbolic function of the law at play in LeTourneau's conviction, in which she becomes the abject, monstrous biological condition, punished to support the dubious assumption that the social order has no responsibility for the horrors that it occasionally brings about. Second, and perhaps more importantly, Žižek's claim that LeTourneau's behavior constitutes an authentic act undermines his own psychoanalytic foundations by reinstating the ego at the center of its own interests. Žižek's redescription of one of the most infamous teacher-student relationships is both romantic and counterintuitive, but it threatens to

The horror of the fantasy made real   89

undermine the Lacanian structure in which Žižek operates, and in which our own desires are at best only partially known to ourselves (Britzman, 1998).

According to Lacan (1999), the ethical commitment of love derives not from an act of personal volition but from the impossibility of sex, the failure of the sexual act to overcome the Aristophanic split that marks human subjectivity with loneliness and desire. The incompleteness of the subject experienced in desire, the relentless return of the drives, the misrecognition suffered by the ego in its attempts to connect: none of these sources of suffering are relieved by the sexual exchanges that seem to promise an overcoming of each through union with another. For Lacan, love is the consolation of sexual failure, a commitment to a way of life, a relationship, a shared project that takes up the two lovers in a detour from their failed attempt to become one. Certainly, LeTourneau's life after prison might be described as a sort of ethical repetition, reliving her transgressive affair through the mundane elements of married life. What Žižek misses, however, is the fantasy of oneness between teacher and student that gives rise to LeTourneau's eventual ethical turn. This fantasy, and the desires it incites, are precisely what are at stake when we consider the teacher's place in the popular imaginary and the effect this place has on teaching ethics.

The effect of film on teachers' identities, desires, and fantasies can be seen in the more tabloid-oriented stories about teacher–student relationships that regularly make their way into the public eye. But the seductive force of film is not limited to sex. Every teacher who views herself as a selfless hero, who believes she can overcome the effects of intergenerational poverty and oppression through *Rumble Fish* (Hinton, 2013), or who breaks with the institutional rules that constitute her professional identity in order to make a human connection with a student, succumbs in some manner to the fantasy of teaching presented in film. Teacher educators, too, who believe that the aim of the teaching relationship is some sort of friendship or caregiving, who view the teacher as a powerfully and positively subversive agent in the lives of young people trapped in a lifeless caste system, have fallen for the lure of the school film.

But if the lure, in this case the ideal fantasy of teaching, is always already present in the practice of teaching, and if, as Lacan (1961, XI.14) states, "The lure [of transference] is reciprocal," this fantasy in which both teachers and students participate may serve as a starting point for desires that are truly pedagogical in addition to those that typically make headlines. Following Plato's claim in the *Timaeus* that Eros is the origin of all things and their opposite, *Election* offers a glimpse of the edifying nature of even the most suspect desires:

*Novotny:*    I know it seems crazy, but Jim, what I'm trying to tell you is that Tracy and I are totally, totally in love.

*McAllister:*  In love?

*Novotny:*    Yeah. It's serious. She inspires me in ways that Linda never has. She even wants to read my novel.

# 90 The horror of the fantasy made real

*McAllister:*   But you haven't written your novel.

*Novotny:*   That's the whole point! I've got the whole thing right here [point-ing to his head] I just need to get it out there. And Tracy wants me to write it so she can read it. It's beautiful.

Outside of the fact that Novotny and Flick are having an illegal, extramarital affair that effectively destroys their relationship as teacher and student, what Novotny describes is by some measure beautiful and might serve as a gesture toward understanding the positive value of the teaching fantasy that has been described here in largely negative terms.

While Novotny short-circuits the pedagogical relationship as a result of mis-reading his own desires, his inspired moment of rededicating himself to his novel demonstrates the connection between the fantasy of the teacher as a knowing subject, shared by teachers and students alike, and a related desire for recognition that is similarly shared. While recognition between teachers and students is inherently asymmetrical—students seek recognition *from* the master while teachers seek recognition *as* the master—the fantasy of teaching sets the conditions of striving in the classroom that make growth possible. The instantly recognizable nature of this fantasy throughout the school films that reflect and reproduce it also propagate the desires that correspond to these fantasies, so that when we walk into a classroom in either role, our expectations are already on. The challenge for teachers and teacher educators is to learn to read the effect that filmic fantasies have on the complex of ideals and desires they bring to the classroom, so that our fantasy of teaching draws us out of ourselves, toward bet-ter versions of ourselves, rather than outside the symbolic order that constitutes the pedagogical relationship.

## Note

1 That teachers' desires and satisfactions are a controversial issue is attested by the fact that their mention is often made in a confessional or deliberately controversial fashion. See (McWilliam, 1995; Gallop, 1997; Higgins, 2003).

## References

*A Teacher*, Hannah Fidell, dir. (USA: Oscilloscope, 2013).

Bauer, D. M. (1998). Indecent proposals: Teachers in the movies. *College English*, 60(3), 301–317.

Britzman, D. P. (1986). Cultural myths in the making of a teacher: Biography and social structure in teacher education. *Harvard Educational Review*, 56(4), 442–456.

Britzman, D. P. (1998). *Lost Subjects, Contested Objects: Toward a Psychoanalytic Inquiry of Learning*. Albany, NY: State University of New York Press.

*The Corn Is Green*, Irving Rapper, dir. (USA: Warner Bros, 1945).

*Dangerous Minds*, John Smith, dir. (USA: Hollywood Pictures, 1995).

*Dead Poets Society*, Peter Weir, dir. (USA: Touchstone Pictures, 1989).

*Election*, Alexander Payne, dir. (USA: Paramount Picture, 1999).

*Freedom Writers*, Richard LaGravenese, dir. (USA: Paramount Pictures, 2007).

Gallop, J. (1997). *Feminist Accused of Sexual Harrassment*. Durham, NC: Duke University Press.

Higgins, C. (2003). Teaching and the good life: A critique of the ascetic ideal in education. *Educational Theory*, 53(2), 131–154.

Hinton, S. E. (2013) *Rumble Fish*. New York: Delacorte Press.

Lacan, J. (1961). *The Seminar of Jacques Lacan: Transference VIII 1960–1961* (C. Gallagher, trans.). Available at karnacbooks.com.

Lacan, J. (1999) *On Feminine Sexuality, The Limits of Love and Knowledge, 1972–1973* (B. Fink, trans.). New York: W.W. Norton & Company.

Lauer, M. (2006) Debra Lafave: Crossing the line. *Dateline NBC*.

McWilliam, E. (1995) *Pedagogical Pleasures*. New York: Peter Lang.

*Notes on a Scandal*, Richard Eyre, dir. (United Kingdom: Fox Searchlight Pictures, 2006).

*The Paper Chase*, James Bridges, dir. (USA: 20th Century Fox, 1973).

*Picnic at Hanging Rock*, Peter Weir, dir. (Australia: Australian Film Commission, 1975).

*Slavoj Žižek: The Reality of the Virtual*, Ben Wright, dir. (United Kingdom: Ben Wright Film Productions, 2004).

*The Sound of Music*, Robert Wise, dir. (USA: Robert Wise Productions, 1965).

*The Teacher*, H. Avedis, dir. (USA: Crown International Pictures, 1974).

*To Sir, With Love*, James Clavell, dir. (United Kingdom: Columbia Pictures, 1967).

Žižek, S. (2000) *The Ticklish Subject*. New York: Verso.

# Chapter 6

## *Down with teachers, up with revolution*[1]
### School violence and fantasies of control

Lindsay Anderson has always acknowledged a debt of influence to Jean Vigo's *Zero for Conduct* (1933) for the final scene of his violent school fantasy, *If . . .* (1968). Both films end in scenes of unnerving and dreamlike triumph: students standing upon the roofs of their respective schools, showering their teachers, administrators, and honored guests of the school below with ammunition drawn from the particularities of their school environments. In *Zero*, the ammunition consists of garbage, old books, and tin cans; in *If . . .* , the ammunition is live bullets, grenades, and mortars. Caught within these formal similarities, both films close with images in which the realization of impossible fantasies solves the problem of schooling. Schooling can only be redeemed, these films seem to suggest, in the fantastical case in which the hierarchical order of the school is reversed and the students come out on top.

In a rather obvious sense, both narratives reach their ends at the close of these fantastical scenes, their violence like a bell signalling the end of class and a release of the mounting tension portrayed in each film. The revolutions planned and executed in both films have reached their respective zeniths and their respective purposes. The revolutions are local, but the authorities that each confronts comprise society itself: teachers, parents, clergy, and the higher ranks of the military. Like Butch and Sundance, we know that the conclusion of these outlaw narratives lies just beyond the final frame. Even if their *coups d'école* could be successful, the students, as victors, would become the oppressors, establishing a new, oppressive law and thereby undermining their deliberately lawless purposes. Like the revolutionaries in *Animal Farm* (Orwell, 2009), their violent overthrow would only violently express their will over others. The only way to keep the revolution alive as a brief escape from the reality of power is to end the film: at the very moment of liberation, maintaining the impossible equilibrium in which the students retain the oppressed status that justifies their violence, before their violence becomes the new regime.

At first glance, the mirrored culmination of these two films seems a perfect opposite of the erotic ideal in education that has framed our discussion of school films in earlier chapters. These films seem to negate and even call into question the validity of a theory of educational relation based in students' desires as the result of the fantasy of transference. Yet, without adding any additional theoretical apparatus to the discussion, we might also come to the conclusion that the student revolutionary is simply subject to the lure of a transferential fantasy that fails to find its object in the school setting and instead looks more broadly, negating its local discursive horizon in favor of some fantasied image of the "real world." In such a fantasy, the teachers, administrators, curriculum, and the entire authorizing discourse of the school become a derided obstacle rather than a desired object, preventing the student from pursuing his desires toward an external authority that offers self-realization. The school itself, regardless of the content of its message, becomes anathema to the erotic goal of self-realization.

The synchronized fantasies of the teacher who knows and the student who erotically strives for knowledge—whether voiced in Alcibiades' confession of love, James T. Hart's desire to take the teacher's place, or Morgan Evans' radical transformation from illiterate miner to Oxford scholar—always contains the possibility of failure through fulfillment. Evident in films such as *Notes on a Scandal* (2006), *A Teacher* (2013), and *The Piano Teacher* (2001), one way for educational eros to fail is through the teacher's acceptance of her status as the object of the student's devotion: a revelation of her own desire by seeking recognition from the student. In order to accept Steven's attention, Sheba must descend to his level, confusing the aim of her work, collapsing the space between the two that the student must traverse in order to engage himself in the world of the teacher.

Yet the realization of the teacher's fantasy is not the only way, and certainly not the most common way in which the failure of the educational relationship is represented on the screen. The student's projection of completeness upon another, extra-scholastic, extra-academic subject—a celebrity, superhero, or even an idea—leaves the teacher entirely without resource, as it is the student's desire that founds the teacher's authority and the potential effect of that authority upon the student. The power of the extra-curricular fantasy stems largely from its impossibility: without a way of working toward a realization of the imagined goal, the misplaced transference promises the student transcendence without pain. Rather than work through desire, building oneself through an authorized discourse, the student draws authority from his fantasy of an alternative discourse to undermine the educational discourse at hand, the ability to say no.[2]

If this alternate discourse can be coherently articulated and its authority structure meaningfully grasped, the contingency of the school power structure is revealed. Without any clear means by which we might choose between two competing power structures, one as arbitrary as another, the students' revolution does not necessarily require violence as much as it relies on the hollowness of the authorized discourse to collapse under its own weight.

Yet part of the problem of being a student is that one is rarely authorized enough even to choose a coherent discourse. This lack of authority seems to be accepted by children, but much of the humiliation of being an adolescent,

# 94 School violence and fantasies of control

with a dawning sense of one's ethical agency, is that alternative discourses in which one might imagine oneself remain hazily imagined greener pastures, drawn with far less detail than the banality of the familiar vistas of home and school. Given the adolescent's incapacity to articulate a compelling, competing discourse, the violence of breaking with the known becomes its own kind of fantasy, as if any reality would be better than the current reality. Or, given the abrupt ending of both films as the fantasy of their violent revolutions are made real, perhaps we should say as if no reality, or only the destruction of reality in violence, can replace the oppression of the everyday.

Many school films set in private institutions, from the melodrama of *Mädchen in Uniform* (1933) to the comedic retellings of *Animal House* (1978) and *Rushmore* (1998), rely upon military themes in order to emphasize the difference between the unyielding expectations of the school's discursive order and the idiosyncratic character of the individuals expected to shape themselves in relation to the school's rules. The ubiquity of the military theme in *If . . .* and *Zero* encourages the characters as well as the audience to view both the problem of the status quo and its solution in terms of strategic violence. As Mick, the central protagonist in *If . . .* muses, "A bullet in the right place can change the world."

By engaging in fantastical violence against the school, *If . . .* and *Zero* demonstrate how the interplay between the transferential fantasy and its erotic effects provides insight into the failure of educational relationships as well as its successes. Throughout the larger part of this chapter, we will focus on connections between these two films, drawing examples from the later film to a larger degree due to the fact that it has more examples to offer in its nearly two hours of narrative than Vigo's 40-minute film with scant dialogue.

In the last section of this chapter, we shift our focus in order to recognize a radical change in school films in the 1970s and 1980s in which schools are no longer portrayed as oppressive, hierarchical regimes, serving as dark contrasts to the bright fantasies of student striving, but as empty spaces where student fantasies are simply realized, often too easily. This change, we argue, makes possible a kind of repetition in the form of the narrative of student revolt in which there is no status quo to overturn. When the violent takeover of the school represented as a fantasy in *Zero* and *If . . .* returns again in Gus Van Sant's *Elephant* (2003), both the historical reference of the film in the Columbine shootings and Van Sant's bleak, dispassionate presentation transform the students' dream of control into a horrific nightmare, no longer focused on an achievable goal of overturning the administration, but steeped in the violence that our learned human conventions attempt to cover up.

## The revolution has already begun

In both *If . . .* and *Zero*, even before the action begins, their titles tell their audiences about significant features of the two films. According to the title *Zero for*

*Conduct*, and the subtitle, *Little Devils at School*—both displayed on the screen with an accompanying soundtrack of chaotic children's screams—the principal characters have already failed before the film rolls, they have already earned their "zero" and will not be let out of school on Sundays. In short, they cannot leave school even before they enter school. But over the course of the title sequence, the chaos of the children's screams coalesces into a marching tune that the children sing together in unison as the opening credits continue. As in the narrative that is about to unfold, the children's voices seem to organize themselves around a purpose of their own: a "zero" according to the measure of the school but not simply nothing.

*Zero's* title begs the attention of the viewer in trying to make sense of the conduct that will be displayed on the screen in terms of the judgment that has already been made. It further suggests that an authorized system is already in place according to which any conduct might be judged and given a score. Chapter titles employed by both films underscore the message that the start of the school year represents not a new beginning but students' repetition of something with which we are all already too familiar: *If . . .* 's "College House . . . return" and *Zero's* "Vacation is over; it's back to school," each suggest that both the students in the films and the audiences watching them already know what to expect.

Yet what the boys in both films take for granted in their returns the audience might find surprising. In *Zero*, from the first scenes at school, the boys discuss "ammunition" in the form of old books and cans that can be found in the attic and that will assist in their attack. *If . . .* accomplishes a similar sense of familiarity and strangeness in relation to violence by showing the walls of the students' dormitories on the first day of term already populated by revolutionary images on posters left over from the previous term: Geronimo, Che Guevara, and Mao Zedong. Allowing the posters to convey the threat of revolution, Anderson puts the question of agency into the mouth of the main protagonist, Mick, as his time spent daydreaming with his friends is interrupted by a whistle announcing the term's first house meeting: "When do we live?"

*If . . .* 's title suggests that it will provide some sort of answer to Mick's question in the form of a fantasy or a conditional mood through which the action upon the screen is intended to be understood. As Hector tells his students in *History Boys* (2006), "You know, the subjunctive? The mood used when something may or may not have happened. When it is imagined." *If . . .*, particularly with its ellipsis dangling unconventionally, heightens its audience's awareness of this possibility and draws attention to the fact that the unknown of possibility and imagination remains both thrilling and terrifying.

The word "if," used as a title, already has a strong point of reference in British culture, one which would undoubtedly have been foremost in the minds of the original audiences of the film, adding another layer of meaning to the title's function. Kipling's (1910) poem, like the film, presents us with a fantastic ideal of manhood with no particular definition other than that of a

# 96 School violence and fantasies of control

restrained superiority in relation to its circumstances. Completing the conditional, the last stanza describes the object of the transferential fantasy:

> If you can talk with crowds and keep your virtue,
> Or walk with Kings—nor lose the common touch,
> If neither foes nor loving friends can hurt you,
> If all men count with you, but none too much;
> If you can fill the unforgiving minute
> With sixty seconds' worth of distance run,
> Yours is the Earth and everything that's in it,
> And—which is more—you'll be a Man, my son!

Kipling's promise is powerfully didactic, promising an ideal of completeness and playing on precisely those desires that are painfully carried by youth: to master any given environment without being mastered by it; to have everything and be able to give it away or destroy it all without fear. Kipling's requirements of manhood, defined by control, vigor, and knowledge, but not necessarily by education, are impossibly idealized. They seem to capture the dream of manhood maintained by adolescent boys and quietly surrendered by grown men: a dream of control and power that is never intended to become real.

## Civilized wars

The given environment in relation to which Mick and his friends are to become men by mastering themselves and the world is the discursive landscape of College House, a highly militarized vision of the English public school, in which the military needs of the nation are transformed into the pedagogical imperatives of the school and dictate highly hierarchical relationships between students. Military themes abound throughout the film: uniformed students march in file through numerous scenes; a Greek lesson involves translating a quotation from Plato's *Republic*, Book VII (537a), in which the value of introducing children to war at a young age is discussed; at one point in the film, the school nurse can be seen standing at the side lines of a rugby match, screaming "Fight fight fight College!" Even the chaplain warns in his sermon, "Jesus Christ is our commanding officer, and if we desert him, we can expect no mercy."

In *Zero*, while the extent of the military symbolism is less pronounced, it is nonetheless present. In the first scene, and regularly throughout the film, students are shown wearing coats and hats patterned after military dress and marching in file. Given the ubiquity of military ideals, it is no surprise that the protagonists in both films adopt military aims even in their refusal of the school's order. In *Zero*, the boys conspire to raise a flag: articulating their revolt in nationalist military terms. Responding to a horoscope suggesting that Mick might find himself on the wrong side in the wrong war, Mick claims,

## School violence and fantasies of control  97

"There's no such thing as a wrong war. Violence and revolution are the only pure acts. War is the last possible creative act."

Various levels of hierarchy in both *If . . .* and *Zero* also suggest the school as both an extension of and a preparation for a military order. In *Zero* this hierarchy exists mainly among the administration and faculty, but in *If . . .* it extends, and finds its strongest realization in characters known as "Whips"—abusive upperclassmen who enforce the rules of the school, shouting their orders in rapid succession and whose collective name derives from the thin wooden canes they carry as a symbol (and occasionally an instrument) of their power.

The Whips' power is exercised directly through their orders and the threat of beatings, but also indirectly as they model an achievement of mastery under the school's authorized discourses. The Whips have become masters of the rules by disciplining themselves in accordance with the rule, in other words, by being mastered. At one with the law, their authority is unquestioned, even by teachers, administrators, and the most rebellious students, and their presence serves as a model for younger aspirants whose peers both mock and respect them for striving toward the position of the Whips. An ambitious junior, aspiring to a role as a Whip, tests and berates a new student, Jute, for not being "word perfect" in his knowledge of College House customs and trivialities. The remarkable element of this scene is not that the older student takes on an abusive role, aligning himself with the powers that be, but that Jute accepts the authority of the older student simply because he invokes the power of an existing authority. Denson—the weakest of the Whips—demonstrates a similar justification of power by invoking a higher authority in disciplining the Crusaders. "I serve the nation," he says, pointing to the school's motto emblazoned on a patch on the breast pocket of his jacket, "You haven't the slightest idea what that means." Mick responds skeptically—"You mean that bit of wool on your tit?"—reducing Denson's symbolic foundation of power to mere materiality while reducing its bearer to stunned silence. Yet despite his show of defiance, Mick nonetheless accepts his beating in the following scene, allowing the violence of the Whips, connected as it is to the oppressive character of the school and the military aims of the nation, to win the day.

From the outset of the film, the Whips bring a brutal message of discipline to their fellow students. Following the Housemaster, Mr. Kemp's benign words of welcome, "Help the House and you'll be helped by the House," Rowntree, the head Whip, tells the students:

> Last summer, this house got itself a reputation for being disgustingly slack. This term things are going to be different. If there's any repetition of that deplorable lack of spirit I shall come crashing down on offenders. We don't intend to carry passengers.

Immediately following Rowntree's speech, the Whips enact their imposition of discipline through a medical inspection in which two Whips interrogate students about communicable diseases and, after their questioning, students drop their pants and turn to an elderly nurse who points a flashlight and inspects each student's groin. Exposure and lack of privacy run as themes throughout the film, extending to students' thoughts and feelings as well as their bodies. A young student writing in his diary is told to "keep it downstairs in the sweatroom," implying that no work on the self is to be anything other than school work. The school's interdiction on anything truly private is matched by its censorship of anything extra-curricular or extra-mural: "The town of course is out of bounds," according to the Whips—a prohibition that also serves as a punishment in *Zero*. The only access the boys have to the outside world seems to be through the magazine images of war and sex that decorate their study carrels and dormitories.

Despite the totalizing discourse that ties the power of the Whips through the authority of the school directly to the character of the nation, cracks and flaws in the ideological commitments of College House remain constantly on display. As if to illustrate the school culture's complicity with a way of life that is hopelessly anachronistic, the history master voices the following prompt to a writing exercise:

> In studying the nineteenth century one thing will be clear: that the growth of technology—telegraph, cheap newspapers, railways, transport—is matched by a failure of imagination, a fatal inability to understand the meaning and consequences of all these levers, wires, and railways, climaxing in 1914 when the German Kaiser is told by his generals that he cannot stop the war he has started because it would spoil the railway time tables upon which victory depends. Or perhaps you fashionably and happily believe that it's all a matter of evil dictators rather than whole populations of evil people like . . . ourselves?

While the history master can address society's and, by extension, the school's ills from a position of smug irony, standing somewhat outside the hierarchical order, the Headmaster is portrayed as having absolutely no understanding of the ideological commitments in which he is sunk. Taking a stroll around campus with the Whips, he offers an extemporaneous string of nonsense as a casual edifying lecture:

> College House is a symbol of many things. Scholarship, integrity in public office, high standards in the television and entertainment world. Huge sacrifice in Britain's wars. Of course, some of our customs are silly. You could say we were middle class. But a large part of the population is in the process of becoming middle class. And many of the middle class's values are values that the country cannot do without. We must not expect to be thanked. Education in Britain is a nubile Cinderella: sparsely clad and much interfered with.

The same failure of meaning that characterizes the Headmaster's speech pervades the order of the school, adding a sense of absurdity to students' meaningless suffering. When Mick and his companions are viciously beaten by the Whips, they are not punished for any particular infraction, but because they "have become a danger to the morale of the whole house." Similarly, in *Zero*, a teacher sleeping in the dormitory room behind a curtain punishes the three protagonists arbitrarily for a crime committed by someone else. These unjustified abuses of power provide both the justification and the model for both films' brutal and arbitrary acts of revolution.

Demonstrating their connection to the tradition of erotic pedagogical relationships in school films, in which a heroic teacher's greatness contrasts sharply against the backdrop of a corrupt institution, both films provide images of teachers who fit the required characteristics for heroism, but nonetheless fall short of the mark. Both of the sympathetic teachers featured in these films bear some of the characteristics that suggest the possibility of igniting their students' desires: both are new, both are young, and each bears idiosyncrasies that prevents him from blending in with the rest of the faculty. But in contrast to the expectations that their presence in the film builds in their audiences, neither makes any difference in his students' education. Huguet, the new teacher in *Zero*, plays ball in the yard with the children and performs impressions of Charlie Chaplin. He spends classroom time teaching one boy to walk on his hands, allowing the rest to wreak havoc pouring glue behind the books in the bookshelf, smoking, and fighting. When the Headmaster enters and stares at Huguet angrily, Huguet smiles and shrugs his shoulders and he is quickly replaced by more authoritarian figures, precipitating the revolution. Despite his outsider status, his inability to transform the energies of the young into a form that the school authorities can recognize as conforming to their measures ends his opportunity to mediate between the rebels and the existing order. It may be that his inability to claim a more authentic form of authority, separate from the brutal exercise of power employed by the administration, means that there can be no authentic or legitimate form of authority over children, only power. John Thomas, the docile new teacher in *If . . .* cannot help himself in relation to the power of the school order. Silenced in relation to the Whips, he gives in to the oppressive discourse of the school. In a mock battle staged on the school grounds, he throws a smoke grenade at the three students and declares: "I've won; you're all dead." His capacity to join the school in delivering the boys to the past by enforcing tradition over the spark of life embodied in youth underscores the conditional mood of *If . . .*'s title as well as Mick's question about when (and how) their own lives are to be lived.

## The revolt of the real

Beneath the simple opposition between the military discourse of the school and the awakening paramilitary fantasies of the students in *If . . .* and *Zero* lies

## 100  School violence and fantasies of control

a more fundamental, if less explicit, force that both the school's order and the boys' fantasy seek to overcome. This more basic force is that of the bodily real of nature, puberty, and the sexual drives: a terrifyingly powerful other at home in the self and suggesting uncertain outcomes for the boys' identities and their positions within the larger world of signifiers reproduced in the school. The discursive order of the school outlaws the students' budding sexuality, intent on making men from boys according to the demands of the nation rather than the demands of nature.

The conflict between boys' bodies and their burgeoning nature in relation to the rules that outlaw their inevitable becoming serves as a repeated theme in *If . . .* and in *Zero*, and in both films is achieved through attention to the pubescent body as well as institutional concerns over students' sexuality. Mick arrives at school in the midst of Whips shouting orders at their inferiors. He rushes past the latter, his face covered, sporting but also concealing an illicit moustache. When Johnny, his accomplice, asks why he grew it, he replies, "To hide my sins," and with this immediately proceeds to shave it off. In the midst of all of this hiding and revealing something is bound to emerge, and the mirror in which Mick shaves provides a way for him to reassert himself as that which remains in the tension between the school rules and the physical growth into manhood that the rules seek to manage. As he stares at his image in the mirror, he reinforces the status of the mirror, the self-image, in the formation of the ego, stating, "My face is a never ending source of wonder to me." Despite his inscription as a failure according to the authorized discourses of the school, despite the body that changes beyond his control, Mick's face remains his own, serving as a guarantor of the fantasy of his ego: the site that negotiates between the real of the body and the demands of discourse by negating both.

In *Zero* the presence and threat of sexuality is less explicitly spoken, but it is nonetheless on display and stands as the primary cause for concern among the school administrators before the revolution begins. In the first scene, when Caussat and Colin play on the train on the way to school, showing off newly acquired toys, tricks, and bad habits in order to pass the time on the journey, Caussat produces a new toy in which a ball pops in and out of a basket. The boys are both clearly delighted playing with the toy for a minute, but as their attention passes to a new object—a balloon blown up and fondled as a breast—Caussat places the toy between his legs with the handle sticking out, and plays with it occasionally over the next few minutes as other games are produced and up until the point that the boys light cigars and the camera angle changes. It is not clear that Caussat, or Vigo, intends the toy to look like a penis, and the presence of the toy between the boy's legs would likely carry less of a phallic significance if it were not for the fact that *Zero* was banned for displaying a boy's penis in a later fantasy sequence in which the boys assemble to revolt against the school. As it stands, the two scenes that feature displays of phallic objects bracket the larger portion of the film that takes place under the oppressive weight of the school's discourse and the punishing presence of the administrators, supporting the idea that the school attempts to suppress or even replace its students' original phallic *jouissance* with its own phallic authority, commanding their desire as a way of claiming their identities.

One means of claiming the students' identities is by directing their desires toward the proper objects and away from degenerate forms of eros. From the moment the boys alight from the train and rejoin their fellow students under the authority of the prefect who waits for them, a concern is raised about the sexuality of a long-haired, traditionally feminine-looking "sissy" named Tabard, whose mother introduces him as being homesick and unable to join the other boys for their first night back in the dormitory. Tabard's return to school occasions a relationship with Bruel that the administration deems as too close. The Headmaster asks the prefect for assurance that "Tabard and Bruel are behaving like little boys and not at all serious," but his plea underscores an anxiety that he expresses in the next breath: "Do you realize the immensity of our moral responsibility?" In a later scene in which the boys pass by huddled under one coat against the rain, he repeats his concern: "This friendship is getting excessive. The Housemaster is right. They must be watched."

The Headmaster calls Tabard into his office and attempts to address the seemingly homosexual relationship, but is still unable to address it directly, circling around the issue instead while becoming increasingly enervated and incoherent: "At your age, there are things . . . isn't that so? Bruel, I mean, is older than you . . . Your sensibility, and then his . . . isn't that so? Neuropaths . . . psychopaths!" Tabard returns to class ashamed by the Headmaster's obvious excitement and unwilling to sit next to Bruel, but his shaming by the Headmaster inspires him to join Caussat and Colin in their plot to undermine the Founder's Day celebrations. His new, sullen attitude becomes the occasion of the boys' declaration of war, as it attracts unwanted and perhaps inappropriate attention from the science teacher, who flirts and asks why Tabard is sullen, touching his hand suggestively. Tabard's response to the teacher, "Merde!" repeated again when Tabard is asked to apologize in front of the students and administration for his earlier vulgarity, becomes the tipping point into fantastical chaos through which the boys make their attack.

In *If* . . . , while the protagonists' physical maturity is further along its way, their capacity to manage their new bodily identities has apparently not quite arrived. Like their precursors in *Zero*, the Crusaders are represented as maintaining a precocious and curious mix of knowledge and ignorance with respect to their own natures. Knightley speaks of having built a hut in the woods over break where he lived away from everyone until he ran out of food after three weeks, the force of nature easily outstripping his own.

Mick speaks of going to a club where they show their "knickers—and then everything else," but the subject is brought up for a laugh and then dropped. Sex is a matter of fascination throughout *If* . . . , but it is often a fascination that is elided or avoided. Two upperclassmen stop Phillips in the hallway: "Come on up, Phillips. We want to stroke you." After chasing them away, Denson scolds,

"You, Phillips. Stop tarting." Just as Tabard's hair confirms his "sissy" status in *Zero*, hair also serves as a signifier of sexuality in *If.* . . . After Phillips, Tabard's mirror figure in *If.* . . is scolded for "tarting," Denson holds his whip to the back of Phillips' neck and tells him that his hair is too long. Even *If.* . . 's Headmaster addresses hair length and its connection to morality, claiming both his admiration for "hair rebels" and a distaste for "scruffiness."

The problem with long hair in both films is that it confers femininity and to be female means to be sexually knowing. While *Zero* offers a few unnoticeable, shapeless mother figures, all three women portrayed in *If.* . . are directly connected to sexual knowledge. The aged nurse inspects the boys' genitals with a flashlight; the Junoesque Mrs. Kemp wanders naked and silent through the empty dormitory, sitting on the boys' beds while they are away playing war games; and the cafe waitress credited as "The Girl" seems to both awaken and guide the protagonists' budding energies, helping to shape them in relation to the fantasy of war. In their first meeting, when Mick's violent wrestling match with The Girl suddenly turns sexual as their clothes disappear, Mick is immediately vanquished, and the scene comes to a close. Throughout the remainder of the film, The Girl represents a sexuality that is not yet ready to be realized.

In a later scene, the Crusaders, now joined by Phillips, who has become Wallace's pet, are inexplicably joined by their female companion as they serve another punishment by excavating the bowels of the school. Breaking the lock on an old cabinet, they come upon a fetus in a jar, staring at it in wonder before The Girl calmly takes the jar from their hands and returns it to the case, returning it to the realm of the unknown and making way for their fantasy to continue. Her sexual knowledge in relation to the boys gives her power in directing their attention and their desires.

The fetus, invoked as a representation of the bodily real, appears earlier in the film as well, when the Crusaders are beaten by the Whips. Scenes of Mick, Johnny, and Wallace alternately waiting in an antechamber and receiving their beatings in the gymnasium are intercut with shots of students looking up from their evening studies at study carrels in quiet awe and horror. Like many aspects of the film, such as the unexplained shifts from black and white to color film stock, the idea that the students studying in the "sweat room" would be able to hear the sound of the whip echoing in the gymnasium seems strange, but it underscores the idea that through the beatings the Whips make a publicly perceptible claim on the Crusaders' bodies. An ostracized character known as Peanuts looks up momentarily from a microscope then returns to watching bacteria grow, alerting the audience to the moment when the Whips' punishment of Mick as an enactment of the law gives way to the execution of punishment as pleasure in going beyond the law: a peek into the workings of the drives. Behind Peanuts, photographs of fetuses at various stages of development reinforce the idea that the Whips' punitive actions are one more expression of a basic, animal drive rather than an execution of the law.

In returning the fetus to its unknown place, locked away in the basement of the school, The Girl reinforces the Crusaders' prolonged sexual ignorance and in doing so makes way for an identity that is neither tied to their drives nor shaped by the demands of nationalism enforced by the school. As *If* . . . makes clear, however, the break that it portrays never loses its relation to the discursive order or the bodily drives that give it shape. To the contrary, the fantasy that it portrays maintains itself in tension between the military discourse of the school and the emerging drives of adolescence, combining the two in a manner that allows the budding adolescent ego to remain in control of both.

## Fantasies of control

Less than ten minutes into *If* . . . , as Mick shaves his moustache and the boys decorate their study, adding new images to those left from the prior term, Johnny shows Mick a magazine photograph of a shirtless, bandaged, black commando firing a machine gun. Mick's response provides a key to understanding the confused and dreamlike action in the remainder of the film: "Fantastic. Put him right in the middle . . . *Fantastic*." The placement Mick suggests for this scene of primal aggression and paramilitary violence is "right in the middle" between a print of Munch's "The Scream" and a photo of three military officers standing for a portrait. The photograph is, as Mick claims, fantastic, providing an image of power and control that draws from the boys' existing discursive context, the nationalist and military order of the school, represented by the photograph of generals to the left, as well as from their feelings of disorder and chaos represented by Munch's painting to the right. The fantastic image stands in tension with those on either side of it, reframing the authorized military discourses of their schooling with the figure of a powerful black man—the colonized body, both defiled and fetishized—shooting back, while at the same time offering a quite different response to Munch's portrayal of existential despair.[3]

Following Freud's (1957) second topology, the fantasy of the ego grows out of this tension, covering over, on the one hand, the subject's incompleteness in relation to the law, and on the other, providing a recognizable and stable identity through which the id seeks fulfillment of its drives. Freud's theory seems to imply that the greater the tension between the drives and the social discourses in which they are limited, the greater the work of the ego in providing a reifying fantasy: not to overcome or reconcile the differences between social norms and the real of the drives, but to stand in denial of both. The fantasy of the self is therefore never a primary impulse, but always derives from an intolerable conflict between two pre-existing and contradictory forces. The ego provides an impossible resolution to the conflict between the body and the world, establishing fantasy as the basis for each person's understanding of him or herself while relegating the demands of the body and the world to extensions of the ego's central place of importance.

Accordingly, in both *Zero* and *If . . .* powerful figures are recast to suit the students' needs for feeling authorized in their overthrow of the status quo. In *If . . .*, the Headmaster is presented, through his own words, as a vapid managerial fool. *Zero*, which makes far less use of words, relies on its visual presentation of the Headmaster, played by a dwarf dressed in a suit, top hat and enormous beard. The character's height is played upon in a series of sight gags, reducing his authority over the teachers and children he purports to rule, and underscoring the idea that his authority is merely put on, and that underneath his affected stature he resembles the very children he purports to educate. In both films, small men control their schools by small means, demonstrating the students' fantasy of unjustified power that in turn justifies their revolutions.

The fantasied caricature of unjustified authority is repeated at a lower level of school hierarchy: *If . . .*'s Housemaster, Mr. Kemp, appears weak, ineffectual, and completely controlled by the Whips. Kemp's weakness in relation to the military masculinity of the school draws attention to his somewhat younger wife, who becomes a convenient object of the schoolboys' sexual fantasies. In a lunchroom scene, the Crusaders sit with her at a communal table, firing falsely polite questions at her:

> "Water, Mrs. Kemp?"
> "Spring greens, Mrs. Kemp?"
> "Salt, Mrs. Kemp?"

"Dead man's leg today, Mrs. Kemp," Mick says, and then, holding a condiment bottle with a phallic shape in front of her face, he asks, "Do you need *this*, Mrs. Kemp?"

Mrs. Kemp's appearance in two dreamlike sequences—both filmed in black and white, in contrast to many of the film's more realistic scenes—underscore the idea that the film is presented entirely within the imaginary frame of an adolescent boy's fantasy. In one scene, she awkwardly guides Mr. John Thomas to his new lodging, her long stares and his total silence suggesting the possibility of something more than professional. In the second, while the rest of the school engages in a mock battle, she drifts naked through the boys' dormitories, silently handling their soaps and towels.

In *Zero*, the prefect is another caricatured, terrorizing fantasy of power without moral authority, rifling through children's belongings, stealing objects from their bags and eating their chocolate while the children are outside for recess. By rewriting the authority of the school as a sneaky but ineffectual tyrant, motivated by his own limitations, the students get to perpetually outsmart him. Returning to class after recess with a large, leather ball, the students continue to play in the classroom. Noticing the Housemaster spying through the window on their game, one boy holds the ball in his upturned palm and it promptly disappears—a magic trick achieved by way of an editing trick. As soon as the Housemaster's face leaves the window, the ball reappears.

Magical and absurd accents such as the vanishing ball appear throughout *Zero* and *If. . .*, reminding the audience that these narratives float above and often deny the punishing power of the school as well as the mysteries of the body and of nature. *If. . .*'s school chaplain, seemingly killed in one scene emerges from a drawer in the Headmaster's office in the following scene, receives a handshake from each of the boys, and is returned to the drawer by the Headmaster, who dismisses the boys' violence as "a quite blameless form of existentialism." In *Zero*, a caricature of the prefect in a swimsuit drawn by Huguet while standing on one hand, becomes animated, seemingly ashamed of his costume, and assumes a more proper style of dress, transforming into Napoleon.

Both films demonstrate the idea that the content of fantasies is not arbitrary, but necessarily draw elements of everyday reality that are made unfamiliar insofar as they are experienced in a way that places the subject back in control, arranging the world according to his wishes. All of the material ammunition that the students use in their armed rebellion, from cans and books in *Zero* to guns and grenades in *If. . .*, is found on the school premises. Just as the tree of wisdom and its fruit are present already in the Garden of Eden, the material possibility of undermining the status quo is already available to the students. It is up to them to take what is given and turn it to their own anarchic advantage.

It follows, therefore, that the first fantastical break in *If. . .* occurs during the students' enforced attendance at the rugby match, in which bodily drives have been co-opted according to the discursive demands of the school. While the rest of the school cheers, Knightley and Mick run off into town—"out of bounds" according to the Whips. Accordingly, the sequence of events in town seems drawn straight from an adolescent boy's imagination. Their escape is filmed as a long-shot, with the two boys running wildly across a village square, handcuffed to one another, as if they were in a movie in which they had just escaped a chain gang. In the next scene, the handcuffs are gone, and after looking briefly at a women's lingerie storefront, a women's clothing storefront, and the women's side of a shoe storefront, the boys stage a pantomime knife fight, drawing the attention of passers by, and then effortlessly steal a British Small Arms motorcycle, and ride out into the countryside where they meet The Girl at a roadside cafe. Mick drops a coin in the jukebox, and the *Missa Luba* that Mick listened to in the dormitory while cutting images of war from magazines begins to play.

After trying to kiss The Girl and getting hit hard across the face, Mick receives an unusual invitation: "Go on. Look at me. I'll kill you. Look at my eyes. Sometimes I stand in front of the mirror and my eyes get bigger and bigger. I'm like a tiger. I like tigers." The Girl growls at Mick and he sniffs at her like an animal. The two begin roaring and scratching at one another, all noise drowned out by a shift in the tempo and volume of the African mass on the jukebox. Tumbling onto the floor, their clothes suddenly and inexplicably gone, she bites Mick on the arm, and the scene ends abruptly: they walk, fully clothed, into the next frame where Johnny is sitting drinking coffee and join him as if nothing has happened.

The Girl remains an important part of the ongoing fantasy that runs throughout the film. Back at school, Mick finds Peanuts peering through a telescope at celestial bodies. Mick looks through it and instead sees The Girl at a window, brushing her hair. She looks back at the telescopic gaze, smiles and waves. After appearing in the basement scene and taking the fetus out of Mick's hands, she joins the Crusaders in exploring the depths of the school basement, where they discover assault weapons. In the final attack, she stands on the roof in fatigues with the other Crusaders, firing a submachine gun, and responds to the Headmaster's appeal to "listen to reason"—a final attempt to return to the authority of discourse—by producing a large revolver from her belt and making an impossible shot to the center of his forehead.

In *Zero*, once a flag is made, war is declared and a plan to bomb the Commemoration Day festivities the following morning is announced, the children break out in a state of total anarchy in the sleeping quarters—a pillow fight in which the resident teacher tries to return the group to order by returning them to their beds, but instead the chaos takes on its own order, a military order that recapitulates the singing that arises out of screaming in the opening credits. In form, the children's regime mirrors that of the school and society, but in content it inverts the relationship between adults and children. The children rise up, marching out of the dormitory in their nightshirts under a blizzard of feathers from their broken pillows. In one scene of the revolution, the children raise a housemaster's bed on its end, leaving the sleeping adult dangling impossibly under his tightly tucked sheets. In another, a boy performs a backflip—again, impossibly—into a chair hoisted on the shoulders of students marching to war.

Contrasting the beauty of the children's march while mirroring its military styling, the Commemoration Day preparations waiting in the school courtyard below are ugly and absurd. One man with a beard, apparently a military leader, sits astride a pommel horse, playing upon its dual meaning by alternately posing with disciplined decorum and making weak attempts at gymnastic techniques. Another man in a suit performs on a set of parallel bars. The crowd assembled to view the events consists of a front row of important looking political, church, and military leaders and a back row of mannequins. When the children begin to shower this moribund caricature of power with tin cans and old books, their rout is total and the film ends in the same mood of a celebratory dream with which the revolution begins.

If the moral attitude of *If . . .* 's finale is less sanguine, the hesitation that it demonstrates is consistent throughout the film. Despite the boys' fantasies of revolution and violence, they are also regularly surprised by the potential reality of their daydreaming and pretended sophistication. Mick speaks with cold certainty to his friends, claiming, "One man can change the world with a bullet in the right place," but in a later scene his face is awed as he uncovers live ammunition in the basement of the school, whispering to himself, "real bullets." Similarly, in a gym class sword fight between the three boys that changes from black and white to color, the boys yell, "Death to tyrants," but when Mick is accidentally cut he is once again surprised at his fantasy made too real. "Blood, real blood," he says astonished, showing his friends the red smear on his hand.

It is therefore not surprising that Anderson draws distinctions between the endings of *Zero* and *If . . .* even as he acknowledges being influenced by Vigo's work. "Vigo's children escape joyfully along the skyline, singing their . . . song of liberty," whereas, "our Mick Travis is left firing desperately, trapped by the massed firepower of the establishment" (Hedling, 1998, p. 96, quoted in Leach, 2004, p. 195). While Vigo allows his narrative to remain on the level of pure fantasy, untouched by the horror of its own realization, Anderson allows us to see a dawning realization of horror in Mick's eyes, similar to the look of awe that accompanies his earlier discoveries of "real blood" and "real bullets," as he comes to understand that his para-educational fantasy was never meant to be realized and that now there is only one way out.

## Revolution and revulsion

As Anderson's commentary makes clear, Mick's terrified stare and desperate firing are directed not only at the school community assembled for Founder's Day, but equally at the viewer, who is positioned as both the potential victim of the Crusaders' rebellion and as something that strikes fear into the young man holding the submachine gun. Mick's face reflects the same awe and terror as earlier scenes in which his violent fantasies stray too close to reality. His terror might have less to do with his own, almost certain, obliteration as with the success of his mission in bringing fantasy into the light of realization. That is, more terrifying than the idea of one's own demise is the idea that the social order, understood as the precondition of one's own existence, might be dismantled through a simple act of violent terrorism, or "a bullet in the right place."

Paradoxically, the committed revolutionary might be especially terrified of his own success, as the oppressive system provides a *raison d'être* and a host of interconnected beliefs and practices that are all linked in some way to the opposition of existing norms. The revolutions in both *Zero* and *If . . .* demonstrate this strong oppositional relationship, recapitulating military tactics as well as religious imagery. The boys in *Zero* turn a sleeping teacher's bed upright, making him look like a crucified Christ. *If . . .* returns to the soundtrack of the Congolese mass in portraying The Girl, standing on top of a speeding motorcycle, her arms outspread in a gesture that suggests both the crucifixion and the glorification of Christ. But alternative interpretations of military masculinity, religion, and sexuality do not provide an actual alternative way of life; they only serve to inspire fantasies of rebellion against an oppressively bleak

108    School violence and fantasies of control

set of educational possibilities. As we suggest at the outset of this chapter, the students' successful realization of their fantasies promises a new social order that their oppositional fantasy cannot deliver.

Yet if *Zero* and *If . . .* attract any attention at all, whether in their initial releases and their growing cult statuses over the decades, they have done so because both films connect to a twentieth-century ideal of cultural revolution led by the interests of the youth, in which the transferential fantasy is turned outward toward competent peers and mythologized celebrity, foreclosing students' erotic attraction to parents and teachers as subjects presumed to know, and instead creating a rule of influence that seems to belong entirely to the youth. This shift not only diversifies the potential thematic elements of the school film but fundamentally changes the nature of adolescent rebellion: the patriarch no longer needs to be killed, as he is already out of the picture. But what happens if the revolution succeeds and the oppressive power of the adult world and its moribund discourses, enforced through the school, no longer poses a threat? By looking at more contemporary films we may be led to the conclusion that films such as *Zero* and *If . . .* are effective insofar as they assign great power and importance to the oppressive adult regimes that the revolutionaries in each film seek to overthrow. That is to say, these films still hold open the possibility of the ideal of transference, the notion that there might be something more toward which the subject might be moved by its desires. In the absence of an oppressive discourse, it may be that the possibility of fantasizing about revolution disappears along with the fantasy of transference.

About a decade before *If . . .* celebrated the fantasy of rebellious adolescence and the negation of the transferential pedagogical relationship, Charles Schultz's comic strip *Peanuts* featured a mockery of the erotic attraction between student and teacher. Teachers, along with all other adults, are visibly excluded from the frames of Schultz's vignettes; the world he discloses through these frames is strictly a world of children, akin to the world of progressive education critiqued by Hannah Arendt, in which children are left to negotiate the world by themselves. Linus, the security-blanket wielding younger brother of Lucy, falls in love with his teacher, Miss Othmar, claiming that he is "fond of the ground she walks on" (October 8, 1959). The trope is easily recognizable, as we have argued in earlier chapters, but it fails to fit the often cold world of Schultz's imagination, where the children's education can have no effect, because their world has no adult discourse to which the children's desires might be directed. Lucy gives voice to Schultz's insistence that his characters should be wary of the adult world: in a strip in which Miss Othmar joins a teacher's union strike, she falls to the ground from exhaustion and Linus runs to her aid (February 26, 1969). Lucy's response: "That blockhead! He's become involved!"

Schultz clearly speaks through Lucy, and reassures his audience that Linus's erotic educational encounter will never be effective in getting him to join the world of adults. Miss Othmar criticizes Linus's attachment to his blanket—a prop that is easily recognizable as a replacement for the mother figure who seems to have abdicated her responsibility. Lucy reports: "Miss Othmar really spoke out against blankets today . . . She said that if a child dragged a blanket around . . . it was a sign of immaturity, and . . . she would never put up with that!" Charlie Brown comments on the difficult choice that this poses for Linus between competing objects of his affection, but the dramatic tension is cut short; Linus walks through a subsequent frame with a swift betrayal: "Who's Miss Othmar?" (October 15, 1959).[4]

Beginning in the 1950s and continuing through a high point in the 1980s, popular films increasingly portray school-aged children in schools or educational outings without authorized adult presences, or in which adults present themselves as weak, foolish, or comically pathetic. While this shift is not total, teachers, principals, and parents lose their status as subjects presumed to know as films featuring young people focus less on *Bildungsroman*-style, socially conservative narratives and shift their focus to youth cultures. The loss of the adult subject presumed to know does not mean a loss of erotic striving on the part of the children. What it does signal is the loss of an ordered, predictable, and measurable sense of how young people's desires serve to reproduce culture, and an accompanying sense of anxiety and chaos insofar as youth desires seem no longer directed toward the staid goals of respectable adult life.

In a series of low-budget films from the late 1970s and early 1980s, the high school becomes a significant backdrop for melodramatic violence, as in *Class of 1984* (1982), *Carrie* (1976), *Prom Night* (1980), and coming of age sex comedies such as *Fast Times at Ridgemont High* (1982), *Rock 'n' Roll High School* (1979), and *Class of Nuke 'Em High* (1986). As the 1980s progress, John Hughes's *Sixteen Candles* (1984), *The Breakfast Club* (1985), and *Ferris Bueller's Day Off* (1986) provide a somewhat more refined narrative and a higher production value to the idea of an adolescent world that seems to operate independently from absent or simply ineffectual adult figures. But if we look more closely at the plot structures of these films, it is clear that they are simply extended oppositional fantasies, exaggerated answers to Mick Travis' question, "When do we live?" The answer, for characters like Ferris Bueller or Joe Spicoli, is "whenever we please," as the adults who would enforce the law have abdicated their positions, or are too incapable to enforce their own law. The important difference between *If . . .* and these more recent films, however, is that the teenage misadventures of the 1970s and 1980s contain no sense of revolution. Adults often stand in the way, in their own, clownish manner, but their slapstick stupidity only underscores the idea that there is no need to overturn them, and maybe more to gain by simply occupying the empty spaces that their excess of power and wealth provide.

Yet even within these safe spaces of privileged adolescent *jouissance*, in which the rules are preserved in order to be broken, and mocked rather than questioned, or engaged at a political level, there remains a horror in the children's fantasy of freedom made real. As Arendt (1961) predicts in her critique of progressive education, the adult's abandoning of the scene of instruction creates an opportunity for the exercise of a more vicious form of power on the part of the students—a phenomenon visible in *Lord of the Flies* (1990), *Kids* (1995) and *Palo Alto* (2013)—in which the settings for these bleak visions of adolescent violence are deliberately outside the ordered settings of the school. One remarkable element of *Elephant* (2003) is that it forces its audience to witness the banality of adolescent violence within a setting normally associated with adult control.

In Van Sant's retelling of the Columbine shootings, the most remarkable element of the film is the unremarkable character of the students' interactions. Adults play minimal, barely functional roles at the edges of students' lives, but the adults are not taking a backseat to students' expressions of freedom or exuberance—just everyday suffering. The mundane banter that occupies the larger part of the film successfully elides serious issues such as parental alcoholism, teen pregnancy and abortion, and bulimia, just as it offers a cover for the teenage killers whose impending attack serves as the occasion for the film. The students' discourse offers no sense of aspiration, no ideal to admire, no desire to change.

As with the low-budget films of the 1970s and early 1980s, and the mainstream work of Hughes and others through the 1980s and 1990s, *Elephant* presents a world devoid of responsible, successful adults toward which students' erotic aspirations might be directed. But while the adolescent-centric visions of earlier films maintain a fantasy in which the failures of adults do not directly affect the lives of children, *Elephant* indicts its adults as failures and causes of the tragedy that the students suffer. The film opens with a boy, John, being driven to school by a father so drunk that he crashes into a parked car and is told by his son John—an unlicensed, unauthorized minor—to move over into the passenger seat so that the child can drive. The principal, who sits John down in his office, presumably to deliver a lecture about John's habitual lateness, says nothing, while a group of adults working in the office can be overheard babbling nonsense. A teacher leading a GSA meeting only speaks to ask the students what they think. Late in the film, as the attacks are underway, the principal begs for his life from one of the teenage gunmen while John continues to parent his father, tracking him down to make sure he's safe.

Van Sant's picture of a life without adults, of a teenage fantasy realized, relies on many of the same structural elements featured in films of the 1970s and 1980s, but with a radically different effect. Teenage girls' obsessions with beauty and bodily image, dramatized in teen dramas, are manifested in *Elephant* in the form of a trio of girls who gossip about physical violence between girls competing for boys' attention, argue over the amount of time spent together at the mall, and vomit their lunch together while discussing their dissatisfaction with their weight. Similarly, Van Sant translates the theme of budding sexuality, often treated as a matter of hilarity in earlier films, as a matter of sadness and secrecy, through a partial communication between a teenage couple over an impending abortion. Finally, the glorification of outsider status that becomes a central theme in all of Hughes' films is redeployed in *Elephant* both through the narrative of the murderers and through images of a sad, ignored girl who drifts through the film, avoided by everyone except the gym teacher and the librarian, and who is the first to be shot.

What makes *Elephant* both terrifyingly bleak and somewhat tedious and boring is that despite its violence, the students in the film are not rebelling against anything, neither do they have anything against which a revolution might be launched. Their lack of moral or intellectual position stands out against the revolutions portrayed in *If . . .* and *Zero* insofar as the students in the latter films take high ground upon the roofs of their schools during high ceremonies in order to attack, whereas *Elephant*'s attackers do so from within the very everyday activities of their school. The difference between these forms of violence is that in the former two cases, the students rebel, because they still believe that there is a difference between higher and lower purposes: their sense of fantasy is still intact and their actions are romantic, linked to an impossible ideal. In the latter, even as the boys draw their experience from first-person shooter games, these games provide only the means to their violence. The ends are non-existent.

While at the outset of this chapter we argued that any discursive structure of power invites its own subversion according to its own limits, *Elephant* suggests that we might be able to go further, claiming that the institution of schooling must, paradoxically, afford students the opportunity to reject the authoritative order into which they are indoctrinated. Like Plato's *Republic*, any full account of educational growth must include both indoctrination and critique. In the next chapter, we explore this tension further with the idea that the proper fulfillment of the student's eros is in the death of the teacher.

## Notes

1 This phrase appears as a subtitle in the film for a phrase that might more directly be translated as "Down with Monitors and Punishment! Long Live Rebellion!" Of course, rebellion—by its very nature—can't be long lived.
2 The connection to Nietzsche's (1956) *Genealogy of Morals* and its take on religious doctrine is significant, not only in the revolutionary power of naysaying, but in the religious imagery that both *If . . .* and *Zero* employ in convincing their audiences of their righteousness.
3 It should be noted that the photo seems to be of an American soldier fighting in Vietnam. The reality of the setting is less important, however, than the "fantastic" quality that allows the boys to reinvigorate what they know of military order with what they see as a more primal, powerful violence.
4 It should be emphasized that in the ten years between Miss Othmar's introduction and the union strike narrative, no child has aged or advanced in school, neither are Miss Othmar or any adult ever seen. Linus's disavowal of his love ten years before he rescues her in her fall should not be taken as a renewal of their love: time in *Peanuts* is not developmental or linear, but pure fantasy.

# References

*A Teacher*, Hannah Fidell, dir. (USA: Oscilloscope, 2013).

*Animal House*, John Landis, dir. (USA: Universal Pictures, 1978).

Arendt, H. (1961) *Between Past and Future: Eight Exercises in Political Thought*. New York: Viking Press.

*The Breakfast Club*, John Hughes, dir. (USA: Channel Productions, 1985).

*Carrie*, Brian DePalma, dir. (USA: Red Bank Films, 1976).

*Class of 1984*, Mark Lester, dir. (Canada: Guerilla High Productions, 1982).

*Class of Nuke 'Em High*, Richard Haines, dir. (USA: Troma Entertainment, 1986).

*Elephant*, Gus Van Sant, dir. (USA: Fine Line Pictures, 2003).

*Fast Times at Ridgemont High*, Amy Heckerling, dir. (USA: Universal Pictures, 1982).

*Ferris Bueller's Day Off*, John Hughes, dir. (USA: Paramount Pictures, 1986).

Freud, S. (1957) *The Standard Edition of the Complete Psychological Works of Sigmund Freud* (Vol. XIX). London: The Hogarth Press.

Hedling, E. (1998) *Lindsay Anderson: Maverick Film-Maker*. London: Cassel.

*The History Boys*, Nicholas Hytner, dir. (United Kingdom: Fox Searchlight Pictures, 2006).

*If . . .*, Lindsay Anderson, dir. (United Kingdom: Memorial Enterprises, 1968).

*Kids*, Larry Clark, dir. (USA: Guys Upstairs, 1995).

Kipling, R. (1910) *Rewards and Fairies*. Garden City, NY: Doubleday, Page & Company.

Leach, J. (2004) *British Film*. Cambridge: Cambridge University Press.

*Lord of the Flies*, Harry Hook, dir. (USA: Castle Rock Entertainment, 1990).

*Mädchen in Uniform*, Leontine Sagan, dir. (Germany: Deutsche Film-Gemeinschaft, 1931).

Nietzsche, F. (1956) *The Birth of Tragedy and the Genealogy of Morals* (F. Golffing, trans.). Garden City, NY: Doubleday.

*Notes on a Scandal*, Richard Eyre, dir. (United Kingdom: Fox Searchlight Pictures, 2006).

Orwell, G. (2009) *Animal Farm: A Fairy Story*. Boston, MA: Houghton Mifflin Harcourt.

*Palo Alto*, Gia Coppola, dir. (USA: Rabbit Bandini Productions, 2013).

*The Piano Teacher*, Michael Haneke, dir. (Arte France Cinema, 2001).

*Prom Night*, Paul Lynch, dir. (Canada: Simcom Limited, 1980).

*Rock 'n' Roll High School*, Allan Arkush, dir. (USA: New World Pictures, 1979).

*Rushmore*, Wes Anderson, dir. (USA: American Empirical Pictures, 1998).

Schultz, C. (1959, October 8) *Peanuts* (comic strip) retrieved from http://peanuts.wikia.com/wiki/Miss_Othmar.

Schultz, C. (1959, October 15) *Peanuts* (comic strip) retrieved from http://peanuts.wikia.com/wiki/Miss_Othmar.

Schultz, C. (1969, February 26) *Peanuts* (comic strip) retrieved from http://peanuts.wikia.com/wiki/Miss_Othmar.

*Sixteen Candles*, John Hughes, dir. (USA: Channel Productions, 1984).

*Zero for Conduct*, Jean Vigo, dir. (France: Franfilmdis, 1933).

# Chapter 7

# End of class
## The death of the teacher and the life of teaching

"You remember your first grade teacher's name. Who will remember yours?"

Featured on a recruitment poster for the New York City Teaching Fellows these words were displayed throughout the New York City subway system during the early 2000s. The purpose of the campaign was obvious: to remind commuting workers of their alienated labor and the likelihood that they will spend their lives suffering what Maxine Greene (1995, p. 16) calls our "fundamental anxiety . . . that we will pass through the world and leave no mark." Teaching, at least according to the advertisement's claim, offers an exception to the loneliness of an anonymous life and inconsequential death, but an exception that is realized in a manner that might seem disappointingly paradoxical. That is to say, teaching can only prevent the feeling of anonymity, not death itself. To the contrary, as many films have demonstrated, the death of the teacher, whether literal or figurative, marks a significant moment in her relationship to her students, serving as a fulcrum upon which both the teacher's commitment to her students and her influence upon them might be registered. Influential teachers throughout the world of school films and through the scope of human history die in various ways, following in the steps of Socrates, who defined his teaching as a living toward death.

*The History Boys* (2006) provides a clear and literal example of the teacher whose death serves as an occasion to witness his influence over his students, as it closes with a funeral for its problematic protagonist, Hector, portrayed in the film as both a beloved beautiful soul and serial fondler. Mrs. Lintott, the history teacher, turns to see Hector's students sitting behind her in the chapel. "Will they come to my funeral?" she wonders aloud, echoing Greene's fundamental fear of oblivion. Her question also reveals something important about teaching and the good that it realizes for the teacher in freeing her from an alienated death, namely that the teacher's influence only takes on significance once the student has left the teacher behind. Only at this point can the teacher's name be remembered or forgotten, and only at this point can the lesson stand on its own, firmly implanted within the student and ready to take on its own life. The teacher fulfills her role in the life of the student through her act of self-annihilation.

## 114   End of class: the death of the teacher

Hector's death is heavily symbolic; he cannot continue his life as a teacher once his secret dalliances have been exposed, relieving him of his position as knowing subject beyond desire, neither is his teaching life one that is possible anymore given the new competitive culture of the Oxbridge exams. Even before his death, he has outlived his time and his way of life has become impossible. Like his namesake, he must die in order for another's lights to shine more brightly. But Hector's death is also a half-serious reference to the deaths of Socrates and Jesus of Nazareth. As with the rest of *The History Boys*, the line between light ironic humor and serious tragedy is subtly maintained, with the effect of creating a productive confusion and raising questions about the relationship between death and teaching. If Hector is upheld as the more influential teacher throughout the film, isn't it precisely because his presence is untimely, because he is not of this world?

Hector introduces the idea of death in the very first scene, quoting *Henry IV* (Part II, Act 3, Scene I) in response to his students' enthusiasm about their futures:

> O, if this were seen,
> The happiest youth, viewing his progress through,
> What perils past, what crosses to ensue,
> Would shut the book, and sit him down and die.

In a similar mood, Hector responds to the complaint of his student, Timms, that "Most of the things that poetry is about haven't happened to us yet," with a promise that the knowledge of poetry will be fulfilled with understanding when life brings about a moment for its fruition, "even when you're dying. We're making our deathbeds here, boys." His students have adapted themselves to Hector's oddly infectious lessons toward death: Akhtar describes his class as "Breaking bread with the dead," while Posner dismisses the physical education teacher's attempts to teach lifesaving techniques with philosophical pretension: "Nothing saves anyone's life, sir, it only postpones their death."

## Teaching death

The death of the teacher in film is not always as literal or total or celebrated as it is in Hector's case, in which the end of his life as a teacher also brings about the end of his life as such, as well as his rebirth in his students' lives. Jean Brodie (*The Prime of Miss Jean Brodie*, 1969) also suffers a scandalous end to her career, but she defiantly and repeatedly cries out "Assassin!" as Sandy, the student who informed on her, calmly walks away through the empty halls of the school in the last scene. Brodie's purpose in life, the idea of herself that she has carefully cultivated has been struck down, but she refuses to die, living on even in her student's traitorous act. In *Dead Poets Society* (1989) Mr. Keating carries out the ideal of Socratic teaching as self-sacrifice, particularly insofar as the scant information the film provides about his background is enough to suggest that his life outside the school is less developed than his relationships to his students. On the other hand, films such as *To Sir, With Love* (1967) and *Freedom Writers* (2007) provide something of a background story for characters like Brodie, Hector, and Keating, by portraying teachers suffering the loss of their lives in the world outside the school in order to become successful, committed professionals. *Freedom Writers* shows Gruwell's marriage eroding, a heroic loss as she devotes her time and attention to her students; *Mr. Holland's Opus* (1995) features the titular character mourning the loss of his career as a composer as he identifies with his teaching; Jaime Escalante (*Stand and Deliver*, 1988) collapses in the stairwell of his school, suffering a heart attack as a result of working too hard on behalf of his students. *To Sir, With Love* has Thackeray abandoning his life's goal of obtaining a career as an engineer after becoming lured by the ideal of shaping young minds. Mr. Chipping (*Goodbye, Mr. Chips*, 1939) walks directly from the scene of his wife's and infant's deaths in childbirth into his afternoon Latin class, where he finds his students transformed. The title character in *Monsieur Lazhar* (2011), struggling with the traumatic loss of his family while reigniting his students' desires after their teacher's public suicide, tells them, "A classroom . . . is where you give your life." Taken together, these films suggest that the practice of teaching swallows the teacher whole, ending her relationship to her life outside her pedagogical relationships, and leaving her in a precarious position should the relationships that establish her identity as a teacher ever fail.

Higgins (2003) has addressed the loss of the teacher's identity outside of the school in the final scene of *To Sir, With Love*, in which Thackeray tears up the job offer that represents his professional aspirations and decides to remain a teacher. Higgins argues that this scene reflects and reinforces an altruistic, ascetic moral culture that persists among teachers, but that is "unsustainable and ultimately undesirable because it tends to collapse into asceticism and lead[s] to teacher burnout" (Higgins, 2003, p. 131). According to Higgins:

> We tend to imagine Thackeray and teachers like him as motivated by the needs of students rather than as caught up in their own possibilities, intrigued by a vision of what they might become through teaching. Indeed, we are prone to estimate the moral worth of such service precisely by the degree to which the person acts selflessly or even self-sacrificially.
>
> (Higgins, 2003, p. 148)

Setting self-interested and selfless goals against one another in the way that he does leaves Higgins only one possible reading of Thackeray's action, namely that "In ripping up the letter, Thackeray makes a choice to prioritize the opportunities of his future students over his own opportunities" (Higgins, 2003, p. 147). A ruined Hector, despairing at the prospect of his career ending in scandal, reflects the binary that Higgins establishes here between selfish and selfless motives, as well as teaching's capacity to destroy the teacher's sense of selfhood: "What made me waste my life away in this godforsaken place? There's nothing of me left."

But this moment of despair works as it does because it stands in stark contrast to Hector's character—buoyed by the recognition he receives from his students—throughout the greater part of the film. Given that so much of Hector's identity derives from the recognition he receives from his students, it may be worthwhile to focus on this idea of relational flourishing as a way of complicating Higgins's binary, while returning the discussion to the transferential relationship as the fantasy that gives meaning to the practice of teaching as it provides motivation for students.

By stepping into the role of the teacher as one who knows and by inspiring the desires of his students, Thackeray feels himself memorialized in the influence he bears. The scene in which he tears up the letter is preceded by a scene in which his students gather to sing to him and give him a gift: a recognition that causes him to hold back tears as he excuses himself from the room, unable to open the gift in their presence. Taking on the role of the teacher has required Thackeray to perform, and in his students' recognition of his performance to become the idealized figure that inspires the desires of his students (Stillwaggon, 2008). In an ideal situation such as the film presents, there is no difference between the figure that the student needs in order to grow and the person the teacher wants to be in the eyes of others. In actual cases, the misrecognitions that color everyday human interactions are also, by necessity, part of pedagogy, providing the alterity that prevents human experience from becoming monolithic. Regardless of the degree of fit between student expectations and teacher desires, the fact that the teacher might be fulfilled and find a substantial identity through her relationships to her students complicates Higgins's construction of the problem as a matter of losing oneself in one's students. While we can certainly say that Thackeray has lost the life he would have lived as an engineer, we cannot do so without acknowledging the positive identity he has gained as a result of delivering himself to the needs of his students.

As the present chapter opens with a quotation from a New York Teaching Fellows advertisement, Higgins's argument makes use of another quotation from the same advertising campaign: "You've made your own dreams come true. Isn't it time you started on someone else's?" While this quotation and the cultural assumptions built into it clearly support Higgins's claim that teaching has become infected with an unhealthy altruism, the quotation at the outset of the current chapter paints teaching as an egotistical, self-interested practice, even if the good that is gained through it is somewhat esoteric. Taken together, however, the two quotations suggest a more complex interplay between altruism and egotism, compelling the teacher to lose herself, her identity, her life to her students in order to gain herself, her name, and her afterlife in the influence she holds in the lives of her students.

According to Blacker (1997) and De Marzio (2007), it is in precisely those ascetic motions critiqued by Higgins that the teacher regains herself *as* a teacher

End of class: the death of the teacher  117

through the recognition she receives from her students. Blacker's (1997) *Dying to Teach* enlightens the relationship between these various, partial deaths and the teacher's identity and motivation by redescribing the self-effacing drive that Higgins critiques as a "longing for immortality," one of teachers' "most powerful motivating factors"(Blacker, 1997, p. 2). Blacker divides this drive for immortality into two distinct parts: the Platonic and the Sophistical, better known to most scholars as the difference between the Christian promise of eternity and the heroic Greek ideal of immortality. The Sophistical drive for immortality describes the afterlife that a teacher enjoys in her influence over her students, both in the fact of one's name being remembered, as in the advertisement quoted above, and in the knowledge that one's work as a teacher changes the lives of one's students, who in turn exert an influence on those they encounter.

The teacher's longing for immortal influence looms large in *The History Boys*, particularly as the beloved teacher is asked to leave in scandal, presumably losing all of the immortal influence he has worked his entire career to cultivate. Immediately after the Headmaster asks him to retire, Hector returns to his classroom and finds himself unexpectedly in a study session with Posner, who recites Hardy's "Drummer Hodge" about a soldier killed and buried in a foreign place. Hector notes that in Hardy's time war memorials first recorded the names of common, private soldiers. "He had a name," Hector says, exposing his own anxieties about being forgotten, or simply categorized as yet another sexual predator. Reflecting the significance of names, Mrs. Lintott asks Irwin if the boys have given him a nickname and explains that he will never achieve anything with them if they haven't. Lintott herself has been given the nickname "Totty" and Hector's nickname is "Hector." In other words, we never know his "real" name, as he has adopted the nickname the students have given him; the recognition he receives from his students is so important that he lives entirely within the identity they have devised.

Both of these scenes recall Irwin's earlier critique of war memorials, in which he has told the boys that the British focus on the names of the dead in remembering the war in order to obscure the fact that their own imperial interests drove the First World War more than any other factor. In unveiling the historical purposes of a sincerely shared sentiment, Irwin has won an intellectual battle with Hector for the boys' imaginations, but his insistence on rationally dissecting and explaining affective human motivations has lost him the war of claiming the boys' hearts and minds. The problem with his thinking is that it could be turned against his own aspirations, easily devaluing the fact that every person remembers his second grade teacher's name. But that same critical spirit not only fails to recognize something significant and pervasive in the human experience; it also erases any need to remember Irwin.

While Blacker's study focuses on the relationship between death and the teaching identity, the immortal death of the teacher also presents itself as essential to the continued growth and flourishing of the student. While the teacher's influence over the student provides the conditions for the student's desires and adherence to recognizable discourses of human flourishing, some limit to the teacher's stature as the subject presumed to know must emerge in order to allow the student a degree of difference from her teacher, a space wherein the student's striving can become her own relationship to the discourse rather than a striving that is constantly mediated by the approval of an authority.

In *The Paper Chase* (1973) Hart's capacity to take the place of the teacher, to see Kingsfield as already dead, begins the moment that Hart finds a break in the contract of Kingsfield's pedagogy, the promise that for every answer there will be another question. In rendering Kingsfield mute, transforming the terror of the classroom into "a goddamned dance," Hart paves the way for his own ascendancy to the crown. This process of placing Kingsfield in the past, eradicating and memorializing him, fulfills itself in Hart's reading of Kingsfield's notes, which contain the formula for the ritual overthrow and subsequent memorializing of authority. "This is the ageless passing of wisdom." Kingsfield, the face of Harvard Law, offers the student the chance to be part of the "unbroken chain."

In Kingsfield's notes, Hart reads, "Can we make a contract with God that is binding to man?" an invitation to the student to negotiate a contract with the teacher that is binding to both, allowing the student to become the "living extension of tradition." Seeing Kingsfield's limits, Hart is invited to take his place: when the class is empty (at the podium) and when the house is empty (with Susan). The king is dead; long live the king. At the close of the film, Hart has moved beyond Kingsfield's class, but not beyond his teacher's authority or influence. He folds his grade report into a paper airplane and throws it into the air over the sea in an act of casual defiance, but the rock from which he throws it is on Kingsfield's property. Like Freud's original, rapacious father, the teacher grows in significance in death, becoming inscribed into the law itself.

## Passing the parcel

Citing Plato's *Phaedo* in support of the link between teaching and death, Blacker asserts another kind of deathlessness that teachers seek to derive from their teaching, namely in identifying with those transcendent principles of learning that are outside of time. From this perspective, "education's ultimate justification lies in its securing of immortality for the lover of learning" (Blacker, 1997, p. 3) and the teacher is understood as a superior student, enthralled in the work of study, and a conduit of his own learning to students, the public, or whoever happens to be around. The audience, as Blacker notes, is less important than the teacher's connection to the transcendent: "The occupation of teaching flesh-and-blood human beings is for the most part secondary" (Blacker, 1997, p. 3).

Elucidating this same relationship to the eternal that Blacker sees as a primary motivational force in teaching, De Marzio demonstrates the historical

End of class: the death of the teacher 119

link, equally central to the *Phaedo*, between the ascetic's retreat from the world and the study of eternal truths that characterizes the teacher. He concludes that:

> [o]ne could not pursue the good life through teaching if teaching did not call upon the self to sacrifice and to transform one's desires. Teaching and being of service for others is a way for one to care for the self, to transform the self, and to enact a special vision of human flourishing.
>
> (De Marzio, 2007, pp. 353–354)

Hector's comparison of teaching to a children's game of "pass the parcel," makes a similar connection between the eternal content of the teaching and the fact that by teaching, we participate in something that necessarily outlives us. In Hector's metaphor, however, he emphasizes the fact that the eternal inspires and motivates teachers and students alike precisely because it resists human understanding. In the game, an object wrapped in multiple layers of paper is passed from one child to the next, stopping occasionally to remove a layer of paper until the object is finally revealed. In keeping with his related claims that he does not understand the poetry he teaches his students, and that the accidents of life afford the opportunity for understanding insofar as our lives provide insight into poetry, Hector underscores a Socratic and Lacanian foundation of teaching that the teacher is capable of teaching something that he does not fully understand. "Pass the parcel. That's sometimes all you can do. Take it, feel it, and pass it on. Not for me, not for you, but for someone."

Blacker's separation of teaching's deathlessness into distinct moments is useful in identifying their respective historical influences, but we can also recognize that, even as early as the *Phaedo*, these drives are inextricably wound together. As Socrates points out early in the dialogue, he intends to fulfill the command of the oracle by practicing poetry, and his arguments that follow throughout the remainder of the dialogue conform to this intention, focusing on the effect that his words manifest in his audience rather than on the logical structure of his argument. The resulting arguments with his interlocutors illustrate this concern. As interpreters of the dialogue have indicated, Socrates' arguments for the immortality of the soul are full of holes, but he returns repeatedly to the effect that believing in the immortality of the soul will have for the living.

Faced with the question of the fate of the soul after the death of the body, Socrates famously sets up the body as the obstacle to the soul's relation to the truth, asking his interlocutors (65b) if they believe it is true, "as the poets are always dinning into our ears, that we neither hear nor see anything accurately?"[1] Combining this idea of the body as a limit with his statement of "firm hope" in the afterlife, Socrates follows his own question with yet another traditional answer from the poets, that neither "absolute uprightness . . . absolute beauty [or] goodness" can be seen or "apprehended . . . with any other bodily sense," (65d). Socrates concludes that "the wisdom which we desire and upon which we profess to have set our hearts

## 120 End of class: the death of the teacher

will be attainable only when we are dead . . . because it is only then that the soul will be separate and independent of the body" (66e).

As Simmias and Cebes agree with Socrates that the body may obstruct truth, Socrates pushes forward to connect the disembodied nature of the philosopher's life to an idea of the moral life, or further, a life of happiness. He begins with an epistemological claim regarding the apprehension of truth: "so long as we keep to the body and our soul is contaminated with this imperfection, there is no chance of our ever attaining satisfactorily to our object" (66b). But this contamination soon spreads to include more than the life of the mind. Socrates claims that too great an attachment to the body produces "distractions," "diseases," "attack[s]," "fears," "fancies," "nonsense," "wars," "battles," and "slave[ry]," (66b–d). While each of these dangers is ultimately presented in relation to the care of the soul beyond the body's death, Socrates successfully introduces a philosophical path in which our relationship to death becomes the governing force of our desires in this life.

Socrates' grounds his justification for his dedication to the eternal truths that have guided his teaching in the life that these guiding principles make possible in the here and now. But the here and now that Socrates ultimately refers to in staking his claim for philosophy is no longer available for him, as he is knowingly and willingly going to end his life within the course of the dialogue. Instead, his relationship to the eternal ideas identified by Blacker and De Marzio as fundamental motivations for the teacher seems contingent upon the influence it promises to manifest in the lives of his students.

Blacker's distinction between the eternity in which a teacher participates as a result of study and the immortality that the teacher lives as a result of influencing students, eventually collapses into the latter case, insofar as beliefs and ideals ultimately serve the poetic purpose of shaping the lives of teachers and students alike. The eternity of intellectual or artistic content in which the teacher participates, as Hart discovers in reading Kingsfield's notes, depends upon the passage of a tradition from one generation to another. The parcel must not only be passed but also received.

Yet if the teacher ultimately looks to the student and depends on the student for her identity and her afterlife, and if this afterlife is what sets teaching apart from other professions, does this mean that teachers desire an afterlife to the exclusion of the more ordinary desires of *this* life? As Dakin explains to Irwin after the new teacher receives extended questions from the students about his extracurricular activities, "What they want to know sir is do you have a life or are we it?" We would expect that students would want the teacher to have a life outside of teaching, but the better part of the genre of school films, whether sympathetic or cynical toward teaching as a practice, tell us that the good teacher has no life of her own. Irwin's description of his activities outside of the school sounds monastic; Hector has a wife, but we only know this because Lintott brings her up as an anomaly. The only images of Thackeray outside of school show him ironing his shirt and commuting to school. Gruwell loses her marriage; LouAnne Johnson's commitment is only possible because her marriage is already over. We are presented with a litany of images of teachers as subjects captivated and moved by strange motivations regarding their own posterity to the extent that they strive to live on in their students' futures, neglecting the here and now of their own lives and the pursuit of what we would typically consider happiness.

## Between two deaths

Freud's (1957) interest in what psychoanalysis comes to call the *death instinct* stems from his interest in cases that feature a similar, inexplicable drive, operating seemingly independently of what he had earlier called the pleasure principle. The cases in question involved empirical studies of soldiers returning from the First World War with what today we would call post-traumatic stress disorder, at the time known as shell shock. The problem with shell shock, for Freud, is that, as a psychological response to trauma, it does not seem to fit in a clean manner within his articulation of the psyche as shaped by the libidinal drives of the pleasure principle and the corresponding limitations upon the drives represented by the reality principle. While the ego typically works to repress elements of the unconscious that will bring pain to the subject, the repetition of painful experiences among shell shock victims fails to repress and in fact seems to promote the subject's return to its own pain.

In order to understand this phenomenon further, Freud discusses two other categories of painful repetition, both of which seem to promote pain in the subject that does not serve any greater sense of pleasure or equilibrium. The first is the well-known Freudian example of the Fort-Da game played by a toddler. The child repeatedly plays a game in which he throws his toys away into a corner, with an exclamation that his mother translates as "Fort" or "Gone." In some instances of this game, he recalls the toys to his own presence, saying "Da," or "There." According to Freud, the game serves as a means by which the child repeats the loss of his mother, both in terms of temporary separations and oedipal interdictions. Freud emphasizes the fact that the game does not always include the recovery of the object, a fact that underscores the child's repetition of painful experiences that do not lead to a pleasurable resolution. At the same time, he allows that the example is not entirely convincing with respect to his argument regarding a separate drive toward death, insofar as the child's repetition allows it to experience mastery of its own experience of loss. "None of this [repetition of pain in children's play] contradicts the pleasure principle; repetition, the re-experiencing of something identical, is clearly in itself a source of pleasure" (Freud, 1957, p. 36).

The pleasure in these repetitions toward mastery derives not only from the fact that the child becomes the agent of the loss but also that the repetition is a representation through the child's toys, not a renewed experience of the actual pain of loss. The imaginary representation fascinates because it provides visual

## 122   End of class: the death of the teacher

coherence in an otherwise incomprehensible chaos (Boothby, 1991, p. 27). A similar understanding of the representation of pain, rather than its actual experience, can be read back as far as Aristotle:

> Objects which in themselves we view with pain, we delight to contemplate when reproduced with minute fidelity: such as the forms of the most ignoble animals and of dead bodies. The cause of this again is, that to learn gives us the liveliest pleasure, not only to philosophers but to men in general.
>
> (Aristotle, 1997, 1448b)

What Freud does not argue explicitly, but that we might read into his claim of non-contradiction, is the fact that the Fort-Da game provides us with an understanding of how the compulsion to repeat or represent a painful experience might reside within any number of non-pathological cases. But in order to consider the death instinct in a less ambiguous manner, he offers a contrasting, clearer category of compulsive repetition that serves no purpose for the subject. "In the case of a person in analysis, on the contrary, the compulsion to repeat the events of his childhood in the transference evidently disregards the pleasure principle in every way" (Freud, 1957, p. 36) The adult neurotic repeats childhood pain by transferring his unresolved feelings toward his parents onto those who he sees as having some sort of power to deny him the fulfillment of his desires, thereby destroying his relationships with friends, lovers, employers, and others as a way of reliving his early disappointments. Clearly, this repetition has no connection to pleasure or mastery and does not help the sufferer reinscribe his own identity into a social discourse in any positive way.

Freud interprets the neurotic's behavior as a clue to the repeated, terrorizing dreams of shell-shocked soldiers and views the two phenomena as linked by a common instinct that operates independently of the pleasure principle and its environing limitations. By Freud's own admission, the remainder of his study is troublingly "speculative," working outside any grounding in empirical evidence, and seems to suggest that the very materiality of the subject's existence serves as a kind of gravitational pull, always drawing the purposes of life back to their inert, inorganic foundations, suggesting a priority based on historical emergence: *"inanimate things existed before living ones"* (Freud, 1957, p. 38, emphasis in original). At times, Freud's language parallels the adolescent fatalism of Posner's Hector-influenced philosophical response to the encouragement of the physical education teacher: "These germ cells, therefore, work against the death of the living substance and succeed in winning for it what we can only regard as potential immortality, though that may mean no more than a lengthening of the road to death," (Freud, 1957, p. 40) and more succinctly, *"the aim of all life is death."* (Freud, 1957, p. 38, emphasis in original).

Given Freud's inability to ground the idea of the death instinct in anything more than speculations about materiality, his theory remains both compelling

# End of class: the death of the teacher  123

and in need of constructive interpretation for anyone interested in making it work. According to Gallop (1985), the idea of the death instinct was both troubling and compelling for Lacan as well, causing him to rework the idea a number of times based on his interests at that time. Gallop states that Lacan's early attempts to interpret Freud's theory describe the death drive as a pre-oedipal nostalgia for unity and later associates it with narcissism and the imaginary order.

Perhaps the best known of Lacan's treatments of the death instinct can be found in his 1959–60 seminar (Lacan, 1997) on the ethics of psychoanalysis, in which he undertakes a reading of Sophocles' *Antigone*, describing her ethical position in burying her brother, Polynieces, as "between two deaths." Lacan's reading of *Antigone* and the death instinct is informed by the Marquis de Sade's reflection on the natural tendency toward crime, death, and destruction. According to Keenan (2005, p. 116), Lacan's reading of Sade distinguishes between murder, or the biological death of the individual, and absolute death, or the destruction of the signifying chain, the discursive social order that grounds one's own being. It is this latter understanding of the death instinct that Lacan associates with Antigone, as her execution of funerary rites over the body of her brother not only challenges the authority of the law, but also calls into question the value of this authority, insofar as her justified transgression of the law condemns her to death. Throughout the play, Antigone exists in the space between her own transgression—an enactment of the second, symbolic death in which her own place in the symbolic order is destroyed—and her own biological death that Creon has already decreed as the punishment for anyone who transgresses his law. As such, Antigone becomes the "sacrifice of the sacrifice" (Keenan, 2005, p. 116) or the sacrificial death by which the symbolic order, in which the individual's desire is sacrificed for the good of the whole, is brought down.

Given the sense of ritualized loss embedded in discussions of teacher identity and filmic representations of teaching, we might be tempted to associate teaching with this sacrificial position. This interpretation of the death instinct matches Keating's (*Dead Poets Society*, 1989) fatalism: he teaches only to lose his position and change his students' lives in the process. From the start, he is marked: given impossible shoes to fill, despite the fact that he seems complete and prepared to challenge authority even as a student. He arrives already dead within the discursive order of the school, as it offers him nothing toward which he might direct his desires. Like Antigone, his desires are attached to something ineffable, neither to the written word nor to the tradition they constitute, but to the fleeting moments he introduces to his students: jumping from his desk, kicking soccer balls while reading triumphant lines of verse, and sounding barbaric yawps. Verse 52 of Whitman's (1892) "Song of Myself," from which Keating quotes the barbaric yawp, demonstrates his willing sacrificial status in the relationship between his ineffable character, his death, and his afterlife:

The spotted hawk swoops by and accuses me, he complains of my gab
    and my loitering.
I too am not a bit tamed, I too am untranslatable,
I sound my barbaric yawp over the roofs of the world.
The last scud of day holds back for me,
It flings my likeness after the rest and true as any on the shadow'd wilds,
It coaxes me to the vapor and the dusk.
I depart as air, I shake my white locks at the runaway sun,
I effuse my flesh in eddies, and drift it in lacy jags.
I bequeathe myself to the dirt, to grow from the grass I love,
If you want me again, look for me under your boot-soles.
You will hardly know who I am, or what I mean,
But I shall be good health to you nevertheless,
And filter and fibre your blood.
Failing to fetch me at first keep encouraged,
Missing me one place search another,
I stop somewhere waiting for you.

(Whitman, 1892)

Emphasizing his untranslatability, Whitman/Keating also refuses success and
mastery according to established norms, as merely mastering the given discourse would also mean being mastered by it. Yet without a place in the
world vouchsafed by a place in words, the subject holds no power except to
"bequeathe [him]self to the dirt" in order to re-emerge everywhere, elusive
and yet at the same time promising the readers/students that by following their
desires and continuing to search, they will at long last arrive at the place where
their impossible author waits for them.

In a less poetic, but equally impossible manner, Lily Moffat (*The Corn Is
Green*, 1945) seems to fit the same sacrificial mold, introducing herself from
the start as a character who has no place in the existing patriarchal discourses
of erudition and power. While her "death" as an empowered subject does
not fundamentally change the ethical landscape of the Welsh mining town in
which she finds herself at the close of the film, it does introduce Morgan to the
world as a potential for change, precisely because of his difference from other
Oxford students. He too is a sacrifice, as he can never return to his home, his
language, or his child, but not as a result of his own agency. Moffatt, on the
other hand, willingly repeats her painful exclusion from the learned world of
men by taking on precisely that role that has historically excluded women from
the public sphere. In taking Morgan's baby, she becomes his de facto wife, losing her public life so that he may live his.

Nonetheless, this purely self-sacrificial reading of the death instinct does not
provide insight into the irreducible peculiarities of Brodie (*The Prime of Miss
Jean Brodie*, 1969) or Hector (*The History Boys*, 2006), to say nothing of the
conservative repetitions of Kingsfield (*The Paper Chase*, 1973). While Hector's

End of class: the death of the teacher 125

momentary expression of despair might cast him as a sacrifice, his portrayal throughout the rest of the film demonstrates a character who lives entirely in and through his transferential relationship with his students rather than in an act of resignation. As Blacker's (1997) and De Marzio's (2007) work, as well as Plato's *Phaedo* make clear, a vision of the teacher as merely a sacrifice fails to do justice to the teacher's own aspirations toward immortality that the teacher seeks through her work.

Gallop (1985) offers a somewhat different reading of Lacan's work on the death instinct that focuses less on the individual's striving to negate the symbolic order in which she is embedded, and draws instead upon an egocentric sense of singularity. She begins by acknowledging the difficulty in interpreting Freud's theory:

> Freud has posited the reactionary nature of all instincts, but the self-preservative instincts do not appear to aim toward a return. The only way he can account for them is to see them working with (in fact, for) the death instincts. He then winds up with what he calls a "paradoxical situation": life is preserved so that the organism can "die only in its own fashion".
> (Freud, 1957, p. 39, quoted in Gallop, 1985, p. 102)

Gallop (1985) reconciles this paradox, and its resultant contradiction, "both that the sexual instincts restore an earlier state and that they do not" (p. 102) with the notion that the death drive is concerned less with "its apparent end-point, death," (p. 103) but with an insistence on the self that is more primary than the distinction between self-preservation and death. "He explains that the repetition of painful experiences in dreams and children's play is an attempt to master an exceedingly painful event by taking over the position of author of this event" (p. 169). That is, "It is more important that a desire pursue the correct path—that is, its own path—to fulfillment than that it be fulfilled" (p. 104).

From Gallop's perspective, the teacher returns to the scene of her own painful educational experiences not as a sacrificial token, lost in order to change the ground of her own being, erasing herself in the process. Instead, Gallop's understanding of the compulsion to repeat more closely resembles the child playing the Fort-Da game, in order to replay the same injuries from a different position. While the return to the classroom as a teacher lacks the aesthetic distance achieved by the child playing the game, it nonetheless allows the teacher to repeat her own incompleteness in relation to knowledge from a position of greater authority. As with the game, here we have no contradiction between eros and thanatos: the teacher's desire to complete herself would necessarily spell her own death if she could achieve it, as there would be nothing for her to strive for; the fact that she cannot achieve the end she desires, that it remains a guiding fantasy, implanted within her before she had reason enough to critique it, allows her to strive ever forward, asymptotically, growing according to her pursuit of something that cannot be reached. Aiding in this fantasy is the gaze of her students, accepting the authority of her words even when she does not and recognizing her as something that she knows she cannot be.

According to Lacan this primacy of recognition is "the necessary and sufficient condition" for "the repetitive insistence of [infantile] desires in the transference and their permanent recollection in a signifier where the repressed returns" (Gallop, 1985, p. 104). To be recognized as a teacher, or a subject presumed to know, by student subjects who presume their own ignorance, allows for the difference that makes teaching a productive repetition of the experience of being a student.

Schneiderman (1983, p. 76) asserts an equivalence between the desire for death and the desire for immortality, reminding us that "Only the living are mortal." He interprets Lacan's emphasis of *Antigone* over Freud's emphasis on *Oedipus* as a shift of the work of psychoanalysis: from coming to understand the operation of unknown desires, to coming to terms with our relationship with the dead. Boothby (1991) also draws a strong connection between death and the fantasy of completeness associated with authority, quoting the master himself: "This image of the master, which is what [he] sees in the form of the specular image, becomes confused in him with the image of death" (Lacan, 1988, p. 149, quoted in Boothby, 1991, p. 22). The same sentiment is reflected in our public imaginary, in which the teachers upheld as an end of desire in a fantasy of knowing completeness are consistently presented as suffering loss and incompleteness in order to pursue their path. How else would we know they were pursuing their own path, unless they pursued it in the face of suffering?

## Authoring one's own death

Returning the question of the teacher's death instinct to the Freudian text, we can recognize two similarities. Assuming that the student's experience, defined by desire as the knowledge of one's own lack, remains within the psyche as a painful inscription, we might also see the student's assumption of the teaching role as akin to the Fort-Da game—a way of repeating a painful experience that reinstates the student-turned-teacher's feelings of mastery and integration. As Freud's argument suggests, this compulsion to repeat does not contradict the teacher's libidinal strivings, but works alongside them, providing a central, egotistical position to which the teaching subject returns as a way of marking its own difference with its past pain. While the teaching position does not guarantee the knowledge that one lacks as a student, it does accomplish goals tangential to this ideal. On the one hand, being a teacher means standing in the place of authority once projected onto others. Occupying this position has two bittersweet benefits: one is the recognition itself, as one gets lured into the transferential relationship through the recognition one receives from students. The other is the knowledge that one's own subjects presumed to know, the venerated teachers, did not know everything we believed they did. On the other hand, this bittersweet knowledge comes with a better and more limited

End of class: the death of the teacher   127

sense of what knowledge is about than we carried around with us as children. Knowing what we do not know, or at least having a better sense of what is knowable, we suffer less the disappointments of our own ignorance.

In this sense, the professional ethics that Higgins (2003) seeks for teachers might be further complicated by teachers' insistence regarding authorship of their own deaths, or at least a claim of authorship over their own limits. As ethics might be read as a way of wholly submitting oneself to the norms of a discourse, what Higgins diagnoses as an ascetic ethical failure might better be understood as an insistence of the idiosyncratic nature of the self, against normal or healthy desires. This desire to stand in control of one's desires, or to stand at the end of one's desires, is particularly resonant with the shared fantasy of trans-ference that founds pedagogical relationships. If the student strives toward the place that she supposes the teacher holds in the symbolic order—a place beyond the problem of mastery—this fantasied position would also hold a privileged place over the teacher's own limits. Socrates' claim of ignorance over the things of this world and over the question of death is a way of standing in a position of authority over his own limits: he knows what he does not know. The teacher, once a student enthralled in the lure of transference, still carries vestiges of those fantasies, believing that, as if magically, she ought to know something simply as a result of standing at the front of the classroom. Her students' credulous attention supports her aspirational fantasy. Nonetheless, standing in front of the classroom, the teacher cannot help but feel that she operates as an impostor, barely two steps ahead of her students yet failing to correct the misguided fantasies of completeness and knowing they project upon her. Reclaiming herself requires her to come to terms with that which she is not.

In *The Browning Version* (1951), Crocker-Harris, known as "the Croc" to his students and colleagues because of his cold-blooded demeanor, is pronounced dead by students, colleagues, and his wife in expectation of his early retirement, discussed as if it were a long-awaited funeral. But Crocker-Harris has apparently been dead for a long time, pronouncing disdain *ex cathedra* and presenting the dead languages as fully dead. Only in being reminded of his death does Crocker-Harris seem to show some signs of life, at first simply by warning his successor of the dangers of an early death in teaching.

Clearing out old papers from his classroom, Crocker-Harris is confronted by the teacher who will replace him: a young, handsome, and personable novice who wears his lack of experience on his sleeve. Surprisingly, glib, Crocker-Harris confesses his inability, after an entire career, "to communicate some of my own joy in the literature of the past. Of course, I failed. As you will fail, nine hundred and ninety-nine times out of a thousand." He asks his replacement to keep his confession of failure a secret, but the audience has also heard his secret confession and can no longer see him in the same way knowing that he is not ignorant of his own failure.

Crocker-Harris also confesses to a middling student named Taplow, who is receiving tutoring from him, that, as a young man, he attempted to breathe

## 128 End of class: the death of the teacher

life into Aeschylus' text by translating it in rhyming couplets. Taplow, whose errant translations also breathe drama and excitement into the ancient Greek text, expresses an interest in both Crocker-Harris's attempted translation of the *Agamemnon* and in Crocker-Harris himself. To express his gratitude, Taplow presents Crocker-Harris with a copy of Browning's translation of *Agamemnon* that Taplow has inscribed in Greek: *God from afar looks graciously upon a gentle master.* Crocker-Harris is overwhelmed by the totally undeserved recognition he has received and breaks down, ashamed of his own emotion. Read through the ascetic ethics of Blacker and De Marzio, in whose work the death instinct of the teacher becomes a struggle with tradition that occasions the pedagogical relationship, his shame and his emotion also emerge from his tragic realization that he has repressed his own desire, failing to repeat the knowledge of his own ignorance that occasioned his beginnings as a great scholar and instead uncannily repeating his beloved *Agamemnon* in his own marriage while performing his teaching at a cold, safe distance. As Gallop (1985, p. 175) argues:

> The Freudian unconscious subjects us to a knowledge we cannot read but which we nonetheless carry with us and which spells our death . . . The death instinct is a knowledge within us, a knowledge of our own path to death, but a knowledge we are not cognizant of.

Becoming aware of his tragic repression of his desire through the recognition he receives from Taplow, Crocker-Harris confesses again, this time publicly, taking full account of his own incompleteness and responsibility for his own desires. Given the opportunity to say farewell to his students at their daily prayer service, attended by the entire school community who wince in expectation, he begins his own eulogy in a familiar, distant tone, then stops and begins again:

> I am sorry because I have failed to give you what you have the right to demand of me as your teacher: sympathy, encouragement, and humanity . . . I claim no excuses. When I came here I knew what I had to do and I have not done it. I have failed.

The students roar in applause, drowning out the rest of the service from the Headmaster. Crocker-Harris has not suddenly become a heroic teacher; his possibilities for achieving something great have already passed. But in recognizing this fact, he has ended the negative repetition of the neurotic in which the compulsion to repeat does not correspond to any productive, erotic drive, as it does in the Fort-Da game. Like Hector admitting that he too does not understand the meaning of the poetry he teaches, and like Socrates, who only admits to knowing something about desire, or his own incompleteness, Crocker-Harris has opened a place of possibility wherein his students might strive to add their own desires to the tradition that keeps ideas alive.

## Note

1 Citations of Plato by Stephanus numbers refer to Hamilton and Cairns (eds) (1961).

## References

Aristotle (1997) *Poetics* (S.H. Butcher, trans.). Mineola, NY: Dover Publications.

Blacker, D. (1997). *Dying to Teach: The Educator's Search for Immortality*. New York: Teachers College Press.

Boothby, R. (1991) *Death and Desire: Psychoanalytic Theory in Lacan's Return to Freud*. New York: Routledge.

*The Browning Version*, Anthony Asquith, dir. (United Kingdom: Javelin Films, 1951).

*The Corn Is Green*, Irving Rapper, dir. (USA: Warner Bros, 1945).

*Dead Poets Society*, Peter Weir, dir. (USA: Touchstone Pictures, 1989).

De Marzio, D. (2007) Teaching as asceticism: Transforming the self through the practice. *Philosophy of Education 2007*. Urbana, IL: Philosophy of Education Society, pp. 349–355.

*Freedom Writers*, Richard LaGravenese, dir. (USA: Paramount Pictures, 2007).

Freud, S. (1957) *The Standard Edition of the Complete Psychological Works of Sigmund Freud* (Vol. XVIII). London: The Hogarth Press.

Gallop, J. (1985) *Reading Lacan*. Ithaca, NY: Cornell University Press.

*Goodbye, Mr. Chips*, Sam Wood, dir. (USA: Warner Bros, 1939).

Greene, M. (1995) *Releasing the Imagination*. New York: Teachers College Press.

Hamilton, E. and Cairns, H. (eds) (1961). *The Collected Dialogues of Plato, Including the Letters*. New York: Pantheon Books.

Higgins, C. (2003). Teaching and the good life: A critique of the ascetic ideal in education. *Educational Theory*, 53(2), 131–154.

*The History Boys*, Nicholas Hytner, dir. (United Kingdom: Fox Searchlight Pictures, 2006).

Keenan, D. K. (2005) *The Question of Sacrifice*. Bloomington, IN: Indiana University Press.

Lacan, J. (1988) *The Seminar of Jacques Lacan, Book I: Freud's Papers on Technique, 1953–1954* (J.-A. Miller (ed.), Forrester, J. trans.). New York: W.W. Norton & Co.

Lacan, J. (1997) *The Seminar of Jacques Lacan, Book VII: The Ethics of Psychoanalysis, 1959–1960* (J.-A. Miller (ed.), D. Porter, trans.). New York: W.W. Norton & Co.

*Monsieur Lazhar*, Philippe Falardeau, dir. (Canada: micro_scope, 2011).

*Mr. Holland's Opus*, Stephen Herek, dir. (USA: Hollywood Pictures, 1995).

*The Paper Chase*, James Bridges, dir. (USA: 20th Century Fox, 1973).

*The Prime of Miss Jean Brodie*, Ronald Neame, dir. (United Kingdom: 20th Century Fox, 1969).

Schneiderman, S. (1983) *Jacques Lacan: The Death of an Intellectual Hero*. Cambridge, MA: Harvard University Press.

*Stand and Deliver*, Ramón Menéndez, dir. (USA: American Playhouse, 1988).

Stillwaggon, J. (2008) Performing for the students: Teaching identity and the pedagogical relationship. *Journal of Philosophy of Education*, 42(1), 67–83.

*To Sir, With Love*, James Clavell, dir. (United Kingdom: Columbia Pictures, 1967).

Whitman, W. (1892) Song of myself. In *Leaves of Grass*. Washington, DC: McKay.

# Chapter 8

# End of term
## The limits of authority and conclusion

In considering the variety of films that constitute this study, from the mainspring of erotic self-overcoming that founds the genre of school films, through the various realizations and failures of transference that bring us, finally, to the teacher's death so that her students may live, it may be useful to draw some of these themes together by considering the limits of transference as a motivating and identifying fantasy shared by teacher and student. Many of the films discussed in this book portray pedagogy in its ideal conditions, and even those narratives in which educational aims don't work out as we would expect still frame the teacher's influence as remarkably powerful. Without diminishing the significance of transference to the educational relationship, in this chapter we focus on a phenomenon in which the shared cultural ideal of teaching—a sort of collective fantasy—has brought our popular imaginary associations regarding the influence of teachers to light.

As a way of drawing this discussion to a close, in this chapter we look at a difficult problem currently at the center of educational policy and practice, namely the idea that teachers might be held accountable for their students' academic success or failure. Recent high-stakes teaching accountability measures, based on students' achievement on standardized tests, suggest policymakers' misunderstanding of the relationship between teaching and learning and, perhaps more importantly, a willful ignorance (Britzman, 1998; Logue, 2009) on the part of legislators to own up to the conditions under which teaching and learning often take place. Given the limited effect that any one teacher's influence has on the actual academic success of a particular student, the only reasonable explanation for teacher accountability movements is that policymakers and academics alike, like many teacher candidates and members of the moviegoing public, participate in the same impossible fantasies about teaching that drive school films.

But as we have claimed from the outset, the point of this study is not to dispel or pull back the curtain on the fantasies of teaching that occupy the public imaginary. Teaching relationships in real schools, after all, rely heavily upon the impossible ideal of "knowing" at the center of transference. Instead, our aim has been to understand what it means to live within these fantasies,

The limits of authority and conclusion    131

moved by ultimately unfounded, but nonetheless productive, desires. With this aim in mind, we argue that overreaching policies such as accountability measures can be helpful in holding a mirror to the imaginary forces that influence so much of our unthought ties to education, insofar as they attempt to realize an impossible fantasy. If accountability measures are so hyperbolic in their expectations, however, we are drawn to the question of how we might better view the connection, if any, between what a teacher teaches and what a student learns. We consider the question of the teacher's pedagogical influence in terms of a fundamental disconnect between teaching and learning that prevents the teacher's effectiveness from being captured by metrics we may use to predict success in other human endeavors.

While the teacher can create a product or performance with specific pedagogical intentions, the ultimate effects of teaching in their influence upon the student can only be addressed as an unknown. The effects may be closely related to the lessons the teacher practices, but even in their fidelity to the message of the teacher they may deliver an outcome impossible to predict or even understand. Teachers too focused on the disconnect of intentionality inherent in any pedagogical relationship may be caught up in a doubled fear over the outcome of their work. On the one hand, the student may fail to become what the teacher desires; on the other, the student might, in bringing the teacher's dreams of influence to reality, reveal the limitations of the teacher's understanding of the world outside the classroom, creating a monster that the teacher cannot control. Alfred Hitchcock's *Rope* (1948) illustrates the latter possibility, insofar as the horror it brings to the screen is premised upon the students' active and literal realization of their teacher's intellectually appealing, but morally damnable lessons.

## Accountability and other teacher fantasies

Accountability measures participate in a naïve fantasy of control at the heart of much educational policy, in which whatever problem can be measured today might one day be fixed. Accountability has been easily critiqued by its opponents for the disruptions it causes across the educational terrain. Teachers feel their authority in the classroom and in society is threatened, their curricula emptied of unmeasurable ideas and non-testable skills, their professional agency limited by the prescriptions of a testing-oriented curriculum. Standardized tests used to measure student outcomes flatten real learning, misrepresent gains in analytical skills, and assume level playing fields between students of vastly different socioeconomic backgrounds. Despite these and more critical evaluations of teacher accountability measures, the idea of accountability has been difficult to challenge in public discourses, partly because it attaches to a fantasy of teaching held by teachers and the public alike, namely, that teachers influence their students, and good teachers bring about intellectual and emotional growth. If this is what we believe about teachers, what could be wrong with verifying that it actually happens? Biesta (2004, p. 241) argues the same point about the difficulty of dispelling the fantasy behind accountability from a different perspective, nonetheless emphasizing that our connection to a fantasy of teaching runs deeper than our political beliefs: "In this respect the idea of accountability may be relatively immune to political ideology, or may even have shaped what is politically 'possible'."

Teachers are especially susceptible to the implicit fantasy informing accountability measures, not only because it suggests that the only teachers who would resist being held accountable are those whose work would not stand up to rigorous scrutiny. Teachers' vulnerability in relation to accountability extends to their own fantasies about their professional efficacy and identity—that which allows teachers to go on teaching even when evidence suggests that what they are doing has no effect. The teacher's fantasy includes an implicit expectation of students' desires in relation to authorized forms of knowledge, and that these desires will move the student to follow the teacher in words and deeds.

The popular teacher fantasy to which accountability measures attach cannot be given up too lightly, therefore, because it is also the fantasy of individual teachers, whose sense of personhood and professional identity depend on the careful balance between the symbolic social function that teachers fulfill and the fleshy continuity that assures their social function is fulfilled, albeit partially, every day. What's more, as we have suggested in previous chapters, the teacher fantasy is only a more complex construction of the student fantasy, in which someone knows something worth knowing and is therefore too much a functioning part of institutional education to sacrifice in order to critique accountability measures. Yet as fantasy is constituted in opposition to its own limits, on the one hand in the insistence of the body and on the other in the demands of the symbolic order, the problem with accountability as a teacher fantasy writ large may not be that it derives from fantasy, but that it tries to take the dream outside its intimate confines and into the symbolic order, like the horror of waking from a wonderful dream of flying only to find that the dream continues in waking life. Borrowing from Freud's formulation, every dream may represent a wish, but not necessarily wishes we wanted to be fulfilled.

The somewhat obvious claim that every teacher has an effect on every one of her students can easily be countered by the equally vacuously true claim that no one knows what this effect will be. As our study has sought to demonstrate, beginning with a single principle such as transference at the center of a pedagogical relationship, the variety of educational outcomes that one might derive is, if not infinite, at least far more complex and revealing of unexpected elements of human relation than is initially evident. Even in this variety, however, the power of fantasy has its limits.

That the fantasy of the teacher as a knowing subject is, like any dream, subject to the limits of its environing conditions can be seen in widely varied and well documented disconnects between teachers and students throughout the history of thought. Of Socrates' three most famous students, none follows his

## The limits of authority and conclusion    133

model: two disobey his rule forbidding writing, thereby immortalizing themselves and their teacher, while the third achieves infamy by taking on only moral skepticism as his primary lesson. The theme of the teacher's limited influence over his best students follows in the long history of students who reject their lessons and thereby apotheosize their teachers and create themselves as thinkers in their own right in the process: Aristotle against Plato, Nietzsche against Schopenhauer, Heidegger against Husserl, Levinas against Heidegger. Students whose thoughts and behaviors are dominated by their teachers are portrayed, alternately, as insignificant, even comic figures, such as Apollodorus and Aristodemus of Plato's *Symposium*, who dress like Socrates in order to pay him homage, but contribute nothing to the discourse on Eros except their ridiculous misunderstanding of what it means to be disciples.

As if in anticipation of this tradition of unknown influence, Plato has Socrates proclaim in the *Meno* that teaching is impossible, a point that Shoshana Felman (1982, p. 21–22) recognizes as echoed in Freud's inclusion of teaching among the three "impossible professions." Socrates' claim is followed almost immediately by a successful lesson in which Socrates teaches geometry to a slave boy, but his success does not negate the limitations he places on teaching. Instead, it demonstrates a difference between Socrates' success at argumentation in the scene of instruction and the questionable influence he holds beyond that intimate scene. The metaphor for shared knowledge with which the *Meno* closes is the statues of Daedalus, who wander about causing havoc if they are not tied down—a vivid illustration of the limits to describing pedagogy as a causal relationship.

Without these limits, however, without the impossibility of teaching, the situation would only be worse. A teacher who taught with the expectation that her students' work would mirror her ideas perfectly might find herself too self-conscious, too prone to endlessly correcting herself, or like a mother irritated at her children for exhibiting characteristics revealingly similar to her own. The refracted misrecognition of transference ensures that the teacher's words will never be simply enacted by the student, but will instead serve as one element in an authorized vision of the world that the student will inhabit as their environment.

Alfred Hitchcock's *Rope* provides an example of how the incomplete, indirect influence of teaching saves teachers from a too literal realization of their teaching. Like many pedagogical narratives, *Rope* is a "true story" dramatization built from the facts surrounding the highly publicized Leopold and Loeb case. Two students, convinced by ideas they have learned in prep school about the natural superiority of some individuals over others and the right of superior individuals to take the life of an inferior with impunity, carry out the murder of a fellow student in the opening scene of the narrative.

Even before this narrative begins, however, an establishing shot behind the opening titles of *Rope* shows a city street as seen from a high-rise window. A tiny adult and children move to cross a street in the middle of the block,

## 134 The limits of authority and conclusion

when suddenly the father reaches out and holds the children back. A car passes and they continue. This is the protective ideal that we, as the viewers, end up wanting in the film: a parent protecting a child from the big city horror that occurs in the next frame. As a reversal of the tiny, peaceful narrative that takes place behind the titles, Hitchcock subjects his audience to the grisly murder of a son mere minutes before his father enters the room, evoking a feeling of sorrow and frustration for the remainder of the film that cannot be undone even when the murderers are caught. In the outside world shown in the view from the window, justice, law, and order prevail. Inside the apartment where the action of the film takes place, the sick intimacies of a fantasy totally at odds with social norms exclude our normal expectations of human interactions.

Critics of *Rope* typically focus on Hitchcock's attempt to create the appearance of a single long shot comprising all the action of the film by splicing together ten reels, each reel a single long shot and spliced with the next behind a clever interposition of an object that completely blackens out the frame. Žižek (1992, p. 42) follows this trend, describing *Rope* as an "artificial, over-strained formal experiment" marked by an "undeniable impression of failure." But Žižek also notes a connection between the forced formalism of the film and its content—a cocktail party thrown in "a psychotic universe without symbolic openness," creating "an almost unbearable tension throughout the film." "In *Rope*, we wait desperately for a cut to deliver us from the nightmarish continuity." Žižek continues:

> *Rope* enacts a psychotic *passage a l'acte* (the "rope" from the film is, of course, ultimately the "rope" connecting "words" and "acts," i.e. it marks the moment at which the symbolic, so to speak, falls into the real . . . the homosexual, murderous couple take words "literally," they pass them immediately to "deeds," realizing the professor's pseudo-Nietzschean theories that concern precisely the absence of prohibition.

The absence of prohibition noted by Žižek suggests that Rupert's words are no mere words, but instead convey to his students a fantasy of living outside the bounds of the law. Spoken as they are by Rupert as the subject presumed to know, Brandon and Phillip interpret Rupert's fantastical parlor game as spoken from a position of authority. What his students fail to understand is that Rupert's authority does not extend beyond the rarefied atmosphere of the dorm room in which they are spoken, neither does his doctrine have any credence as a way of life in the real world. In Brandon's and Phillip's attempt to transport the closed circles of their dorm room "bull sessions" into the light of the outside world, they instead create an enclosure in which the fantasy shared with their teacher is played out as a reality, bringing about the closed psychotic universe described by Žižek. The absence of lapses in time or space within the narrative creates a feeling of interiority, even claustrophobia, as the viewer has been closed inside the apartment with Brandon, the madman and murderous mastermind, his neurotic and weak sidekick Phillip and the body of David, the boy whose murder we witness in the very first scene. From the strangling death of David until Rupert opens the window and fires the three shots, ending the film, the apartment is sealed with the viewer inside.

Hitchcock's depiction of this private, interior space is echoed by the guests' discussions of private schooling and privileged, intellectual life, by Brandon and Phillip's closeted homosexual relationship, and by the fact that the victim's friends and relations are drawn into the apartment with the dead in order for Brandon to commit "the perfect murder" as a work of art, "a masterpiece" in which his control of the environment proves his right to commit murder. Within the closed space of his own design, Brandon attempts to realize his fantasy of power and superiority. But even before the party is over, the telephone rings, a link to the world outside, bringing the message that David has not come home and something might have gone wrong. Similarly, the first clue suggesting David's whereabouts comes to Rupert when he prepares to exit Brandon's constructed fantasy and is handed a hat from the coat closet that doesn't fit. The initials printed inside the hat, D. K. (David Kentley) suggest that David has been drawn inside the machinations of Brandon's scheme and has been unable to leave. Rupert continues with his departure, but a few minutes later he returns from the outside, eventually destroying Brandon's construction and the fantasy upon which it is based by opening the window and exposing his students to the outside world as murderers.

Rupert's transformation at the end of the film into a detective and moral judge draw our attention because they expose and destroy a space of interiority and fantasy nearly identical to that which Rupert shared with the boys as their prep school hall master. The scene of the murder ideologically reproduces the quasi-Nietzschean revaluation of moral values and noble distance that Rupert taught the boys and that he glibly reproduces at the cocktail party, to the horror of the dead boy's father. Mr. Kentley uncannily registers the seriousness of the amoral prescriptions even as Rupert delivers them in a sort of dark humor, and even before a hysterical telephone call from Mrs. Kentley alerts the guests to David's absence as a matter of concern.

Rupert's growing concern and transformation into the role of detective and moral judge in the last scenes of the film demonstrate an undermining of two related fantasies: on the one hand, the idea of his own intellectual superiority, on the other, the confirmation of his superiority in the influence he holds over the boys. Both of these fall apart, because they have been taken beyond the walls of the dormitory into a world where neither can continue in its original form. The emergence of horror in these imaginary relationships—through his students, to himself—is not because either fantasy is inherently corrupt but because any fantasy denies the symbolic order, the order of the law that also serves to hold back every person's murderous instincts. Rupert comes to realize the damage he has done in Brandon's reflection of his own teachings, claiming "He [Phillip] and I have lived what you and I have talked." When Rupert

## 136 The limits of authority and conclusion

finally gathers the strength to open the chest in which David's dead body has lain throughout the party, serving as buffet and as display library, the books stacked upon the chest fall to the ground. Rupert's lessons, his bookish charm, his ideas all fall away as he looks in horror at what today we would call their educational outcome.

While Rupert ends the film as its hero, what stands out as especially strange about Rupert's character is his ability to stand at polar opposites on a single issue. With a drink in his hand, sitting next to the murdered boy's father and aunt, Rupert proclaims that he is quite serious about his defense of the idea of justified murder, not only as an idea but as an actionable ethic. Minutes later, holding a gun, he condemns Brandon's and Phillip's actions and initiates their public judgment by summoning the law. His position seems hopelessly self-contradictory, insofar as he does not play his judgment of his students' actions as a horrific realization of his own teachings; he suggests no shame or change of heart in his condemnation. Instead, it seems that, to Rupert, the distinction is obvious: an ethical ideal that can be discussed and championed in the private company of the school, the academic publishing house, or a dinner party of like-minded guests, might still be morally unthinkable in the public sphere.

Hitchcock underscores the distinction between intellectual spaces and the rest of the world by building a degree of unworldliness into Rupert's character. Played by James Stewart, Rupert is established as an inconsequential, oddball, scholarly type despite, and perhaps as an explanation of, his Übermensch beliefs and the profound effect these teachings have had on his students. What we know of him is that he has spent his adult life in prep school dorms and scholarly publishing houses that don't make any money. In other words, he has no experience of or significance in the world and neither do his fantasies. While almost all the characters in the film are paired with another in realized romantic relationships, Rupert engages in flirtatious banter with Mrs. Wilson, Brandon's aging housekeeper, suggesting a sort of arrested development.

A similar theme of the classroom as a kind of separate realm, populated by teachers who are better suited for the world of books than the real world outside can be seen in many school films, including *The Browning Version* (1951), *Dead Poets Society* (1989), and *The History Boys* (2006). The theme is especially pronounced in *Term of Trial* (1962), which opens with a boy, Thompson, leaving the abuses of his all-too-real homelife, running through the streets of a working class English neighborhood and into the closing doors of a school chapel. The scene quotes the opening scene of *The Browning Version* in its portrayal of urgency and the fear of the child being locked out of the temple of learning, but even in the first seconds of *Term*, it is clear that Thompson is running from his home rather than because he is afraid of being late.

Thompson's presence in the film serves as an establishing backdrop to the tragic teacher's life of Graham Weir (Laurence Olivier), a middle-aged scholar whose honors degree would grant him access to teaching in the best public

The limits of authority and conclusion 137

schools if it were not for his criminal record as a conscientious objector. Instead, he teaches at the East Secondary Modern School, a government sponsored inner-city high school characterized by the same unruly students featured in all films about inner-city schools. His bitter wife, Anna (Simone Signoret), claims that he hides from the world in his pretentions of non-violence, taunting him about his lack of a better teaching position: "Who would want to employ a man who has no guts?" He doesn't argue, describing himself instead as "more than a little afraid of life." Weir's unrealized life as a scholar is mirrored by his fruitless marriage to Anna, who accuses him of resenting her for being unable to have children.

Yet it is Weir's lack of fitness for anything but the scholarly life that brings about the tragic narrative told by the film. His social and political ineptitude is shown early, through a suggestion from a departing deputy headmaster that Weir may be named as his successor. The suggestion seems hopeful, but is clearly doomed. When Mitchell, a hoodlum, takes an indecent photo of Shirley, a fellow student, and passes it in class, Weir intercepts it and, incensed with moral rage, breaks with his ethic of non-violence, whipping Mitchell's hands. When asked to justify his use of corporal punishment by the Headmaster, Weir is unable to produce the offending photograph, realizing that in his rage he had ripped it up. The Headmaster offers only a warning, but the warning is enough to suggest that Weir will not win the position he was promised.

At the same time, Shirley's desires for a better education bring her closer to her teacher; Weir offers her free tutoring after school, knowing there is no way she can pay for it. Shirley visits Weir's house for tutoring when her own home is overrun by a family party. Her reaction upon stepping into his study demonstrates the distance that the teacher stands from the world of his students: "Have you read all these books then?" When Weir explains that he spends most of his time reading them, Shirley's tone shifts to judgment: "You don't have much of a life, do you?" Her question has already been answered by the film itself, in which the audience never catches Weir studying, but instead sees him moving back and forth between equally harrowing school and home settings, fortifying himself each time he leaves the school and returns to the world by stopping off at a neighborhood bar, often late into the night.

Unable to face the world without being numbed, Weir is insensitive to Shirley's obvious, growing fascination with him as someone unlike any of the people she knows. When she presents him with a gift of a rolodex with her name already written in it, Anna warns him, "Seriously Graham, she's stuck on you. So be careful: she might get hurt." Unheeded, the warning fails to save Weir from stopping Shirley's advances until she has gone too far, exposing her desires for her teacher and leaving her devastated when he refuses to reciprocate. Humiliated by her failure, Shirley turns to Mitchell and sets out to save face by ruining Weir, accusing him of inappropriate advances. Found guilty and facing sentencing, Weir is helpless in relation to the world and the law that prevails outside of his classroom. In a dramatic reversal, Shirley takes pity on

## 138    The limits of authority and conclusion

Weir and recants, allowing him to retain his livelihood as a teacher, even in a highly reduced capacity as the survivor of a scandal.

Rupert and Weir are of a kind: charming and noble in their ascetic, scholarly existence, but totally incapable of getting by in the world. But if male teachers are more often portrayed as fairly incapable of managing reality, too focused on their studies to be of any practical use, female teachers regularly appear as posing a threat to the real world due to their unmanageable, insatiable desires. *Mademoiselle* (1966) features a "pyromaniacal provincial schoolteacher who perpetrates a series of catastrophes on the village where she lives and works: fires, floods and poisonings" (Ross, 1997), because of her inability to realize her desire for a local laborer. Similarly, in *The Piano Teacher* (2001), the teacher in question carries out violent acts in order to control the fate of her student as a means of securing him as the object of her desire.

A similar horror in the teacher's expression of unusual desire defines *The Prime of Miss Jean Brodie* (1969), in which the titular character provides a complete world of facts and values dominating the minds of her students, by replacing an objective account of the world, for which the school serves as a formal, if partial, preparation, with a more romantic, entirely fantastic narrative of her own making, in which Mussolini and Franco are great men and the study of history and geography correspond to narratives of Brodie's love life. Questioning her students on the name of the greatest Renaissance painter, Brodie dismisses her students' answers of Michelangelo and Da Vinci with a definitive statement: "The answer is Giotto. He is my favourite." She continues the description of her travels in the Tuscan countryside. In a similar fashion to *Rope*, *Brodie* suggests that the idle fantasies of a teacher with little connection to reality can be viewed as humorous or even charming so long as those fantasies never have any bearing on the lives of students. When those same fantasies are transposed into the lives of young people, however, as in the case of Mary MacGregor who travels to Spain at Brodie's suggestion and dies trying to join the Franco forces, the charming oddity of the teacher in her distance from the real world becomes a tragic, even menacing presence.

While these masculine and feminine stereotypes seem to portray opposing problems, they are simply obverse sides of the same coin: the public expectation that the teacher remain at a distance from the world, engaged in books rather than in life. At first glance, this expectation is hardly ennobling to the profession, casting teachers as outcasts and strangers with unrecognizable desires and reinforcing the old adage that "Those who can, do; those who cannot, teach." But perhaps a more productive way of seeing the teacher's strangeness is in its capacity to respond to society's need for difference.

The teacher's unworldliness connects to commonly held ideals of liberal learning. To dismiss Rupert's study of Nietzsche, Hegel, or any other thinker whose work yields impracticable or distasteful results would work against the purposes of schools as places where the possibilities and limits of human experience are explored. Schools and other academic sites stand apart from the rest of the world, because they are not held to the political or economic forces that define the status quo and therefore offer a better vantage point on the limits of current norms. If schools are designed to stand out in this manner, however, we are also tied to the corresponding idea that teachers, as intellectuals, stand at a distance from the world. Rupert and Weir provide vibrant examples of this distance.

Another perspective on the unworldliness of the teacher comes from Hannah Arendt's (1961) critique of progressive education, which offers an argument for keeping education at a distance from the world. For Arendt, the essence of education is natality, the fact that human beings are born into the world belatedly rather than designed to fit its existing social structures, and as a result need to catch up on the language and laws that precede them and define them.

Arendt's critique depends heavily on her association of modern, particularly American democracy with an:

> [e]xtraordinary enthusiasm for what is new, which is shown in almost every aspect of American daily life, and the concomitant trust in an "indefinite perfectibility"—which Tocqueville noted as the credo of the common "uninstructed man" and which as such antedates by almost a hundred years the development in other countries of the West—would presumably have resulted in any case in greater attention paid and greater significance ascribed to the newcomers by birth, that is, the children, whom, when they had outgrown their childhood and were about to enter the community of adults as young people, the Greeks simply called οἱ νέοι, the new ones.
>
> (Arendt, 1961, p. 176)

This "pathos of the new" leads Arendt to view contemporary democratic society as perpetually revolutionary, forever "founding . . . a new world against the old" (p. 175).

The question Arendt asks, and to some extent answers, is what educational model properly serves democratic society's insistence upon the new? Arendt cautions that:

> Even the children one wishes to educate to be citizens of a utopian morrow are actually denied their own future role in the body politic, for, from the standpoint of the new ones, whatever new the adult world may propose is necessarily older than they themselves. It is in the very nature of the human condition that each new generation grows into an old world, so that to prepare a new generation for a new world can only mean that one wishes to strike from the newcomers' hands their own chance at the new.
>
> (Arendt, 1961, p. 177)

Her analysis here echoes her dismissal of Plato's *Republic* as a poetic rather than a political work (Arendt, 1958), emphasizing the fact that in order for young

# 140    The limits of authority and conclusion

people to engage in political action of their own, they must have the freedom to operate in an unscripted manner, without expectations of purpose or end. The critique of progressive education that she derives from this analysis is:

> Anyone who refuses to assume joint responsibility for the world should not have children and must not be allowed to take part in educating them . . . The teacher's qualification consists in knowing the world and being able to instruct others about it, but his authority rests on his assumption of responsibility for that world. Vis-a-vis the child it is as though he were a representative of all adult inhabitants, pointing out the details and saying to the child: This is our world.
>
> (Arendt, 1958, p. 189)

Arendt's argument against an accountability movement she could not possibly have predicted comes to its destination:

> Our hope always hangs on the new which every generation brings; but precisely because we can base our hope only on this, we destroy everything if we so try to control the new that we, the old, can dictate how it will look [and that therefore] the function of the school is to teach children what the world is like and not to instruct them in the art of living.
>
> (Arendt, 1958, pp. 192, 195)

Biesta's (2004, p. 250) response to accountability measures follows a similar trajectory, as he argues that:

> [r]edefining our relationships on the basis of responsibility might also be a way to regain and reclaim the political dimension of accountability, in that we can understand "the political" as taking responsibility for that which is of common concern (the *res publica*). After all, to take political responsibility is precisely to take responsibility for what is not directly of interest to us (as consumers), and may not even be of interest to us at all.

Biesta's reframing of accountability follows Arendt's understanding of the political purpose of education insofar as it sets the teacher's responsibility in relation to the world that educational discourses are intended to represent, rather than to the lives of students that are both impossible to predict and in no way controlled by teachers' work.

Brodie, by contrast, typifies both an inability to faithfully represent the world and an attempt to instruct in the art of living, or even to live through her girls. "I am in the business of putting old heads on young shoulders, and all my pupils are the *crème de la crème*. Give me a girl at an impressionable age and she is *mine for life*," Brodie tells her students, encouraging them to be claimed as hers and shaped in her image.

The limits of authority and conclusion    141

If the fundamental lesson that we learn from films about pedagogical relationships is that teachers occasion desires in their students, and that these desires in turn produce the students as subjects who stand in relation to their teachers' authority, the caveat offered by *Rope* and *Brodie* is to remember the significance of the disconnect between the student's and teacher's respective views of the world. The teacher, after all, attempts to produce herself, through her teaching, as the completed subject she believed she encountered in her own teacher, and therefore spends more time looking backward rather than forward.

It should be clear that the teacher's commitment to her students is not a commitment to ensuring that her students engage in a simple reduplication of her desires and attachments, as in the case of Brodie, or the desires appropriate to her particular generation, class, or personality. Contrary to the concept of accountability, the appropriate outcome of an educational relationship, at least in a democratic society, is something that the teacher could not have predicted. Bauer (1998) for instance, is spot on in diagnosing Mr. Keating in *Dead Poets Society* (1989) with an inappropriately dominating relationship toward his students, insofar as he desires that they reinstate his forbidden club, address him as Whitman addresses Lincoln, and otherwise live according to a set of rebellious, but nonetheless academic, principles that are not applicable to the world outside of the classroom.

## Now my heart is full

Appropriate to Arendt's limitation of the teacher's authority to the representation of the world, school films present a remarkable number of moments in which the teacher is pulled up short, silenced in the face of some experience that stands outside her capacity for representation. While the teacher is presented as the master of a discourse, that discourse itself is not unlimited, and typically fails at those moments when the seemingly infinite permutations of language confront the limitations of the real world. More often than not, the occasion for the teacher's silence is in the response she has brought about in her student. In *La Maternelle* (1933) Rose falls silent when Marie asks for a kiss. Bernburg is similarly silent in *Mädchen in Uniform* (1931) during the "thousand tongues" classroom scene that follows her passionate kiss with Manuela. Thackeray finds himself alternating between silenced and stammering twice in *To Sir, With Love* (1967). In the beginning of the film, when he and a colleague are caught watching the students dance between classes, Dare invites him to join. Thackeray mumbles, unable to put together a sentence, and departs, obviously ashamed of the fact that he has come to the gymnasium out of his own desire for a spectacle. At the end of the film, after finally accepting Dare's invitation to dance and managing his desires in relation to hers, Thackeray is once again caught off guard, too emotional to speak in receiving the film's title song and a memento as a gift from his students.

Crocker-Harris, in *The Browning Version* (1951) similarly collapses into speechless emotion when presented with a gift from his student. Significantly,

## 142    The limits of authority and conclusion

the book he receives from Taplow is not only a token of the latter's awakening desire; the imperfect mirror it holds to their relationship provides Crocker-Harris with a reminder of what he once intended to be. The inscription Taplow has written: "God from afar looks graciously upon a gentle master," demonstrates both Taplow's developing mastery of the Croc's discursive discipline and a praise of his teacher that is totally undeserved. The roles, if not reversed, are shifted, demonstrating the teacher's lack in relation to the student's inchoate understanding of the proper end of humanistic study.

Kingsfield (*The Paper Chase*, 1973) who has told his class, "In my classroom, there is always another question—another question to follow your answer," falls silent at Hart's thorough analysis of *Carlill v. Carbolic Smoke Ball*, the morning Hart decides to "join the fray." The case involves an institution that fails to follow through on its promise; Kingsfield similarly cannot follow through on his promise to respond to every question with another question. The setup is a bit clumsy, with Kingsfield's silence followed by exuberant music and Hart running across campus to kiss Susan, but the significance of the scene is similar to that in *Browning*: the teacher finds himself awed by his student's erotic self-overcoming in relation to a belated start.

*My Fair Lady* (1964) closes with a silent Professor Higgins listening to a recording of Eliza's voice upon her first visit to his home. On the record, Higgins and Colonel Pickering describe Eliza as "low" and "dirty," but by the time the film ends her education has been completed, and the voice on the recording that gave Higgins a purpose has been erased. Only when Eliza returns, assuming the stature of the low and dirty by declaring, "I washed me face an' 'ands before I come, I did"—can he in turn take up the position of the one who speaks, crying out, "Where the devil are my slippers?"

In the last moments of *The Corn Is Green* (1945), teacher and student, their tasks completed and their respective identities erased, stare silently at one another as the distance between them grows, closing the film and their connection.

These silences not only reveal something about our cultural expectations of teachers' identity, they also provide a way of relating to the fantasies that these films offer. As the teachers demonstrate through their silence, the fantasy only extends so far. Regardless of the student's feelings for the teacher, her influence over the student cannot ultimately decide the student's "educational outcomes" or who the student becomes in relation to the world.

Despite an authoritative presence as a teacher, Lacan himself seemed to embrace the idea that he would have little control over those who chose to follow him. He famously claimed, "C'est à vous d'être lacaniens, si vous voulez. Moi, je suis freudien," (It's up to you to be Lacanians, if you want. Me, I'm a Freudian) emphasizing the idea that while a student can exercise direct discursive power in relation to his teacher's message, magnifying, diminishing, or misreading the message in a new direction, the only way a teacher can hold influence over her student is by becoming the impossible object of his desire.

## References

Arendt, H. (1958) *The Human Condition*. Chicago, IL: University of Chicago Press.

Arendt, H. (1961) *Between Past and Future*. New York: Viking Press.

Bauer, D. M. (1998) Indecent proposals: Teachers in the movies. *College English*, 60(3), 301–317.

Biesta, G. (2004) Education, accountability, and the ethical demand: Can the democratic potential of accountability be regained? *Educational Theory*, 54(3), 233–250.

Britzman, D. P. (1998) *Lost Subjects, Contested Objects: Toward a Psychoanalytic Inquiry of Learning*. Albany, NY: State University of New York Press.

*The Browning Version*, Anthony Asquith, dir. (United Kingdom: Javelin Films, 1951).

*The Corn Is Green*, Irving Rapper, dir. (USA: Warner Bros, 1945).

*Dead Poets Society*, Peter Weir, dir. (USA: Touchstone Pictures, 1989).

Felman, S. (1982) Psychoanalysis and education: Teaching terminable and interminable. *Yale French Studies*, 63: 21–44.

*The History Boys*, Nicholas Hytner, dir. (United Kingdom: Fox Searchlight Pictures, 2006).

Logue, J. (2009) The unbelievable truth and dilemmas of ignorance. In R. Glass (ed.) *Philosophy of Education 2008*. Urbana, IL: Philosophy of Education Society, pp. 54–62.

*Mädchen in Uniform*, Leontine Sagan, dir. (Germany: Deutsche Film-Gemeinschaft, 1931).

*Mademoiselle*, Tony Richardson, dir. (France: Procinex, 1966).

*La Maternelle (Children of Montmartre)*, Jean Benoit-Lévy, dir. (France: Photosonor, 1933).

*My Fair Lady*, George Cukor, dir. (USA: Warner Bros, 1964).

*The Paper Chase*, James Bridges, dir. (USA: 20th Century Fox, 1973).

*The Piano Teacher*, Michael Haneke, dir. (France: Arte France Cinema, 2001).

*The Prime of Miss Jean Brodie*, Ronald Neame, dir. (United Kingdom: 20th Century Fox, 1969).

*Rope*, Alfred Hitchcock, dir. (USA: Warner Bros, 1948).

Ross, K. (1997) Schoolteachers, maids and other paranoid histories. *Yale French Studies*, 91: 7–27.

*Term of Trial*, Peter Glenville, dir. (United Kingdom: Romulus Films, 1962).

*To Sir, With Love*, James Clavell, dir. (United Kingdom: Columbia Pictures, 1967).

Žižek, S. (1992) *Looking Awry*. Cambridge, MA: MIT Press.

# Glossary

**All Things Fair** or **Lust och fägring stor** (1995) Directed by Bo Widerberg. Sweden: Per Holst Filmproduktion. Color. Starring Marika Lagevcrant John Widerberg. A 15-year-old has a relationship with his married, 37-year-old teacher.

**Animal House** (1978) Directed by John Landis. USA: Universal Pictures. Color. Starring John Belushi. A college fraternity is home to humorous miscreants and their lewd pranks.

**Blackboard Jungle** (1955) Directed by Richard Brooks. USA: Metro-Goldwyn-Mayer. Black and white. Based on the book of the same title by Evan Hunter. Starring Glenn Ford, Sidney Poitier. A new teacher to a rough inner-city school tries to tame the student body.

**The Breakfast Club** (1985) Directed by John Hughes. USA: Channel Productions. Color. Starring Emilio Estevez, Molly Ringwald, Ally Sheedy. Five students from differing high school cliques spend detention together, forming friendships and flirtations.

**The Browning Version** (1951) Directed by Anthony Asquith. United Kingdom: Javelin Films. Black and white. Based on the play of the same name by Terence Rattigan. Starring Michael Redgrave. An aging classics master at a British public school is forced into retirement and into confronting his pedagogical and marital failings.

**Carrie** (1976) Directed by Brian DePalma. USA: Red Bank Films. Color. Based on the book of the same name by Stephen King. Starring Sissy Spacek, Piper Laurie. An introverted and bullied teenage girl uses her psychokinetic powers to seek revenge upon classmates, teachers, and mom.

**The Children's Hour** (1961) Directed by William Wyler. USA: The Mirisch Corporation. Black and white. Based on the play of the same title by Lillian Hellman. Starring Audrey Hepburn, Shirley MacLaine. Two teachers' lives and careers are radically disrupted when accused of lesbianism by a student at a private school for girls.

**The Class** or **Entre les murs** (2008) Directed by Laurent Cantet. France: Haut et Court. Color. Based on the book of the same title by François Bégaudeau. Starring François Bégaudeau. A French teacher attempts to bring order and inspiration to a group of ethnically diverse students.

**Glossary** 145

**Class of 1984** (1982) Directed by Mark Lester. Canada: Guerilla High Productions. Color. Starring Perry King, Roddy McDowall, Timothy Van Patten. In a school overrun by violence, a new teacher abandons the dream of starting an orchestra to instead hunt down the student gang members who raped his wife.

**Class of Nuke 'Em High** (1986) Directed by Richard Haines. USA: Troma Entertainment. Color. A runoff from a nuclear power plant has the greatest influence on students, turning them monstrous.

**Conrack** (1974) Directed by Martin Ritt. USA: Twentieth Century Fox Film Corporation. Color. Based on the book *The Water is Wide* by Pat Conroy. Starring Jon Voight. A young white teacher attempts to educate poor black teenagers on an isolated island off South Carolina.

**The Corn Is Green** (1945) Directed by Irving Rapper. USA: Warner Bros. Black and white. Based on the play of the same title by Emlyn Williams. Starring John Dall and Bette Davis. After founding a school in a Welsh mining town, a middle-aged teacher endeavors to send her star student to Oxford.

**Dangerous Minds** (1995) Directed by John Smith. USA: Hollywood Pictures. Color. Starring Michelle Pfeiffer. A former Marine enlists all her reserves to educate the poor, disadvantaged and vicious youth of an inner city.

**Dead Poets Society** (1989) Directed by Peter Weir. USA: Touchstone Pictures. Color. Starring Robin Williams. At an elite New England boarding school, a teacher's unorthodox style inspires students and outrages administrators.

**Different from the Others** or ***Anders als die Andern*** (1919) Directed by Richard Oswald. Germany: Richard-Oswald-Produktion. Black and white, silent, incomplete print. Conrad Veidt, Fritz Schulz, Reinhold Schünzel. A gay violinist is blackmailed over his relationship with a younger student.

**Election** (1999) Directed by Alexander Payne. USA: Paramount Pictures. Color. Based on the book of the same name by Tom Perrotta. Starring Matthew Broderick, Reese Witherspoon. An annoyingly enthusiastic and accomplished student elicits the scorn of her teacher to his detriment.

**Elephant** (2003) Directed by Gus Van Sant. USA: Fine Line Pictures. Color. A fictionalized school shooting loosely based on an actual one at Columbine High School, Colorado in 1999.

**Fast Times at Ridgemont High** (1982) Directed by Amy Heckerling. USA: Universal Pictures. Color. Based on the book of the same name by Cameron Crowe. Starring Sean Penn. Sex and drugs and rock n' roll, and abortions.

**Ferris Bueller's Day Off** (1986) Directed by Jerry Hughes. USA: Paramount Pictures. Color. Starring Matthew Broderick. A high school senior plays hooky in downtown Chicago with his girlfriend and best friend in the vintage Ferrari of his best friend's father.

**Freedom Writers** (2007) Directed by Richard LaGravenese. USA: Paramount Pictures. Color. Based on the book *The Freedom Writers Diary* by Erin Gruwell. Starring Hilary Swank. A white teacher wins over the trust of her poor, angry and racially diverse class by discussing the Holocaust.

## 146 Glossary

**Goodbye, Mr. Chips** (1939) Directed by Sam Wood. USA: Warner Bros. Black and white. Based on the book of the same name by James Hilton. Starring Robert Donant. A retired Latin teacher and former headmaster reflects upon his career and life teaching boys at a British boarding school.

**Half Nelson** (2006) Directed by Ryan Fleck. USA: Hunting Lane Films. Color. Starring Ryan Gosling. In Brooklyn, a drug-addicted teacher (white, male) befriends a black, female student with troubles of her own.

**The History Boys** (2006) Directed by Nicholas Hytner. United Kingdom: Fox Searchlight Pictures. Color. Based on the play of the same name by Alan Bennett. Starring Richard Griffiths. At an English boarding school for boys, the intelligent and irreverent interactions of teachers and students both underscore and belie the ultimate goal: admission to Cambridge or Oxford.

**If. . .** (1968) Directed by Lindsay Anderson. United Kingdom: Memorial Enterprises. Color and black and white. In a truly cruel English boarding school for boys, students appear to find a cache of guns and ammunition and possibly stage a revolt.

**Jonah, Who Will Be 25 in the Year 2000** or *Jonas qui aura 25 ans en l'an 2000* (1976) Directed by Alain Tanner. France: Galimont. Color and black and white. Starring Miou-Miou. Inspired and upended by the social upheavals in France after May 1968, eight characters in their late twenties and early thirties attempt to navigate their lives and find meaning.

**Kids** (1995). Directed by Larry Clark. USA: Guys Upstairs. Color. Starring Chloë Sevigny. Set in New York City, the film follows a group of untethered teenagers as they abandon themselves to lives of sex, drugs, alcohol, and violence.

**Lolita** (1962) Directed by Stanley Kubrick. USA: Metro-Goldwyn-Mayer. Black and white. Based on the book of the same title by Vladimir Nabakov. Starring Sue Lyon, James Mason, Peter Sellers. A middle-aged teacher's infatuation with a teenage girl leads to murder, among other things.

**Lord of the Flies** (1990) Directed by Harry Hook. USA: Castle Rock Entertainment. Color. Remake of the book of the same title by William Golding. Starring Balthazar Getty and Chris Furrh. American military cadets deserted on an island following a plane crash resort to war between rival factions.

**Mädchen in Uniform** (1931) Directed by Leontine Sagan. Germany: Deutsche Film-Gemeinschaft. Black and white. Based on the play *Gestern und Heute* (*Yesterday and Today*) by Christa Winsloe. Starring Hertha Thiele, Dorothea Wieck. An orphaned teenager at an all-girls boarding school falls in love with her teacher with dramatic consequences.

**Mademoiselle** (1966) Directed by Tony Richardson. France: Procinex. Black and white. Starring Jeanne Moreau and Ettore Manni. A repressed schoolteacher causes a series of deliberate "accidents" to the inhabitants of her rural French village.

**La Maternelle** or *Children of Montmartre* (1933) Directed by Jean Benoit-Lévy and Marie Epstein. France: Photosonor. Black and white. Based on the book of the same name by Léon Frapié. Starring Madeleine Renaud, Paulette Élambert. A recently abandoned bride becomes a successful maid at a nursery and adopts the recently abandoned daughter of a Parisian prostitute.

**Mikaël** (1924) Directed by Carl Dreyer. Denmark: Universum Film (UFA). Black and white, silent. Based on the novel of the same name by Herman Bang. Starring Benjamin Christensen, Nora Gregor, Walter Slezak. An older painter takes a young male model under his wing and roof, only to be swindled when the youth instead falls in love with a woman.

**Monsieur Lazhar** (2011) Directed by Philippe Falardeau. Canada: micro_scope. Color. Based in the play *Bashir Lazhar* by Évelyne de la Chenelière. Starring Mohamed Fellag, Sophie Nélisse. At a Montreal grade school, an Algerian immigrant without teacher training is a successful hire until the truth is revealed.

**Mr. Holland's Opus** (1995) Directed by Stephen Herek. USA: Hollywood Pictures. Color. Starring Richard Dreyfuss. The demands of teaching and of parenting a deaf child compete with a music instructor's desire to compose.

**My Fair Lady** (1964) Directed by George Cukor. USA: Warner Bros. Color. Based on the play *Pygmalion* by George Bernard Shaw. Starring Audrey Hepburn, Rex Harrison. A professor of speech is at a loss for words when an undereducated flower seller blossoms into a lady.

**Notes on a Scandal** (2006) Directed by Richard Eyre. United Kingdom: Fox Searchlight Pictures. Color. Based on the book of the same name by Zoë Heller. Starring Cate Blanchett and Judi Dench. An unattractive, older teacher uncovers an affair between a 15-year-old boy and his appealing but incompetent female art teacher.

**Oleanna** (1994) Directed by David Mamet. USA: Bay Kinescope. Color. Starring Debra Eisenstadt, William H. Macy. A struggling student seeks help from her teacher, but then accuses him of sexual harassment.

**Palo Alto** (2013) Directed by Gia Coppola. USA: Rabbit Bandini Productions. Color. Starring Jack Kilmer, Emma Roberts. High school parties lead to drunken sexual escapades, a car crash, and a tree carving.

**The Paper Chase** (1973) Directed by James Bridges. USA: 20th Century Fox. Color. Based on the book of the same title by John Jay Osborn, Jr. Starring Timothy Bottoms, John Houseman, Lindsay Wagner. The chronicles of a first-year student at Harvard Law School, who attempts to win the recognition of his demanding professor.

**The Pervert's Guide to Cinema** (2006) Sophie Fiennes. United Kingdom: ICA Projects. Color and black and white documentary. Speaking from various film locations and within reconstructed tableaus, the philosopher Slavoj Žižek offers psychoanalytic interpretations of both masterworks and lesser-known titles.

**The Piano Teacher** or *La Pianiste* (2001) Directed by Michael Haneke. Arte France Cinema. Color. Based on the book of the same name by Elfriede Jelnek. Starring Isabelle Huppert, Benoît Magimel. In Vienna, a sexually

## 148 Glossary

repressed, sadomasochistic music professor dominates and is dominated by her younger, male student and by her own desires.

**Picnic at Hanging Rock** (1975) Directed by Peter Weir. Australia: Australian Film Commission. Color. Based on the book of the same name by Joan Lindsay. Starring Dominic Guard, Rachel Roberts. During an outing at a private girls' school, several students and one teacher vanish, leaving survivors confused and haunted.

**The Prime of Miss Jean Brodie** (1969) Directed by Ronald Neame. United Kingdom: 20th Century Fox. Color. Based on the book of the same title by Muriel Spark. Starring Maggie Smith. At an all-girls school in Edinburgh, a teacher's unorthodox approach has great influence upon her students, for better and worse.

**Prom Night** (1980) Directed by Paul Lynch. Canada: Simcom Limited. Color. Starring Jamie Lee Curtis, Leslie Nielsen. An accidental death and purposeful cover-up make for a bloody night of dancing when revenge—six years in the making—is exacted.

**La Robe du Soir** (2009) Directed by Myriam Aziza. France: Mille et Une Productions. Color. Starring Alba Gaïa Kraghede Bellugi, Lio. A young girl becomes inspired, enamored, and obsessed with her teacher.

**Rock 'n' Roll High School** (1979) Directed by Allan Arkush. USA: New World Pictures. Color. Starring P. J. Soles, Mary Woronov. An oppressive school administration is blown away—musically and literally—by punk-loving students.

**Rope** (1948) Directed by Alfred Hitchcock. USA: Warner Bros. Color. Based on the play of the same name by Patrick Hamilton. Starring John Dall, Farley Granger, Jimmy Stewart. A prep school teacher inspires students to commit murder only to summon the law when they do.

**Rushmore** (1998) Directed by Wes Anderson. USA: American Empirical Pictures. Color. Starring Bill Murray, Jason Schwartzman, Olivia Williams. At a private school, an eccentric student competes with an industrialist to win the love of a first grade teacher.

**Sixteen Candles** (1984) Directed by John Hughes. USA: Channel Productions. Color. Starring Molly Ringwald. The adventures and misadventures, frustrations and flirtations of a high school sophomore as she navigates her sixteenth birthday.

**Slavoj Žižek: The Reality of the Virtual** (2004) Directed by Ben Wright. United Kingdom: Ben Wright Film Productions. Color. Speaking from behind a desk, Žižek remains seated as he waxes philosophic about a multitude of subjects.

**The Sound of Music** (1965) Directed by Robert Wise. USA: Robert Wise Productions. Based on the memoir *The Story of the Trapp Family Singers* by Maria von Trapp. Color. Starring Julie Andrews, Christopher Plummer. Failing to become a nun, an Austrian woman wins over the affections of a widower and his seven children through song.

# Glossary 149

**Stand and Deliver** (1988) Ramón Menéndez, R. USA: American Playhouse. Color. Starring Edward James Olmos, Lou Diamond Phillips. At a struggling Hispanic school in Los Angeles, a teacher inspires his students to learn calculus and pass the Advanced Placement exam.

**A Teacher** (2013) Directed by Hannah Fidell. USA: Oscilloscope. Color. Starring Will Brittain, Lindsay Burdge. An English teacher's relationship with her student spells trouble.

**The Teacher** (1974) Directed by H. Avedis. USA: Crown International Pictures. Color. Starring Angel Tompkins. Attracted to their female teacher, three high school boys learn to stalk, have sex, and murder, but little else.

**Term of Trial** (1962) Directed by Peter Glenville. United Kingdom: Romulus Films. Black and white. Starring Sarah Miles, Laurence Olivier, Simone Signoret. A constantly dispirited and often inebriated teacher is falsely accused of sexual molestation when he tries to help a female student.

**To Sir, With Love** (1967) Directed by James Clavell. United Kingdom: Columbia Pictures. Based on the book of the same title by E. R. Braithwaite. Color. Starring Sidney Poitier. An elite, black teacher saves broken white youths from lives of poor desperation in the East End of London.

**Vingarne** or *The Wings* (1916) Directed by Mauritz Stiller. Sweden: Svenska Biografteatern AB. Based on the book *Mikael* by Herman Bang. Black and white, silent, largely lost. Starring Lili Bech, Egil Eide, Lars Hanson. An older sculptor, his younger model, and a crafty countess compete for affection in perhaps the first openly homoerotic film.

**Whiplash** (2014) Directed by Damien Chazelle. USA: Bold Films. Color. Starring J. K. Simmons, Miles Teller. At a New York conservatory for music, a bandleader's aggressive approach both motivates and obliterates his students, including a talented drummer.

**Zero for Conduct** or *Zéro de conduite* (1933) Directed by Jean Vigo. France: Franfilmdis. Black and white. Starring Jean Dasté. At a repressive French boarding school, four students stage a revolt.

# Index

accountability 131-3
Achilles 12-13
Alcibiades 22-4, 26, 28, 46, 48, 76, 79
*All Things Fair* 35
*Animal House* 56 (note 7), 94
Antigone 17, 123, 125-6
Arendt, Hannah 17, 108, 110, 139-41
Aristotle 13, 122, 133
asceticism 17, 55, 115-19
authority: and teacher's identity 5-9, 34,
    38-9, 41-6, 51-5, 60-6; in discourse 73
    (note 2); of film 2
Ayers, W. 6

Bauer, D. M. 6, 16, 58, 75, 141
Berlin, I. 58
belatedness 45-6, 55 (note 5), 139, 142
Beyerbach, B. 6
*Blackboard Jungle* 13, 40, 69
Blacker, D. 17, 116-120, 125, 128
Boothby, R. 2, 122, 126
Borromean knot 84
*Breakfast Club, The* 109
Britzman, D. 5-8, 18 (note 1), 36 (note 2),
    46, 68-70, 86, 89, 130
*Browning Version, The* 35, 127-8, 136,
    141-2
Brooke, R. 9, 18 (note 1), 36 (note 1)
Burbach, H. 6
Burmester, B. 60-1
Butler, J. 66

Camus, A. 13
*Carrie* 109
Chennault, R. 7

*Children's Hour, The* 7
*Class, The* 70
*Class of 1984* 109
*Class of Nuke 'Em High* 109
Cohen, S. 6
*Conrack* 69, 71
*Corn is Green, The* 9, 13, 58, 61-9, 72-3,
    81, 124, 142

Dalton, M. 7, 38
*Dangerous Minds* 13, 69-70, 75, 121
Davis, R.C. 9, 18 (note 1), 36 (note 1)
*Dead Poets Society* 17, 86, 114-15, 123-4,
    136, 141
death of the teacher 16, chapter 7 *passim*
death drive 17, 121-3
De Marzio, D. 17, 116-20, 125, 128
desire 2, 4-5, 9-11, 22-3, 45, 55 (note 4)
*Different from the Others* 11, 21, 24-6
discourse *see* language
divorce 63, 79, 87-8, 115, 121, 128, 137
domination 10, 12, 57-61, 67, 87
Dyer, R. 29
Dylan, B. as signifier of whiteness 70-2

Ebert, R. 49
ego 55 (note 4), 84, 88-9, 100, 103, 121;
    ideal 80
*Election* 9, 15, 35, 86-90
*Elephant* 16, 55 (note 2), 94, 110-11
Ellsworth, E. 59
Eng, D.L. 66
Eros/erotic: and drives 26, 45, 51, 53, 59,
    86, 89; and education 4-5, 8-9, 11-3,
    18 (note 1), 22, 24, 31, 34, 36 (note 1),

Index  151

38; and fantasy 22, 31, 89; and Lacan
4-5, 9-10, 22, 45, 55 (note 1), 89. 126;
44-55, 75, 80, 84, 86; and Plato 4, 10-1,
22-3, 45-6, 89, 133; and students 11, 13,
15, 22, 26, 31, 72, 93, 101, 111;
and teachers 26, 125, 133
heterosexuality 49-50
homosexuality 21, 24-6, 29

Farber, P. 7
fantasy: made real 14-5, chapter 5 *passim*,
94,107; student 1-2, 5, 16, 22-3, 26, 28,
30-1, 34, 39, 57, 116, 126-7, 130, 132,
134-5; teacher 1, 4, 8, 15, 17, 24, 26,
35, 73, 116, 125, 127, 130-2, 135, 142
*Fast Times at Ridgemont High* 16, 109
Felman, S. 9, 18 (note 1), 36 (note 1), 133
*Ferris Bueller's Day Off* 109
Figgins, M. 6
Fort-Da game 121-2, 125-6, 128
Frank, A.W. 18 (note 1), 38
*Freedom Writers* 13, 17, 69-70, 84,115,
120-1
Freud, S. 2, 9, 18 (note 1), 80, 103,
132-3; death drive 17, 121-8;
melancholia 66-73; pedagogy 4, 22,
69, 118
Fried, R. 38

Gallop, J. 8, 18 (note 1), 38, 90 (note 1),
123, 125-6, 128
Giroux, H. 71
*Goodbye, Mr. Chips* 9, 115
Greene, M. 113

*Half Nelson* 71-3
Hedling, E. 107
Hegel 18 (note 1), 71-3, 138
Heidegger 133
Higgins, C. 17, 90 (note 1),
115-17, 127
Hinton, S.E. 89
*History Boys, The* 16, 21, 35, 55 (note 1),
56 (note 7), 136; and the death of the
teacher 113-14, 117, 124
Hitchcock, A. see *Rope*
hooks, b. 38
Hughes, J. 16, 109-11

id 103
*If...* 16, chapter 6 *passim*
ignorance: student's 8, 45-6, 48, 59, 61,
70, 101, 103, 126 ; teacher's 85, 119,
127-28, 130
imaginary 2, 4-5, 84-5, 123

*Jonah, Who Will be 25 in the Year 2000*
1-2, 9
jouissance 13-4, 77, 101, 109: of the other
55 (note 4)

Keenan, D.K. 123
Keroes, J. 7, 38, 41, 43, 48
*Kids* 110
Kipling, R. 95-6
Kristeva, J. 67

Lafave, D. 88
language: and desire 9, 45-7, 51-5, 62-3;
and fantasy 83; and the law 45, 47, 51-5,
83, 139; and subjectivity 39, 80
Leach, J. 107
LeTourneau, M.K. 88-9
lesbian 101, 134-5
Logue, J. 8, 130
*Lolita* 34-5
*Lord of the Flies* 110

*Mädchen in Uniform* 11, 28-31, 34-5, 94,
141
marriage 33, 41, 49, 62
master 21, 27, 39, 90, 126, 141
*Maternelle, La* 11-12, 31-36, 141
melancholia 12, 66-73
McGowan, T. 8
McWilliam, E. 90 (note1)
Metz, C. 8
*Mikaël* 11, 26-8, 30-1
Mitchell, C. 3
*Monsieur Lazhar* 115
*Mr. Holland's Opus* 17, 115
*My Fair Lady* 5, 142

name of the father 52
Nietzsche, F. 17, 111 (note 2), 133-5, 138
*Notes on a Scandal* 9, 15, chapter 5
*passim*, 93

## 152 Index

Oedipus/oedipal 121, 123, 126
*Oleanna* 60-1
Orwell, G. 92

Palo Alto 110
*Paper Chase, The* 9, 12, 35, 39, 44-54, 81, 118, 120, 124, 142
Paragraph 175 24-6,
*Pervert's Guide to Cinema, The:* see Žižek, Slavoj
Peters, M. 57
*Piano Teacher, The* 35, 93, 138
*Picnic at Hanging Rock* 85
Plato: cave allegory 59-61; culture 2, 4, 9, 46, 61, 85-6; dialogues 2; Eros 4, 9, 11, 22-3, 31, 46, 59, 89, 111, 133; *Meno* 133; *Phaedo* 118-19, 125; *Republic* 59, 96, 111, 139; *Symposium* 4-5, 8-11, 22-7, 31, 45-6, 48, 51, 85, 133
*Prime of Miss Jean Brodie, The* 78, 114-15, 124, 138, 140-1
*Prom Night* 109

real 2, 10, 84-5
repetition 1, 6, 89, 94-5: and the death drive 121-2, 125-6, 128
*Robe du Soir, La* 21, 35
*Rock 'n' Roll High School* 16, 109
*Rope* 17, 34, 131, 133-6, 138-9, 141
Ross, K. 138
*Rushmore* 35, 94

sacrifice 42, 114, 119, 123-5
Sade, Marquis de 123
Schleifer, R. 9
Schneiderman, S. 126
Schopenhauer, A. 133
Schultz, C. 108
Sedgwick, E.K. 49
sex scandals 3, 5, 11, 21, 30, 80-90, 114-15, 117, 137-8
*Sixteen Candles* 109
Socrates: death 16-17, 113-14, 119-20,127; Alcibiades love for 22-4, 26, 28, 46, 48, 76, 79; impossibility of teaching 59, 128, 132-3
*Sound of Music, The* 75
*Stand and Deliver* 9, 115
St. Pierre, E. 57

student: desire 1-2, 4-5, 21-4, 45-9, 51-3; fantasy 1-2, 4-5, 13-15, 22-4, 77, 93-4, 100, 103-4 *see also* transference; revolt 92, 94, 97, 106-8, 111; sexual drives 99-102
superego 34
symbolic 4, 77, 84, 123
symbolic order *see* language

Taubman, P. 18 (note 1)
teacher: authority 2, 5-9, 12, 14-17, 27, 29-30, 34, 38-44, 46, 51-5, 59-61, 73 (note 1), 75-7, 79, 80, 83-7, 93, 97-9, 101, 104, 106, 118, 123, 125-7, 131, 134, 140, 141; death 16-17, 26-8, 111, chapter 7 *passim*, 130; identity 5, 6-7, 17, 26, 39, 41-3, 54, 77, 80-1, 89, 115-17, 120, 132, 142; preparation 5-9; savior 22-5, 55, 57-68, 82
*Teacher, A* 76, 93
*Teacher, The* 76
*Term of Trial* 136
*To Sir, With Love* 1, 9, 12, 17, 35, 38-44, 69, 71, 76-7, 81, 85, 115-16, 120, 141
Todd, S. 38
transference: and desire 4-5, 12, 22-3, 28, 77, 84, 86, 89, 93, 108, 122, 126-7, 132; as fantasy 4-5, 10, 12, 16, chapter 2 *passim*, 77, 83-6, 89, 93, 108, 127, 130-32; Lacan's definition of 4-5, 22-3 84-6, 89, 126; Plato's description of 4-5, 22-4, 28
trauma 70

violence: gang 70; revolutionary 92, 94, 97, 106-8, 111; in schools chapter 6 *passim*
*Vingarne* 26

Weber, S. 3
*Whiplash* 21, 44, 55
Whitman, W. 123-4, 141

*Zero for Conduct* 9, 16, 92, chapter 6 *passim*: Vigo, J. 92, 94, 100, 107
Žižek, Slavoj 2-4, 8, 14, 16, 73 (note 2), 75-6, 88-9, 134: *Pervert's Guide to Cinema, The* 3-4, 8; *The Reality of the Virtual* 75